Battlefields of Europe

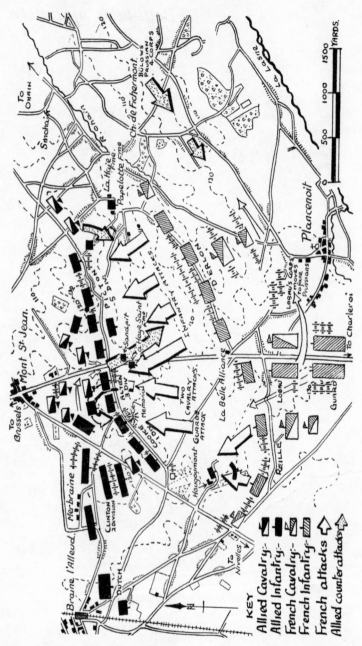

WATERLOO 18th June 1815

A PROJECT OF DIMENSION BOOKS

A Guide to the

Battlefields of Europe

EDITED BY DAVID CHANDLER

Volume I Western Europe

CHILTON BOOKS — A DIVISION OF CHILTON COMPANY

PUBLISHERS PHILADELPHIA AND NEW YORK

Published by Dimension Books, Wilkes-Barre, Pennsylvania in association with Chilton Books and simultaneously in Toronto, Canada by Ambassador Books, Ltd.

Library of Congress Catalog Card Number: 66-17192

© 1965 Hugh Evelyn Ltd.

Table of Contents

List of Contributors Vols. I & II

(in alphabetical order)

J. E. ADAIR, M.A., Senior Lecturer, Department of Military History, R.M.A. Sandhurst

A. R. BIRLEY, M.A., Research Fellow in Latin, Birmingham University

B. J. BOND, M.A., Lecturer in Modern History, the University of Liverpool

E. A. BRETT-JAMES, M.A., Senior Lecturer, Department of Military History, R.M.A. Sandhurst

D. G. CHANDLER, M.A., Senior Lecturer, Department of Military History, R.M.A. Sandhurst

C. J. DUFFY, M.A., D.Phil., Senior Lecturer, Department of Military History, R.M.A. Sandhurst

Major-General H. ESSAME, C.B.E., D.S.O., M.C. (retd.)

Captain C. FALLS, M.A., Sometime Chichele Professor of the History of War, the University of Oxford

Major-General J. F. C. FULLER, C.B., C.B.E., D.S.O. (retd.)

Professor N. GIBBS, M.A., D.Phil., Chichele Professor of the History of War, the University of Oxford

Professor M. E. HOWARD, M.C., M.A., Professor of War Studies in the University of London

J. D. P. KEEGAN, M.A., Senior Lecturer, Department of Military History, R.M.A. Sandhurst

H. G. MACINTOSH, M.A., Deputy Secretary of the Associated Examining Board for the G.C.E.

W. L. McELWEE, M.C., T.D., M.A., Head of Department of Modern Subjects, R.M.A. Sandhurst

Professor P. PIERI, Silver and Bronze Medals of Valour, Member of the Italian and Spanish Academies, Head of 'Facoltà di Magistero', the University of Turin

Professor M. ROBERTS, M.A., D.Phil., F.B.A., Professor of Modern History, the Queen's University, Belfast

D. D. ROONEY, M.A., B.Litt., Headmaster, King's School, Gutersloh, B.A.O.R., Westphalia, West Germany.

J. M. SELBY, T.D., M.A., Senior Lecturer, Military History, R.M.A. Sandhurst

Lieutenant-Colonel G. A. SHEPPERD, M.B.E. (retd.), Librarian, R.M.A Sandhurst

Brigadier P. YOUNG, D.S.O., M.C., M.A., F.S.A. (retd.), Reader in Military History, R.M.A. Sandhurst

Illustrators
Colonel R. W. S. NORFOLK, O.B.E., T.D., D.L.

T. STALKER MILLER, M.S.I.A.

Introduction

Almost a century ago General Hamley wrote in his introduction to the *Operations of War* that 'no kind of history so fascinates mankind as the history of wars'. This fascination has steadily developed, and in recent years there has been a perceptible increase in popular interest in military history. A glance at the book lists of many publishing houses reveals a remarkable growth over the last decade in the number of titles relating to the military affairs of the past. This growing awareness of the interest and importance of the subject has been long overdue; too many historians have tended to dismiss military history as rather a trivial 'poor relation' of the great constitutional, economic and social fields of study, or at best a subject only suitable for study by soldiers in the furtherance of their professional knowledge. Today it would appear that the close connection between military and other historical subjects is becoming more fully appreciated.

The purpose of this book is three-fold. In the first place it plans to provide the reader with a series of glimpses into the past, giving him some idea of the ways in which warfare has changed as weapons and tactics have developed down the ages, of how the essential attributes of leadership have remained unaltered, and at the same time offering him the opportunity of widening his knowledge through sampling the recommended reading. Secondly, the book is designed to furnish a store of valid factual information which will assist the serious student as a minor work of reference. Lastly, but by no means least, it is hoped that the following pages will encourage more travellers to visit the sites of historic battlefields at home and abroad for nostalgic or educational reasons, there to indulge in the fascinating and instructive pastime of attempting to reconstruct the events of the past and solving some of its many remaining mysteries: the study of history does not need to be confined to reading alone.

Owing to printing considerations, *A Traveller's Guide to the Battlefields of Europe* is being published in two parts, the division being determined on a purely geographical basis. Thus volume one relates to those European countries situated west of the Rhine; volume two covers those states lying to its east. In round terms, 23 national sections are incorporated (8 in the first part, 15 in the second), the colony of Gibraltar being included as a separate entity for reasons editorial convenience. The allotment of space varies considerably from country to country, ranging from forty subjects in the case of Great Britain to only one in the case of Gibraltar. Two countries in each part receive a generous allocation of space —namely Great Britain and France (Vol. One) and Italy and Germany (Vol. Two)—and these states consequently form the focal points for the complete *Guide*.

To keep this two-part *Guide* to manageable proportions, it has proved necessary to confine its scope to the description of 245 battles. The task of selection has not by any means been easy, for owing to the regrettably blood-stained history of Europe over the past two millenia more than 2,000 possible subjects are available. In making the final choice, a series of considerations have been balanced against one another. As one prime purpose of the book is to provide a *Guide* in the practical as well as the philosophical sense, foremost among these ranked the regional distribution and present availability of battlefield sites, and the interest of the subjects for expert and amateur alike. In consequence of practical considerations of this kind, it was obvious that the countries of western Europe were more amenable for this purpose than their eastern neighbours, where a different interpretation might be placed upon foreigners armed with binoculars and maps examining the countryside. At the same time, however, it was impossible to exclude these regions completely and still present a reasonably comprehensive picture of battles through the ages. Next, the particular interests of the team of contributors had to be taken into account, and another form of balance maintained. The practical difficulties of pin-pointing the sites of many ancient and mediaeval battlefields—besides the problem of finding accurate information about the contests—also suggested a strong weighting of the chronological allocation in favour of the comparatively well-documented period from 1500 onwards. It was also decided to associate each country with particular periods and great generals; thus in the case of England, the Scots, Baronial and Civil Wars receive fuller attention, whilst the German and central European countries record the battles of Gustavus Adolphus, Frederick the Great and Napoleon; Belgium follows Marlborough's fortunes, France is seen as the location of the Hundred Years' War and the three great struggles of 1870, 1914–18 and 1939–45 against Germany—and so on. However, provision has also been made to include representative battles from other periods in each National Section. Inevitably, any limited selection leaves important gaps unfilled; indeed, in the interests of economy, the Scandinavian countries have been totally omitted, although the deeds of the greatest Swedish soldiers emerge in the pages on Germany and Russia. The causes of the conflicts and the events leading up to the battles are often only briefly sketched, but it is hoped that the selection of suggested reading on each subject, and the more general list relating to the art of war appended below, will between them help the reader to remedy these obvious deficiencies.

This *Guide*, therefore, is designed for the use of three categories of people who are all, in their various ways, interested in exploring the dim corridors of the past. First are the serious students, whether at work in the library or out in the field equipped with binoculars, compasses, map and notebook. Secondly, we hope to cater for the traveller, whether at home or abroad, whose interest is aroused by the non-committal symbol of crossed-swords and date found on his map, or whose attention is attracted to a roadside monument; this volume should go some way towards answering the natural questions of 'Who?', 'Why?' and 'How?'. Lastly, there is the arm-chair campaigner, who enjoys browsing and speculating by the comfort of his own hearth, recreating and analysing in his mind the events of yesteryear which have done so much to shape the present and may well forecast part of the future. No one would deny that all wars and battles are regrettable acts of human folly, causing unjustifiable agony and distress to combatants and non-combatants alike—but these considerations should not preclude their serious study, if only to avoid the mistakes of the past which made such tragedies inevitable. If battles can be described as the punctuation marks on the pages of history then the study of their causes, course and results must be vital to any understanding of our common European heritage. It is hoped that this *Guide to the Battlefields of Europe* will in its own way make a small contribution to that comprehension, and prove both interesting and useful.

D.G.C.

List of General Books on the Art of War

Colin, J., *Les Transformations de le Guerre* (English Edition) London, 1912.

Delbruck, H., *Geschichte der Kriegskunst*, 4 vols., Berlin, 1900–20.

Falls, C., *The Art of War from the Age of Napoleon to the Present Day*, London, 1961.

Fortescue, J. W., *History of the British Army*, 10 vols., London and New York, 1899.

Fuller, J. F. C., *The Decisive Battles of the Western World*, 3 vols., London, 1954–6.

Fuller, J. F. C., *The Conduct of War, 1789–1961*, London, 1961.

Liddell Hart, B. H., *Strategy: the Indirect Approach*, London, 1954.

Lot, F., *L'Art Militaire et les Armées au Moyen Age*, 2 vols., Paris, 1946.

Oman, C. W. C., *History of the Art of War in the Middle Ages*, *A.D. 378–1485*, 2 vols., London, 1924.

Oman, C. W. C., *The Art of War in the Sixteenth Century*, London and New York, 1937.

Preston, Wise and Warner, *Men in Arms*, Aldershot, 1956.

Spaulding, Nickerson and Wright, *Warfare*, New York, 1925.
Several of these volumes contain useful bibliographies.

List of Maps and Diagrams

For information on the format of the Maps and Diagrams see Editor's Note.

Editor's Note

As has already been briefly mentioned in the Introduction, *A Traveller's Guide to the Battlefields of Europe* is being presented by the publishers in two volumes. Volume one relates to *Western Europe*, and deals with battlefields in Belgium, Eire, France, Gibraltar, Great Britain, Holland, Portugal and Spain; Volume Two covers selected battlefields to be found *East of the Rhine*—namely in Austria, Bulgaria, Cyprus, Czechoslovakia, Germany (East and West), Greece, Hungary, Italy, Malta, Poland, Switzerland, Turkey, U.S.S.R., and Yugoslavia. In both volumes the countries are placed in alphabetical order, as are the battles within each national section. For the general convenience of readers, the list of contributors, introduction, campaign chronology and general index (all suitably annotated where necessary to distinguish between work presented in the respective volumes) appear in full in each part.

In order to assist the reader in the use of this book, several points concerning the presentation of the battle descriptions and the format of the accompanying maps and diagrams require brief explanation.

CLASSIFICATION   After the name of each battle—whether on the 'data tables' or, in the case of the shortest items, in the body of the text—a classification symbol comprising a capital letter followed by between one and four asterisks will be found throughout the volume. The capital letter signifies an estimate of the suitability of the battlefield for a visit to the ground, ranging from an 'A' site (easily accessible and practically unchanged) to a 'D' site (difficult to reach and practically unrecognisable). Similarly the asterisks relate to the historical and military interest of each battle or siege, four asterisks denoting a very important action, one a conflict of comparatively minor significance.

DATA TABLES   In the second place, the 'data tables', which introduce some 75 battle descriptions in each volume, are intended to provide a minimum of vital information in a form that can be assimilated at a glance. The greatest possible care has been taken in preparing these sections, but in several instances the exact size of the forces engaged or casualty figures have been difficult to verify. Particularly in the case of the more ancient battles, accurate information is not always forthcoming —contemporary chroniclers being especially prone to overexaggeration—and where there is any reason to doubt the authenticity of the figures shown the prefixes 'estimated' or 'approximate' have been liberally employed.

READING   Each contributor has provided a list of suggested reading for the guidance of any who may wish to pursue particular subjects. As a general rule, only those titles that are likely to be obtainable through public libraries or book shops have been cited. Thus manuscript sources have generally been omitted and, for the convenience of the general English reader, whenever possible preference has been accorded to books published in English. In certain cases, however, where no notable English work is readily available, foreign authorities have been listed. For those readers who may prefer a rather 'lighter' approach, reputed historical novels have been included in a number of instances.

SHORT TREATMENT   In the case of the 45 or so battles and sieges in each volume which have been restricted to the very briefest of treatments for reasons of space, an abbreviated format has been adopted. The name of the battle is followed by its classification, date, approximate location and map reference number, title of war, brief description of the event and one suggested authority for consultation.

CAMPAIGN CHRONOLOGY   Although the battles are listed in alphabetical order within the relevant national sections, the campaign chronology tables at the end of the book will enable a reader to follow up any particular period or war in which he is interested.

MAPS   The general maps have been designed to show the approximate locations of the battlefields together with the most convenient means of approaching the sites by road. Limitations of size have made it impossible to show any more than the minimum of relevant information, although for the convenience of travellers the main population centres and major roads have been included. Please note that *modern* boundaries and state names have been employed throughout the volume.

In addition, a number of diagrams, illustrating a selection of important and accessible battlefields, have been included with the interests of the present-day visitor in mind. In each case, the symbols indicating the approximate position of the troops on the ground have been superimposed on a simplified modern map showing the terrain and local landmarks as they exist today. By this means it is hoped that the visitor will be helped to find his way over battlefields which often extend for miles. Where important topographical changes have taken place since the action, both the original and the present locations are indicated. Thus in the diagram relating to Blenheim (see

Vol. II) the ancient and the modern courses of the river Danube are both shown. Of course the accurate positioning of the troops on the ground has often been difficult to discover, but the reconstructed dispositions of the forces engaged should bear at least an approximate resemblance to the truth and provide a useful guide. The contour heights on the diagrams are shown in feet for battles in Great Britain, and in metres for sites on the Continent. Visitors to the actual battlefields may wish to procure good maps in advance. For the majority of actions down to 1914, a scale of 1/25,000 is the most convenient; the size of more recent battles makes 1/100,000 more practical. Many maps may be purchased from E. Stanford Ltd., 12 Long Acre, London W.C.2, who are the official agents for sale of Defence Department maps and can also often procure foreign maps.

DATING 'New Style' dating has been used throughout each volume.

HOLLAND
1   Heiliger-Lee
2   Bergen
3   Alkmaar
4   Haarlem
5   Zutphen
6   Arnhem
7   Brille

BELGIUM
8   Laffeldt
9   Ostend
10 Oudenarde
11 Landen
12 Rocoux
13 Flanders
14 Courtrai
15 Steenkirk
16 Waterloo
17 Ramillies
18 Fontenoy
19 Mons
20 Fleurus
21 Malplaquet
22 The Ardennes

NORTH SEA

Groningen
Leeuwarden
Winschaten
Den Holder
Bergen Alkmaar
Haarlem
AMSTERDAM
Zwolle
DEN HAAG
Utrecht
Zutphen
Rotterdam Arnhem
Rhein Nijmegen
HOLLAND
Breda
Tilburg
Vlissingen
Oostende
Nieuwpoort
Gent
Antwerpen
Coutrai Aerschot
Ypres Oudenarde
Halle BRUXELLES St. Truiden
Tournai Maastricht
Mons Liege
BELGIUM
Namur
Charleroi
Marche St. Vith
Bastogne
LUXEMBOURG
Luxembourg

0   10 20 30 40 50
Miles

Belgium

The Ardennes (A***)

Date: 16 December 1944–1 February 1945.

Location: From Marche take Route 4 (E 40) to Bastogne; thence Route 28 to St. Vith. **22.**

War and campaign: The Second World War: North-west Europe Campaign, 1944–5 (see p. 197).

Object of the action: The Germans were making a desperate bid to reach Antwerp, isolate 21st Army Group and thereafter induce Great Britain and the U.S.A. to offer a negotiated peace.

Opposing sides: (a) General Eisenhower, Supreme Commander Allied Powers Europe. (b) Field-Marshal von Runstedt, Supreme Commander West.

Forces engaged: (a) Allies: 18 infantry divisions; 7 armoured divisions (1,100 tanks); 2 airborne divisions (U.S. 1st and 3rd Armies). *Total*: 400,000. (b) Germans: 14 infantry divisions; 9 Panzer divisions (1,000 tanks) (6th S.S. Panzer Army, 5th Panzer and 7th Armies). *Total*: 250,000.

Casualties: (a) 77,000 men; 733 tanks. (b) 90,000 men; 600 tanks.

Result: Complete defeat of Hitler's 'final gamble' and the restoration of the American front, but it delayed the Allies from reaching the Rhine for six weeks.

Nearby accommodation: Luxemburg or Namur.

Suggested reading: General Works: Wilmot, C., *The Struggle for Europe*, London, 1952. Bradley, O., *A Soldier's Story*, London, 1949. Eisenhower, D. D., *Crusade in Europe*, London, 1948. von Manteuffel, H., 'The Fatal Decisions', (Part VI), London, 1956. Biography: Wellard, J., *The Man in the Helmet*, London, 1947

Throughout November 1944 Eisenhower continued his efforts to close with the Rhine on a broad front. The 80-mile Ardennes sector was thinly held by the U.S. 8th Corps consisting of 2 veteran divisions, 2 fledgling divisions and an inexperienced armoured division. Bradley later described this as 'a calculated risk'.

In fact Allied intelligence with regard to German intentions and resources was surprisingly bad. It was accepted that the Germans lacked fuel for an offensive and that von Runstedt was unlikely to consider the narrow winding roads and involved country of the Ardennes in the mists and snow of winter as a promising line of advance. As early as the first week of November, however, Hitler had decided to stake everything on a counter-offensive here to restore German morale and give him the respite he needed to transfer reserves later to the Russian front. He hoped thus to secure a negoti-ated peace or win time to put his new weapons into action.

The plan aimed at the capture of Antwerp and the destruction of the Allied armies north of the Ardennes. It was to be carried out by the strategic reserve—the 5th and 6th S.S. Panzer Armies. On the right the 6th S.S. Panzer Army under Sepp Dietrich, consisting of 4 Panzer and 5 infantry divisions, was to cross the Meuse on either side of Liège and make for Antwerp. On the left the 5th Panzer Army under von Manteuffel, crossing the Meuse between west of Liège and Namur, was to head for Brussels. The 7th Army was to protect the southern flank. The infantry divisions with heavy artillery support were to make the initial attack. The armour was then to drive through, heading due west without a pause straight for the Meuse. Strongly held villages and defensive positions were to be by-passed. The plan included two further novel features: the dropping of a parachute unit to block the roads north of the Ardennes; and Skorzeny's force, equipped with captured American vehicles and including English-speaking volunteers in American uni-form, which was to pass through the advance guards and seize the Meuse bridges.

The preparations were carried out in extreme secrecy. The assaulting divisions were assembled behind the Aachen front to create the impression that they were to be fed into the battle there. Headquarters were given deceptive signs. Panzer officers were even dressed as infantry. Night fighters were flown overhead to drown the noise of the move up of the artillery. Newly arrived divisions were marched north and east in daylight and then doubled back on their tracks at night. Non-German soldiers were evacuated from the front line. Full advantage was taken of the long hours of darkness.

The Germans waited for a period of bad weather. Low cloud on 12 December and for the next week hampered Allied air reconnaissance. Then at 0530 hours on 16 December 14 infantry divisions supported by 2,000 guns advanced through the mist against the thinly held American line. In

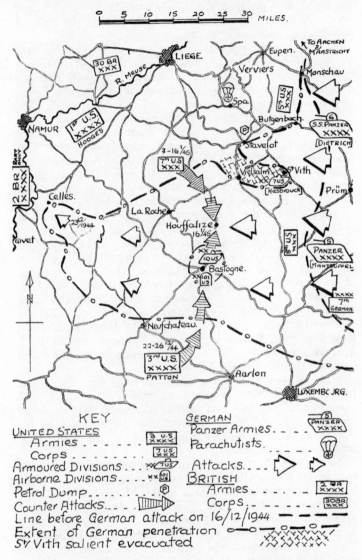

the extreme north, between Monschau and Butgendach, the 6th S.S. Panzer Army struck firm resistance by two divisions of the U.S. 5th Corps. Dietrich, selected to command on account of his bravery and loyalty to Hitler, soon found himself faced by a task beyond his ability. One of his armoured groups, however, Task Force Pieper, nearly got through to the big American petrol dump at Stavelot. It was south of Butgendach

3

where the collapse occurred. Here, von Manteuffel's 5th Panzer Army swamped the widely extended U.S. 28th and 106th Divisions and, moving-on that night by the light of searchlights, continued the breakthrough.

American confusion was immediate and impressive. Late on the 16th Eisenhower and Bradley had only received fragmentary reports. Bradley considered it a spoiling attack designed to forestall Patton's offensive in the south. Eisenhower took a more realist view and ordered the 7th U.S. Armoured Division from the 9th Army in the north and the 11th U.S. Armoured Division from the south into the Ardennes. That night German paratroops, landing near Spa, produced something like paralysis behind the American lines. Late on 17 December the 7th U.S. Armoured Division, under Brigadier-General Hasbrouck, occupied the important road junction at St. Vith. Here it blocked Dietrich till the 23rd. It was not till the evening of the 17th that Eisenhower ordered forward the celebrated 82nd and 101st Airborne Divisions from his theatre reserve. By this time von Manteuffel's 3 leading Panzer divisions were within 15 miles of the key road centre of Bastogne. The first American troops to reach this place were a battle group of the 10th U.S. Armoured Division on the evening of the 18th. The 101st Airborne Division in a lightning move of 100 miles by road arrived there during the night. At dawn on the 19th Bayerlein, with Panzer Lehr, found Bastogne strongly held. Von Manteuffel therefore decided to encircle the place and continue the drive to the Meuse.

With Dietrich halted and von Manteuffel with the ball at his feet, Model now proposed to reinforce the latter with Dietrich's 2 uncommitted panzer divisions. Hitler would not agree. He wished the decisive blow to be struck by the S.S. divisions on Dietrich's front and not by the Wehrmacht under von Manteuffel.

Meanwhile Montgomery, thoroughly informed of the situation by his liaison officers, had on his own initiative switched his 30th Corps to the west bank of the Meuse between Liège and Namur. Here with 3 battle-hardened divisions, 1 armoured division and 3 armoured brigades, admirable lateral communications and the best tank going in Belgium, he viewed the prospect of a German irruption over the Meuse with an equanimity which his American colleagues did not share. At his headquarters at Luxembourg Bradley was completely out of touch with the situation. It was left to Eisenhower to rise to the level of events. Meeting Bradley, Patton and Devers at Verdun on the 19th, he placed all American troops north of the line Givet–Houffalize–Prum under Montgomery's command and ordered Patton to swing his army north towards Bastogne. Patton's drive got going on the 22nd.

On the following day the spearhead of the 5th Panzer Army got to within 4 miles of the Meuse near Celles. The sky now cleared and the Allied Air Forces were once again able to intervene. Immobilised for lack of petrol, the Germans failed to make further progress. Here the battle ended on 26 December when the U.S. 2nd Armoured Division crushed the 2nd Panzer Division at Celles. Late on the same day Patton's 4th Armoured Division punched a narrow corridor into Bastogne. Throughout the next week the Germans made an all-out effort to take Bastogne and its corridor but Patton, thrusting in newly arrived divisions straight into battle and aided by the 19th Tactical Air Force under abominable flying conditions, held his ground.

In the north Montgomery proceeded to tidy up the front and restore balance, despite American objections, by evacuating the St. Vith salient and withdrawing the U.S. 7th Corps into reserve to reorganise for the counter-offensive. This went in on 3 January. By this time much of the 6th S.S. Panzer Army's strength had been dissipated at Bastogne. Driving through bitter German opposition, storms and waist-deep snow, the U.S. 7th Corps cut the vital La Roche–Vielsalm road on the 7th. Next day Hitler, no longer able to deny that most of his surviving armour was in danger of being trapped between Montgomery's and Patton's thrusts, authorised Model to give up the area west of Houffalize. The Germans waged a fighting retreat, but on 16 January the U.S. 2nd and 11th Armoured Divisions linked up at Houffalize and re-established a solid front. It was not till the end of January, however, that the last Germans were driven out of the Ardennes.

Unquestionably, Eisenhower's decision at the crisis to place the northern armies under Montgomery and to send the 101st Airborne Division to Bastogne saved the day. In abandoning the St. Vith salient and creating a reserve before turning to the counter-offensive, Montgomery showed a grasp of the situation superior to that of his American colleagues. Time was needed to regroup, reorganise and make the necessary administrative preparation. Once the skies cleared and the Air Arm could come into its own the issue was never in doubt.

H.E.

Courtrai (B**)

Date: 11 July 1302.

Location: Courtrai is 27 miles south-west of Ghent (Route 14 (E 3)) The battlefield lies near the Groeninghebeke stream. 14.

War and campaign: Flemish Revolt against the French (see p. 194)

5

Object of the action: The French were trying to relieve their garrison in the town.

Opposing sides: (a) Guy of Namur and William of Juliers leading the Flemish insurgents. (b) The Count of Artois commanding the French army.

Forces engaged: (a) Flemings: details uncertain, but mostly pikemen. *Total*: perhaps 12,000. (b) French: details uncertain, but a large number mounted. *Total*: perhaps 15,000.

Casualties: (a) Uncertain, but not heavy. (b) 63 nobles; 700 knights.

Result: Defeat of the French expedition.

Nearby accommodation: Courtrai or Menin.

Suggested reading: General Work: Van der Linden, H., *Belgium: The Making of a Nation*, Oxford, 1920. On the Battle: Oman, C. W. C., *A History of the Art of War in the Middle Ages*, Vol. II (2nd Edn.), London, 1924.

In May 1302 the Flemings arose in revolt against King Philip of France, who had imprisoned their Count and annexed his lands. Courtrai was one of the few towns the French succeeded in retaining. The Flemish army fell back to Courtrai when Count Robert of Artois invaded the country with a royal French army, composed of the feudal array of north France, Italian mercenaries and Gascon javelin soldiers.

Behind the Groeninghebeke outside Courtrai the Flemish army under a son of the Count, Guy of Namur, and William of Juliers his cousin, stood ready for battle. The Flemings were armed mainly with pikes, which they relied upon to hold off the French cavalry. They were arrayed in a long tightly packed phalanx, with a small reserve under John van Remesse behind and another 1,200 men still farther to the rear on guard in case the French garrison in Courtrai sallied forth.

On the morning of 11 July, after an exchange of cross-bow fire across the stream, Robert of Artois ordered his cavalry to charge at the Flemings. The three lines of men-at-arms were thrown into disorder by their own infantry as they reached the brook. The marshy ground on both sides of the stream caused the 10 squadrons of heavily armoured men even more trouble. Before they could form ranks again the Flemish phalanx advanced, pikes levelled, and thrust them back. The main force of French cavalry fared no better against the pikemen, who presented them with an unbroken front. Van Remesse reinforced the Flemish centre with his pikemen, and the French third line and infantry were unwilling to renew the conflict. Artois lost his life along with large numbers of his cavalrymen.

The battle is more important from the military than the political point of view, for it demonstrated that determined pikemen were more than a match for unsupported cavalry. It represented the first major victory of infantry over mounted warriors since Adrianople, 1,000 years before.

J.E.A.

Flanders (B****)

Date: Continuous fighting, 1914–18.

Location: The battlefield extends from Nieuport (Belgium) to Vimy (north France); the most famous area is around Ypres. **13.**

War and campaign: The First World War; the Campaigns on the Western Front (see p. 197).

Object of the action: Continuous Allied and German attempts to achieve a breakthrough towards Berlin or Paris respectively, and thus to solve the impasse of the trench war.

Opposing sides: (*a*) The British, French and Belgian armies. (*b*) The German army.

Forces engaged: Several million men on each side.

Casualties: Several millions, details incalculable.

Result: Little ground won or lost by either side, but the battle of attrition fought along the front contributed largely to Germany's final collapse.

Nearby accommodation: Ypres, Lille or Nieuport.

Suggested reading: General Work: Cruttwell, C. M. F., *A History of the Great War*, Oxford, 1936. On the Campaigns: Edmonds, J. E.(ed.), *Military Operations, France and Belgium*, London, 1922–39. On the Campaigns: Mottram, R. H., *Through the Menin Gate*, London, 1932. Wolf, L., *In Flanders Fields*, London, 1959.

At the end of the German retreat from the Marne in the autumn of 1914 their open flank came to rest upon the sea at Nieuport, just within the borders of the Flemish province of West Flanders. Held there by Belgian inundation of the estuary of the Yser, the line they established ran south-eastwards into France, passing in front of Ypres, between Lille and Armentières, through the mining villages around Lens to the edge of the Artois uplands at Vimy. Between Dixmude and the sea the line was held throughout the war by the Belgian army, but the sector around Ypres and southwards was from the first essentially and memorably British. Most of the place-names along this line are ominously familiar to British ears and it is possible to note only the more important. The battles for the Ypres ridges are the most notorious. In November 1914, May 1915, July–November 1917 and April 1918 there was bitter fighting for their possession. In the First Battle of Ypres the old British regular army held a foothold upon them in the face of ferocious assaults. In the Second the Germans employed gas for the first time in war and caused a temporary panic but, surprised by the extent of their own success, were unprepared to consolidate it. The Third Battle, better known as Passchendaele, is one of the half-dozen great battles of the Western Front, during which the British army suffered over 200,000 casualties for negligible territorial gains. The German offensive of April 1918 extinguished them completely and they were recovered only in the general advance of the autumn. Other significant battles are those of Neuve Chapelle (May 1915) and Loos (September 1915), both inconclusive but costly assaults, and Messines (June 1917), a classic limited offensive preceded by mine explosions so large that the contours of Messines ridge were permanently altered.

A tour of the battlefield is still a poignantly moving experience for the British visitor. The 60,000 names of the unfound dead of the Ypres salient recorded on the New Menin Gate and the numerous and enormous cemeteries are an almost unbearable reminder of the sufferings of the British and Commonwealth armies in Flanders between 1914 and 1918.

J.D.P.K.

FLEURUS (C**); battle of, 1 July 1690; 7 miles north of Charleroi; **20**: War of the League of Augsburg. A French army under Marshal Luxembourg signally defeated the Dutch and German army of the Prince of Waldeck, inflicting 14,000 casualties and taking 49 guns. See Spaulding, Nickerson and Wright, *Warfare*, New York, 1925.

Fontenoy (B****)

Date: 11 May 1745.

Location: Five miles south-east of Tournai, turn left at Antoing from the Mons road (Route 61). **18**.

War and campaign: The War of the Austrian Succession; Netherlands Campaign of 1745 (see p. 195).

Object of the action: The Allied army was attempting to interrupt the French siege of Tournai.

Opposing sides: (*a*) The Duke of Cumberland commanding the Anglo-Dutch-Austrian army. (*b*) Marshal de Saxe (accompanied by Louis XV) commanding the French.

Forces engaged: Allies: 56 battalions; 87 squadrons; about 80 cannon. *Total*: 53,000. (*b*) French: 93 battalions; 146 squadrons; perhaps 70 guns. *Total*: 70,000. (N.B. Of these forces 27 battalions and 17 squadrons were before Tournai.)

Casualties: (a) Possibly 7,000 Allies. (b) Possibly 7,000 French.

Result: A hard-fought victory for the French leading to the conquest of much of the Austrian Netherlands (Belgium).

Nearby accommodation: Tournai.

Suggested reading: General Works: Fortescue, J. W., *A History of the British Army*, Vol. II, London, 1910. Colin, J., *Campagnes de Maurice de Saxe*, Paris, 1901–6. Biography: Whitworth, R., *Field-Marshal Lord Ligonier*, Oxford, 1958. Biography: White, J. M., *Marshal of France; the Life and Times of Marshal de Saxe*, London, 1962. On the Battle: Skrine, F. H., *Fontenoy and the War of Austrian Succession*, Edinburgh and London, 1906.

The Battle of Fontenoy is notable on several accounts. For the French it is the masterpiece of the Marshal de Saxe, and a victory with wide strategic consequences. The British have long recalled the stout-heartedness of the infantry, and look back with no less pride on the dash and sacrifice of their opponents in the Irish Brigade in the service of France.

In the spring of 1745 the commanders of the Allied army in the Austrian Netherlands rejected the project of the British general Ligonier for a thrust into France, and merely waited upon events. So it was that the initiative was left entirely to the French, whose commander was not a man likely to neglect such an opportunity; the Marshal de Saxe had already achieved a considerable reputation, both as military thinker and rake of prodigious powers, and in April 1745 he directed a feint north-east towards Mons, and then pounced with his powerful army upon the fortress of Tournai and sealed up the unsuspecting garrison.

At Brussels the Allies were taken aback at the news that de Saxe was on the move, and still more so when they later heard that the gateway to western Flanders was as good as within his grasp. They accordingly marched south and then west by circuitous and ill-directed marches, largely under the impression of the feint on Mons, and thus gave de Saxe ample time to prepare a position where he would be all too delighted to receive them.

Leaving a force to contain Tournai, de Saxe arrayed the rest of his army in a carefully chosen defensive line 5 miles to the south-east of the fortress. In outline the French position was a sharp salient extending eastwards from the Scheldt at Antoing for just over a mile to the apex at the hamlet of Fontenoy, and then turning at right angles north to the Wood of Barry and the village of Ramecroix. Both flanks were securely anchored—the one on a river and the other on a wood—but de Saxe improved this strong position still further by studding it with redoubts of his own devising: these were compact earthworks furnished with artillery, which could

9

direct a heavy fire against an enemy advancing from the front or around the flank, and yet leave the French troops wide gaps through which they could launch their own attacks—a decided improvement upon Villars' entrenchments at Malplaquet (q.v.). Three such redoubts were thrown up on the French right wing between Antoing and Fontenoy, and a further battery was cunningly ensconced on the far bank of the Scheldt.

FONTENOY *11th May 1745*

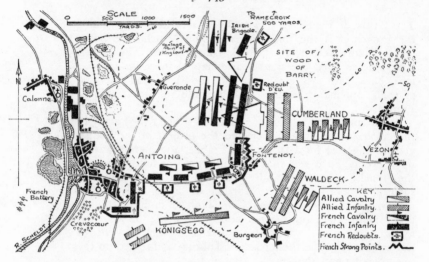

To the left of his line, however, de Saxe devoted his greatest attention, for here he expected the assault of the British, whom he accounted the most formidable troops of the Allied army. On his far left he lined the Wood of Barry with sharpshooters, and constructed two redoubts on the fringes of the wood: the southernmost of these earthworks became famous as the Redoubt d'Eu. Two lines of infantry, supported by two further lines of cavalry, were disposed behind a sunken road leading northwards from Fontenoy across a low plateau in the direction of Ramecroix: the French troops would be out of sight of the enemy until the last moment, and to get this far the Allies would have had to cross the natural glacis formed by the gentle and open eastern slopes of the plateau. A reserve of fine troops, including the 6 regiments of the Irish Brigade, was placed behind the Wood of Barry, and Fontenoy itself was converted into a miniature fortress.

The Allied plan of attack for 11 May was clear and simple, but based upon a faulty reconnaissance undertaken the day before. The Austrians and Dutch were to tackle the French right between Antoing and Fontenoy, while the British were to press home their assault against the apparently clear ground between Fontenoy and the Wood of Barry. The advance in the early hours of the 11th had already begun when Cumberland learnt for the first time of the existence of the Redoubt d'Eu. The strength of the flanks of the French left was only now appreciated, and their clearing became a matter of the greatest importance. The Dutch assault against Fontenoy was, however, thrown back by a murderous fire, as were the attacks of the Austrians and of the rest of the Dutch against the French right; no less fatally, the muddles and delays of Brigadier Ingoldsby prevented a detached command of British and Hanoverians from carrying the Redoubt d'Eu. The continued resistance of these two strongpoints was a thorn in the side of the British for the remainder of the battle.

Meanwhile the British cavalry had completed its passage of the broken country around Vezon, and at about 6 am it deployed in the plain beyond in full view of the French gunners, who began to rain down shot on the motionless squadrons. The cavalry endured its torture until Ligonier brought the British infantry through the intervals, and arrayed the foot in two lines in front. At last, at 10.30, Cumberland took the head of the beautifully dressed lines, and led them to the beat of drum against the plateau. Neither a destructive artillery fire, nor the first volley of the French infantry were able to break or hasten the steady controlled pace of the British, and the depleted redcoats finally delivered one appalling blast of fire which reduced the French lines to a shambles.

The two British lines pressed on into the French camp, gradually coalescing under the effect of the enemy fire into one monstrous column against which even the Maison du Roi and the Irish regiment of Dillon threw themselves to no purpose. A renewed Dutch assault on Fontenoy having failed, the British withdrew to the crest of the ridge to reform, and then came on again. The French gunners were in a frenzy, loading their pieces with stones and glass when their grape-shot was exhausted, and now that the crisis of the day had come de Saxe did not hesitate to commit his last reserves to the fight: the 5 remaining regiments of the Irish Brigade charged yelling against the British right, while a number of line regiments and the French and Swiss Guards closed in on the left. Early in the afternoon Cumberland had to order his drummers to beat out the order to fall back. The British accomplished their retreat in admirable order, the rearguard facing about at measured intervals to drive away the pursuers.

The Battle of Fontenoy had established the clear superiority of the French in force and high command, and September found the Allies in the north of Belgium, concerned only with preserving their communications with Antwerp. Tournai, Nieuport, Ostend, Bruges and Ghent: all had fallen to de Saxe, and with the outbreak of the Jacobite rebellion the British were forced to look for a time to their own defences.

C. J. D.

Laffeldt (C***)

Date: 2 July 1747.

Location: Immediately south-west of Maastricht on the Belgo-Dutch frontier, between the rivers Jaar and Demer. **8.**

War and campaign: The War of the Austrian Succession; Netherlands' Campaign of 1747 (see p. 196).

Object of the action: Cumberland was seeking to regain territory lost in the Netherlands.

Opposing sides: (a) Marshal de Saxe in command of a French army. (b) The Duke of Cumberland commanding an Allied army.

Forces engaged: (a) Approx. 120,000 French. (b) Approx. 90,000 Allies.

Casualties: (a) 14,000 French killed and wounded.
(b) Nearly 6,000 Allies (including 2,000 British); Lord Ligonier was captured.

Result: An extremely costly victory for de Saxe. Stalemate ensued on the Meuse for the rest of the year, but the French detached a force which took Bergen-op-Zoom.

Nearby accommodation: Maastricht.

Suggested reading: As for Rocoux (see p. 000).

In 1747 Cumberland sought to inflict a decisive defeat on the French, as a means of recovering the territory lost in the Netherlands in the year before. The isolation of the corps of the Prince de Clermont seemed to offer the desired opportunity, but de Saxe hurried down from the west to join his subordinate, and a clash between the two main armies became inevitable. The Allies held an extended position facing south, and just as at Rocoux, de Saxe skilfully concentrated his forces for a heavy blow against the enemy left. The British infantry, however, distinguished themselves as well as in any other battle of the century, and the French had to make four attacks before they could win the village of Laffeldt. The field was lost for Cumberland, but a suicidal charge of three British cavalry regiments, led by Lord Ligonier, enabled the Allies to retreat in good order.

C.J.D.

LANDEN (D**); battle of, 28 July 1693; 7 miles south-west of
St. Truiden; **11**; War of the League of Augsburg. King William
III (50,000) offered battle to the French Marshal Luxembourg
(80,000) but over-extended his front and eventually the weak
point was penetrated by the superior French cavalry. See
Renier, G. J., *William of Orange*, London, 1932.

Malplaquet (B***)

Date: 11 September 1709.

Location: The actual battlefield lies exactly on the Franco-Belgian
border, 10 miles south of Mons. **21**. Malplaquet village itself is in
France, but Aulnois lies in Belgium.

War and campaign: The War of the Spanish Succession: Netherlands Campaign of 1709 (see p. 195).

Object of the action: The Allies hoped to crush Marshal Villars
and the last large French army and thus open the road to Paris.

Opposing sides: (*a*) The Duke of Marlborough and Prince
Eugene leading the Allies. (*b*) Marshals Villars and Boufflers at
the head of the French army.

Forces engaged: (*a*) Allies: 128 battalions; 253 squadrons; 100
guns. *Total*: 110,000. (*b*) French: 96 battalions; 180 squadrons;
60 guns. *Total*: 80,000.

Casualties: (*a*) 24,000 killed and wounded. (*b*) 12,000 killed and
wounded.

Result: A technical victory for the forces of the Grand Alliance
leading to the capture of Mons; its most lasting effects, however,
were to rally French national morale and damage Marlborough's
reputation in England.

Nearby accommodation: Mons.

Suggested reading: See Oudenarde (p. 18). On the Battle:
Belloc, H., *Malplaquet*, London, 1911. Sautai, M., *La Bataille
de Malplaquet*, Paris, 1904. Article: Bowen, H. G., 'The Dutch
at Malplaquet', *Journal for S.A.H.R.*, March 1962. Work of Fiction
(on the period): Sterne, L., *Tristram Shandy*, London, 1760-5
(and many more recent editions).

The Battle of Malplaquet was the last major battle jointly
fought by Marlborough and Prince Eugene and was by no
means their best action. In the spring of 1709 it had appeared
that nothing could save France from defeat, but the so-called
victory of Malplaquet did little to secure final victory for the
Grand Alliance.

After the fall of Tournai on 5 September, only the city of
Mons lay between the Allies and the road to Paris. Louis XIV
ordered Marshal Villars to take any risk to save the fortress,

and sent the ancient hero, Marshal Boufflers, to join France's last army in a desperate bid to avert national disaster.

Villars set out to court battle—but, mindful of his great inferiority of numbers, selected a strong position north of the village of Malplaquet for his stand. He placed his flanks in two woods and fortified the gap dividing them, keeping all his cavalry in reserve. There he awaited the Allied onslaught.

Marlborough and Eugene advanced their armies from the direction of Mons, confident of their ability to destroy Villars at their leisure. The plan they adopted was hardly subtle: a series of massed attacks against the French flanks in the woods might induce Villars to weaken his centre, through which the Allied cavalry would charge to deliver the *coup de grâce*. On the morning of the 11th the preliminary attacks were launched at 8 am, but for several hours very little progress was made owing to the difficulty of the terrain and the gallantry of the French. The Allied right suffered heavy casualties penetrating Taisnières wood, while on the left the Prince of Orange's heedless attacks from Aulnois against Boufflers were decimated by a cunningly sited French battery which enfiladed the advancing Dutch troops. Shortly after midday, however, a small body of Allied cavalry appeared on the extreme French left near La Folie after passing round the forest, and this development led Villars to weaken his centre exactly as Marlborough had hoped. By 1 pm Orkney's 19 battalions had taken possession of the undefended redoubts in the French centre, and the full splendour of the Allied cavalry—30,000 strong—swept through the entrenchments to engage the French horsemen drawn up beyond. A tremendous mêlée developed, during which Villars was himself wounded, but the Allies were too weary to clinch their victory. Consequently Marshal Boufflers was able to withdraw the bulk of the French army in excellent order.

Allied casualties were horrific—25 per cent of their effective strength was laid low—but the French had fared far better. Both sides claimed a victory, but the long-term advantages favoured the French cause. The near-success rallied French morale whilst Marlborough's political foes used the casualty figures to weaken his position.

D.G.C.

Mons (and *Le Cateau* and the *Marne*) (B****)

Date: 23 August–8 September 1914.

Location: The initial action was fought along the banks of the Mons–

Condé Canal, but the final crisis took place 100 miles to the south on the River Marne. **19.**

War and campaign: The First World War; Flanders Campaign of 1914 (see p. 197).

Object of the action: The German army was attempting to break through the left flank of the Allied armies and envelop them.

Opposing sides: (*a*) Sir John French commanding the B.E.F. and Marshal Joffre leading the French. (*b*) 1st and 2nd German Armies under von Kluck and von Bulow.

Forces engaged: (*a*) 100,000 men of the B.E.F.; 400,000 French troops. *Total*: c. 500,000. (*b*) 1st and 2nd German Armies. *Total*: c. 600,000.

Casualties: (a) B.E.F. approximately 15,000, (1,600 at Mons). (*b*) Not accurately known.

Result: The final result was a victory for the Allies as the Germans were forced back to the river Aisne.

Nearby accommodation: Mons.

Suggested reading: General Work: Cruttwell, C. R. M. F., *A History of the Great War*, Oxford, 1936. On the Campaign: Churchill, W. S., *The World Crisis*, Vol. I, London, 1923. On the Battle: Terraine, J., *Mons*, London, 1960. Asprey, R. B., *The First Battle of the Marne*, London, 1962.

The Battle of Mons has perhaps become more famous than it deserves, but the individual glory gained there cannot be questioned as it is substantiated by the large number of V.C.s awarded.

The B.E.F. under Sir John French had taken up a position on the left of the French army—having concentrated at Maubeuge. With them it proposed to advance against Germany in accordance with the French Plan 17. When Belgium was violated the British on the exposed left met the full force of the strong German right wing in the form of the 1st German Army under von Kluck. Luckily the leading corps of von Kluck's army were scattered, and the force which met the British 2nd Corps at Mons was less strong than it might have been, or, in fact, than it is sometimes made out to be.

The region which contains the battlefield of Mons is an unattractive one, consisting of an almost continuous built-up area stretching some 16 miles to the west of Mons bisected by the Mons–Condé canal. The canal running straight on an east–west line marked the front along which the B.E.F. was mainly engaged on 23 August. The canal, about 7 feet deep with an average width of 64 feet, was crossed by 18 bridges in its length of 16 miles. The bridges shaped the fighting.

General Smith-Dorrien's 2nd Corps, covering the long front

of 21 miles, lined the canal. The 5th Division under General Fergusson held the canal line to the west of Mons, and some of the regiments who fought so well there were the Duke of Cornwall's Light Infantry, the West Kents, the Northumberland Fusiliers and the Royal Scots Fusiliers. The 3rd Division under General Hamilton held the right of the front, including the town of Mons and the awkward salient which the canal made to the north-east of it. Here the Royal Fusiliers, the Middlesex and the Royal Irish distinguished themselves. General Haig's 1st Corps, facing almost east, covered the right flank of the 2nd Corps with the 5th Cavalry Brigade. The rest of General Allenby's cavalry division was behind the 5th Division.

It was a curious battle. Sir John French, the British Commander-in-Chief, was away when it started and played no part when he returned. General von Kluck seemed to have exercised little control, permitting his army corps to stumble into the British army one by one as they arrived with no co-ordination of their activities at all.

The British dug in among the houses and slag heaps covering the bridges, and it was the infantry's shooting which dominated the day. The Germans advanced in solid blocks, making easy targets, but the British suffered from the massed German artillery fire. The British rifle fire was so accurate and deadly that the Germans were convinced that the British had brought into action great numbers of machine guns.

The crux of the battle lay in the salient. Here the enemy crossed the canal in force and enveloped the Middlesex, and both the Middlesex and the Royal Irish supporting them had to withdraw covered by the Gordons on their right. The Royal Fusiliers, too, had to be withdrawn after gallant fighting in defence of the Mons' bridges which won them two V.C.s.

The whole British line to the left also began its withdrawal west of Mons. Here the Sappers won two V.C.s for gallant persistence in blowing bridges.

After withdrawing to a better position 2 or 3 miles south of the canal, a general retreat from Mons began covered by cavalry actions by the 9th Lancers and 4th Dragoon Guards, and well-organised rearguard actions with excellent support from the Royal Artillery.

The casualties at Mons as finally estimated were 1,600 killed, wounded and missing, and 2 guns abandoned. Almost half the casualties were sustained by two battalions: the Middlesex with over 400, and the Royal Irish with over 300. The casualties in the 1st Corp were only 40. Mons was entirely a 2nd Corps battle.

Three days later at Le Cateau the 2nd Corps fought another celebrated battle after they had become separated by the Forest of Morny from the 1st Corps.

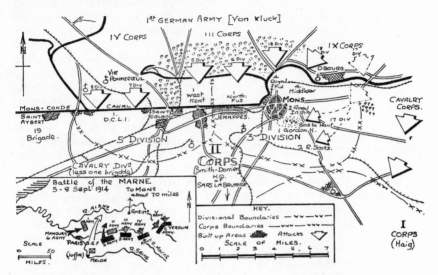

Le Cateau followed the pattern of Mons, but this time the field of battle lay on open rolling country with few obstacles and less cover for the British fighting their rearguard action. Again the enemy penetration came on the British right, this time round the town of Le Cateau itself and up the valley of the Selle. The main feature on the Allied side was the very close support given to the infantry by the Royal Field Artillery which was right up alongside them, in many instances firing over open sights and at almost point-blank ranges. Many of the honours of the battle went to the gunners who manned their weapons to the last and then took them away in the face of the enemy.

The losses at Le Cateau were more serious than at Mons, and are estimated at 7,800 men and 38 guns.

After this, rapid retreat alone saved the B.E.F. of 70,000 men under Sir John French and the French 5th Army under General Lanrezac from destruction. An unhappy lack of co-operation between General French and Lanrezac seemed likely to make disaster more certain until Lord Kitchener, the Secretary of State for War, visited France and put things on a better footing.

The French Rhine offensive had failed, and everywhere their armies fell back. In the west the German armies now pressed on towards Paris. It appeared as if the Germans must be successful when there occurred what came to be known as the 'Miracle of the Marne'. Winston Churchill says of it: 'One must suppose upon the whole that the Marne was the greatest battle ever fought in the world . . . but it was less like any other battle ever fought. Comparatively few were killed or wounded, and no great recognisable feat of arms, and no shock proportionate to the event can be discerned.' To begin with the Russians had mobilised quicker than had been expected, and, to relieve the pressure on France, had invaded East Prussia. The Germans withdrew two corps from their right wing in the west to meet this danger, and thus weakened their forces at a critical moment. Then von Kluck swung south-east. Joffre, in the meantime, by a clever appreciation of strategy, built up a new 6th Army on the west of Paris under General Manoury, which, supported by General Galliéni, governor of Paris, struck at the German right flank. To meet this von Kluck drew forces from his centre and left, and created a 30-mile gap, filled only by cavalry, between him and von Bulow's 2nd German Army on his left.

It was into this gap that the B.E.F. and some French forces pushed forward. The B.E.F. advanced none too vigorously into the vitals of the German right wing; but the British were the only army to cross the Marne before the German retreat; the only Allied force which advanced continuously throughout the four days from 5 to the 8 of September; and because of it the Germans found it necessary to retreat from the River Marne, and they found no secure resting-place till they reached the northern side of the river Aisne. Paris was safe.

J.M.S.

OSTEND (B**); siege of, 1601–4; **9**; 80 Years' War (or Dutch Revolt against Spain). The garrison defied all attempts to take the town for three years, inflicting perhaps 70,000 casualties on the Spanish besiegers; only when the famed General Spinola took charge were the Dutch compelled to capitulate. See Campaign Chronology, p. 194, and Geyl, P., *The Netherlands Revolt*, London, 1947.

Oudenarde (A***)

Date: 11 July 1708.

Location: The town lies on the river Scheldt, 19 miles south-west of Ghent (Route Nationale 58) and 37 miles west of Brussels (Route Nationale 9). **10**. The battlefield area lies north of the town.

War and campaign: The War of the Spanish Succession; Netherlands Campaign of 1708 (see p.195).

Object of the action: Marlborough was trying to regain the territorial losses of early 1708 by forcing action on the French army.

Opposing sides: (a) The Duke of Marlborough and Prince Eugene leading the Allied army. (b) Marshal Vendôme and the Duke of Burgundy commanding the French.

Forces engaged: (a) Allies: 85 battalions; 150 squadrons. *Total*: 80,000. (b) French: 90 battalions; 170 squadrons. *Total*: 85,000.

Casualties: (a) 4,000 Allied killed and wounded. (b) 15,000 French casualties, including some 9,000 prisoners.

Result: A heavy defeat for the French which ultimately led to the Allied recapture of Ghent and Bruges and the fall of Lille.

Nearby accommodation: Oudenarde.

Suggested reading: General Works: Churchill, W. S., *Marlborough, His Life and Times*, Book II, London, 1947. Atkinson, C. T., *Marlborough and the Rise of the British Army*, London, 1921. Article: Atkinson, C. T., 'Oudenarde—the missing order of battle', *Journal of the S.A.H.R.*, 1924. Work of Fiction (on the period): Thackeray, W. M., *The History of Henry Esmond*, London, 1852.

The Battle of Oudenarde came in the nick of time to rally the morale of the Grand Alliance after a series of disasters which lasted throughout 1707 and into the early months of 1708. The Duke of Marlborough was extremely despondent about the general situation until he was joined by Prince Eugene (though not the Imperial Army) on 9 July at Aasche. Heartened by the Prince's robust confidence, Marlborough devised a bold plan to defeat Vendôme's army as it prepared to besiege Oudenarde. On the night of 10 July the Anglo-Dutch army made a forced march to surprise the French.

The ensuing battle was more a contact action than a set-piece engagement and in this lies much of its modern interest. Marlborough took a great risk when he ordered the main body of the army to follow Cadogan's advance guard over the Scheldt at a point half-way between the town and the French forces drawing up behind the River Norken, but the gamble succeeded. At first the French were too surprised to react, and the Duke profited from their inaction to hurry fresh battalions over the pontoon bridges. He was further aided by dissension between the two French commanders—Vendôme and Burgundy—which resulted in half their army being kept out of the battle; this gave Marlborough just enough time to reinforce Cadogan sufficiently and enable him to hold his own against first General Biron and thereafter Vendôme in person. A bitter and fluctuating struggle developed around the villages of Eyne, Heurne and Groenewald which lasted from 3 pm to nightfall, but the Duke was always at hand with fresh units to extend the Allied battle line as new French formations came into action. Command of the crucial right flank and centre was entrusted to Prince Eugene.

Marshal Vendôme, infuriated by Burgundy's intransigence, forgot his rôle of commander-in-chief and plunged into the fighting, pike in hand. Judging the moment for victory to be close, Marlborough sent General Overkirk and the young Prince of Orange on a long detour through Oudenarde to the Boser Couter high ground. This move through dead ground went unnoticed by the French right and centre, who suddenly found themselves assailed in flank and rear by the Dutch and Danish troops, whilst Eugene launched a desperate charge against their left. By 8 pm almost half the French army was virtually surrounded, but Marlborough was forced to call a halt as dusk deepened into night, and many of Vendôme's men escaped through a gap in the encircling troops. Nevertheless, the result was a notable victory which once again shattered French morale and eventually led to the recapture of Ghent and Bruges and to the fall of Lille, the second city of France.

D.G.C.

Ramillies (A****)

Date: 23 May 1706.

Location: From Namur follow Route Nationale 22: the village of Ramillies-Offus lies 4 miles beyond Eghezée. **17.** This formed the centre of the French position.

War and campaign: The War of the Spanish Succession; Netherlands Campaign of 1706 (see p. 195).

Object of the action: Marlborough was undertaking the conquest of the Spanish Netherlands.

Opposing sides: (a) The Duke of Marlborough commanding the Allied army. (b) Marshal Villeroi in command of the French army.

Forces engaged: (a) Allies: 74 battalions; 123 squadrons; 120 guns. *Total*: 62,000. (b) French: 70 battalions; 132 squadrons; 70 guns. *Total*: 60,000.

Casualties: (a) 3,600 Allied killed and wounded. (b) 18,000 French casualties, including 6,000 prisoners.

Result: A complete victory for the Allies, leading to the capture of the north and east of the Spanish Netherlands.

Nearby accommodation: Namur or Brussels.

Suggested reading: General Works: Churchill, W. S., *Marlborough, his Life and Times*, Book II, London, 1947. Atkinson, C. T., *Marlborough and the Rise of the British Army*, London, 1921. On the Battle: Trevelyan, G. M., *England under Queen Anne: Ramillies*, London, 1932. Article: Burne, A. H., 'Ramillies and Oudenarde', in *The Fighting Forces' Review*, August 1933. Article: Atkinson, C. T. and Wijn, J. W., 'Ramillies' in the *Journal of the Society for Army Historical Research*, Vol. 32, 1954.

The Battle of Ramillies was perhaps the Duke of Marlborough's

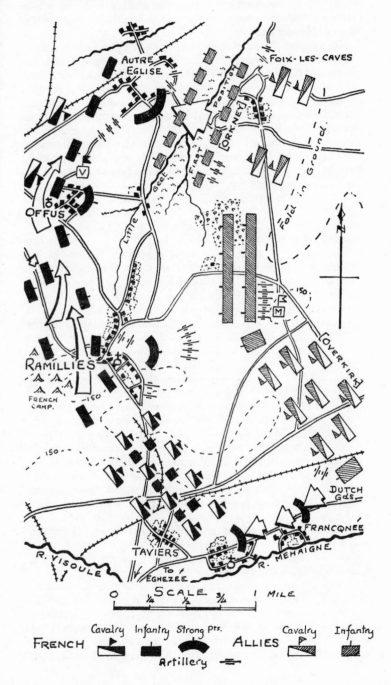

AUTRE EGLISE

FOIX-LES-CAVES

[ORKNEY]

First Posiion

Position

OFFUS

Little Gcctc

Fold in Ground

N

[OVERKIRK]

[M]

RAMILLIES

150

FRENCH CAMP.

150

150

DUTCH Gds.

FRANCQNEE

R. VISOULE

TAVIERS

R. MEHAIGNE

To EGHEZEE

SCALE

0   ¼   ½   ¾   1 MILE

Cavalry   Infantry   Strong Pts.

FRENCH   ALLIES

Cavalry   Infantry

Artillery

21

most successful action. On this one occasion he was in sole command of the Anglo-Dutch army, and earned the whole credit for both the victory and the subsequent conquest of the Spanish Netherlands.

The year 1705 and the early months of 1706 were a period of deep frustration for the Duke. Allied over-confidence after his triumph at Blenheim (q.v., Vol. II) had resulted in a breakdown of co-operation and an abortive campaign in Flanders (1705), affording Louis XIV enough time to reorganise his disrupted forces. In consequence, Marshal Villars's offensive on the Rhine thwarted Marlborough's first plan for 1706—a march to north Italy in support of Prince Eugene. The Duke, however, soon adjusted his schemes to meet the new situation, and, abandoning his original intentions, marched from Liège in early May into enemy territory, hoping to lure Marshal Villeroi into accepting battle. Marlborough was not very confident that the battle-wary French would take up the challenge, but on this one occasion Louis XIV was equally determined that a battle should be fought so as to restore the prestige of the French army, and consequently goaded his commander in the Netherlands to seek out 'Monsieur Marlbrouck'. Whilst the latter trailed his coat near the Lines of Brabant, Villeroi suddenly advanced from Louvain and crossed the River Dyle. Reports of these moves caused a surprised and gratified Marlborough to concentrate his forces and march with all speed for the plain of Ramillies, where he intended to camp on the night of Whit-Sunday, 23 May 1706. However for once the French forestalled the Allies, and Marlborough's advance party found the chosen site already occupied by Marshal Villeroi's 60,000 men. As soon as it was light on the 23rd the Duke reconnoitred the French position and decided to attack with his 62,000 troops as soon as they came up from Merdorp.

Villeroi's army was deployed along a low ridge, two-thirds of which was protected by the marshes of the Little Geet, whilst the right flank was sheltered by the River Mehaigne. A series of villages provided a line of useful strongpoints: slightly advanced before the extreme right stood the hamlet of Francqnée (Franquenay), supported by the village of Taviers. The centre of the line was formed around Ramillies and Offus, and the left flank pivoted on the village of Autre Eglise. On the open ground stretching between Taviers and Ramillies, Villeroi stationed 82 squadrons supported by infantry brigades. In many respects, the position bore a remarkable resemblance to the one occupied by the French at Blenheim.

Marlborough's eagle eye, however, at once noted several important errors in the French dispositions. To cover the entire 4-mile ridge Villeroi had been compelled to over-extend his forces. Moreover, his front stretched in a long concave curve which would delay movements from one flank to the other. The Allied army, on the other hand, was drawn up on a shorter front inside the two horns of the French crescent, and possessed an additional advantage in a convenient fold in the ground which would effectively conceal any Allied transfers from the right flank to the centre. In addition Villeroi had stationed 50 squadrons on his left flank, where the marshes of the Little Geet would inevitably obstruct their employment. Taking into account these errors, the Allied army's slightly superior numbers and far stronger artillery, the advantages of 'interior lines' and the invaluable area of dead ground, Marlborough was in a commanding position.

At one o'clock the batteries went into action, and an hour later the Allied forces attacked both French flanks simultaneously. General Orkney launched a determined attack with the English infantry across the Little Geet against Autre Eglise. This assault soon attracted Villeroi's attention. He was under specific instructions from Versailles 'to have particular attention to that part of the line which will endure the first shock of the English troops', and accordingly immediately transferred several units from his centre to the threatened area. Meanwhile on the other flank the Dutch Guards, assisted by 2 cannon, stormed the villages of Francqnée and Taviers with such vigour that the French garrisons fled precipitately. To stabilise this sector Villeroi was forced to draw still further on the infantry reserves of his right centre. Thus within an hour of the opening of the battle Marlborough was already imposing his will upon his adversary, compelling him to weaken his centre to strengthen his flanks.

Shortly after three in the afternoon the crisis of the day took place. The French cavalry on the right charged Overkirk's 69 squadrons and almost routed them. This event constituted a dire threat to Marlborough's centre, but was remedied by the Duke in person at the head of first 18 and then a further 21 squadrons drawn from his centre and right wing by way of the concealing reverse slope. During the bitter cavalry action that ensued Marlborough had a narrow escape. General Orkney recorded: 'Milord Marlborough was rid over, but got other squadrons to his aid which he led up. Major Bingfield, holding his stirrup to give him assistance onto his horse, was shot by a cannon ball that passed through Marlborough's legs.' In due course the French cavalry were severely repulsed, the *Maison du Roi** losing their silver kettle-drums and Negro drummer in the mêlée.

Although Orkney was still making great progress on his side Marlborough now knew that the battle would have to be won in the centre, for the marshes on the right made it practically impossible to support Orkney's battalions with cavalry.

* *Special note:* See glossary, p.192.

Consequently the Duke called off the assault—much to Orkney's indignant amazement: 'The village of Autre Eglise was in our grip, but as I was going to take possession I had ten Aides-de-Camp to me to come off, the last being the Adjutant General himself.' Under Cadogan's eye the English infantry withdrew to its earlier position. Reaching the crest of the opposite ridge half the battalions halted in full view of the foe, whilst on Marlborough's order the remainder disappeared from sight into the dead ground, turned to their left, and marched off to reinforce the *coup de grâce* against the French centre. To deceive the French command into believing that the whole of Orkney's force still faced Autre Eglise, the colour-parties of these battalions were left just below the crest.

At five in the evening the great assault against Ramillies and Offus was launched. In desperation, after the final rout of the remnants of his cavalry near the Tomb of Ottomond, Villeroi tried to form a new line at right angles to his centre, but his troops became inextricably involved with the tents and wagons of the camp area. A renewed attack all along the crumbling line finally shattered French resistance, and by eight in the evening the pursuit was well under way. Before dawn the following morning the fleeing remnants of Villeroi's army had been chased 15 miles towards Louvain, its cohesion shattered.

The fruits of victory were most rewarding for the Grand Alliance. Town after town fell to the Allies during the ensuing weeks: Louvain, Brussels, Antwerp, Ghent, Bruges, Ostend and Menin all opened their gates. 1706 indeed proved a memorable year for the Allies; for besides the victory of Ramillies and the conquest of the Spanish Netherlands, Prince Eugene won the Battle of Turin (q.v.) in north Italy and cleared the French from the Po valley. Little wonder that contemporary observers forecast a speedy end to the war. But, once again, a combination of diplomatic bungling, overconfidence and lack of Allied co-operation was to throw away the many advantages gained by Marlborough and his men at 'this great and glorious day at Ramillies'.

D.G.C.

ROCOUX (C***); battle of, 11 October 1746; near Liège; **12**; War of the Austrian Succession. The French Marshal de Saxe (120,000) defeated Charles of Lorraine (80,000 Allies) by penetrating his extended left flank; each side lost approx. 5,000 men. See Campaign Chronology, p. 196, and Fortescue, J. W., *A History of the British Army*, Vol. II, London, 1910.

STEENKIRK (C**); battle of, 3 August 1692; near Enghien on the river Senne; **15**; War of the League of Augsburg. King

William III (70,000) attempted to surprise the camp of the French Marshal Luxembourg but was repulsed after a hard fight costing each side more than 7,000 casualties. See Renier, G. J., *William of Orange*, London, 1932.

Waterloo (A****)

Date: 18 June 1815.

Location: Waterloo village is situated 9 miles south of Brussels on the road to Charleroi via Genappe. The battlefield lies a further 3 miles south. **16.**

War and campaign: The Hundred Days—or final campaign of the Napoleonic Wars. (see p. 196).

Object of the action: Napoleon, having defeated the Prussians at Ligny, was intent on crushing Wellington's Allied army, thus opening the way to Brussels.

Opposing sides: (*a*) The Duke of Wellington commanding an Anglo-Dutch army. (*b*) The Emperor Napoleon in command of the French army.

Forces engaged: (*a*) Allies: 50,000 infantry; 12,500 cavalry; 5,600 artillerymen; 156 guns. *Total*: approx. 68,100. (*b*) French: 49,000 infantry; 15,750 cavalry; 7,250 artillerymen; 246 guns. *Total*: approx. 72,000.

Casualties: (*a*) The Allies lost 15,000; the Prussians suffered a further 9,000 casualties in the later stages. (*b*) The French lost 25,000 killed, wounded and prisoner.

Result: Complete victory for the Allies and the final defeat of Napoleon, leading to the firm restoration of the Bourbon dynasty on the throne of France.

Nearby accommodation: Brussels.

Suggested reading: General Works: Hall, *Studies in Napoleonic Strategy*, London, 1918. Hamley, Sir E., *The Operations of War* (7th Edn.), Edinburgh, 1922. On the Campaign and Battle: Naylor, J., *Waterloo*, London, 1960. Ropes, J. C., *The Campaign of Waterloo*, 1893. Fuller, J. F. C., *Decisive Battles of the Western World*, Vol. II, London, 1955. Brett James, A., *The Hundred Days*, London, 1964.

On 1 March 1815 Napoleon landed at Cannes after his escape from Elba. On 20 March he entered Paris and Louis XVIII fled. In response the four Allies—Great Britain, Russia, Austria and Prussia—agreed that each would put an army of 150,000 men into the field and that, as in 1813–14, Napoleon would be overwhelmed by sheer weight of numbers. Allied strategy was for the Anglo-Belgian-Dutch forces commanded by Wellington, and the Prussian forces commanded by Blücher, to invade France from the north. The Russian army was to attack across the middle Rhine, and the Austrian across the lower Rhine. Wellington and Blücher were ready for operations first.

By the end of May 1815 Napoleon had nearly 300,000 men under arms and, of these, 125,000 formed the Armée du Nord under his personal command. He decided to deal with his enemies piecemeal if possible, and to start by attacking Wellington and Blücher who were advancing from the Netherlands and the lower Rhine. His reasons for this choice were that the eastern and south-eastern frontiers of France were strong and could be held with relatively few troops for the time being. The Franco-Belgian frontier, on the other hand, was open except for a few fortresses, and they had not prevented the enemy from invading France in 1814. Finally, Wellington's and Blücher's forces were already in the neighbourhood of Brussels and Liège and, therefore, most directly menacing Paris.

Having made his choice, Napoleon's strategy was, broadly, of the kind he had used on several earlier occasions with great success, that is to strike at allies at the point where their armies joined. If those allies had divergent lines of communication, then success against them at this critical point would almost certainly drive them apart. This strategy had succeeded against the Austro-Sardinian forces in 1796. Now, in 1815, the Prussian line of communication lay north-east via Liège to Cologne; Wellington's lay north-west on the line Mons–Ghent, that is south-west of Antwerp and west of Brussels.

Napoleon therefore decided to advance along the axis of the Charleroi–Brussels road which led directly to the area where Wellington's left wing joined the right wing of the Prussian army.

By 14 June the French army had concentrated in the area Maubeuge–Avesnes–Roçroi–Chimay. At this point Blücher's advance guard was at Charleroi, but his army as a whole was spread over the area Charleroi–Liège. On 16 June Napoleon attacked Blücher's army, still not fully concentrated, at Ligny, some 10 miles north-east of Charleroi. But the Prussian army, though driven back, was not fully engaged and withdrew in comparatively good order. Moreover, instead of withdrawing eastwards, away from Wellington, Blücher retreated northwards towards Wavre, fully complying with the agreement reached between himself and Wellington that they would not allow their armies to lose contact. Having begun the campaign in his best style, Napoleon at this point committed two grave mistakes. First, had he kept d'Erlon's corps with him at Ligny, then the Prussians must have been much harder hit. Second, when the Prussians withdrew, Napoleon assumed and continued to assume that they were moving away from Wellington. And Grouchy, sent to pursue Blücher, failed to do his job properly.

In the meantime Wellington, who had been taken by surprise by the speed of Napoleon's advance, had himself advanced towards Quatre-Bras. There he made contact with Ney, who had been ordered by Napoleon to hold the British in check, on the afternoon of 15 June. On 16 June Ney and Wellington watched each other at Quatre-Bras and some indecisive action took place. On 17 June Wellington heard of Blücher's temporary reverse and withdrawal, and himself decided to withdraw also to the Waterloo position. Unaccountably, Ney failed to strike swiftly with his concentrated force at this stage and thus lost the opportunity of defeating Wellington before he was ready to fight.

WATERLOO
18th June 1815

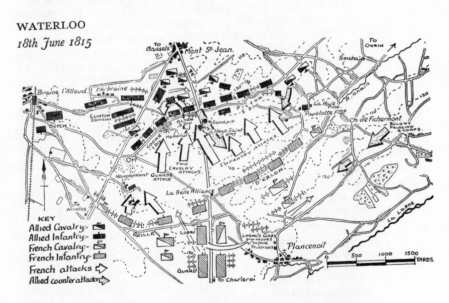

KEY
Allied Cavalry:-
Allied Infantry:-
French Cavalry:-
French Infantry:-
French attacks
Allied counter attacks

On 18 June the two armies, with the French now concentrated under Napoleon who had joined with Ney, lay opposite each other on the Waterloo battlefield. Wellington also was determined to accept battle, because he received a message telling him that at daybreak on 18 June two Prussian corps would set out to join him and that two more would be held in readiness to follow.

The battlefield of Waterloo was comparatively small, stretching about $2\frac{1}{4}$ miles from north to south and no more than 4 miles at its extreme width. It was divided by the

Charleroi–Brussels road. On the north, where Wellington's main line ran, there was a low ridge nearly a mile south of the village of Mont St. Jean and extending about a quarter of a mile west of the road and a mile and a quarter east of it. Wellington, as on other occasions, gave his line the protection of the dead ground behind the ridge until the action began. His front centre was reinforced by the farm and sandpit at La Haye Sainte, and his right flank by the Château of Hougomont.

On the south of the battlefield was another low ridge, the ground between the two ridges never dipping more than about 50 feet. Here Napoleon drew up his line, stretching from the Brussels–Nivelles road, from a point about a mile and three-quarters south of Mont St. Jean, south of Hougomont to the hamlet of Frichermont.

The fighting, which lasted from 11.30 am until about 8 pm, consisted of four main phases. Napoleon's overall tactical plan was to strike at the centre of Wellington's army, to penetrate there and exploit the penetration. In the first phase Reille's division advanced at 11.30 am against Hougomont, as a diversion, before Ney's attack in the centre with d'Erlon's corps began the main operations. From the beginning the diversion in fact tended to absorb more French than Allied forces. At 1.30 pm d'Erlon's main attack began and ran into immediate trouble because the French columns were too densely packed to deploy into line as they approached the Allied position between La Haye Sainte and Papelotte. The result was that they suffered very heavy casualties from the delayed and concentrated musket fire of Picton's division and were then driven back by Uxbridge's cavalry. In the process, however, Wellington's forces themselves suffered heavily, particularly since the cavalry drove on too far and became disorganised.

The second phase began at about 4 pm at a time when Napoleon was already beginning to be distracted by the appearance of the forward Prussian troops debouching from the Paris Wood. Ney led a great cavalry attack covering the whole area between La Haye Sainte and Hougomont. Unsupported by infantry and with no preparations to spike the Allied guns, Ney's cavalry broke through only to beat themselves vainly against the infantry squares, and then, turned back by Uxbridge's cavalry, were decimated by the Allied guns quickly brought back into action again.

In order to restore the morale of his army Napoleon now ordered another cavalry attack, led by Kellerman, at about 5.30 pm. This, again unsupported by infantry and, this time, with very little help from the French artillery, met with the same fate as the earlier cavalry attack. But it was far from a complete failure. Wellington's centre had been weakened so much that he was almost without reserves and himself led forward the Brunswickers to re-establish the centre of his whole position.

At about 7 pm the fourth and final phase took place. Napoleon brought forward the Guard and attacked diagonally between Hougomont and La Haye Sainte towards Wellington's right centre. Again, packed too tight to deploy against concentrated musket fire, this attack also failed, this time against Maitland's Brigade of Guards. As the French were repulsed, so the Prussians had established full contact with Wellington's left, and the retreat of the French began.

Waterloo was won—apart from the vital co-operation of the Prussians at the critical phase—by Wellington's superior tactics. As before he depended upon concentrated fire by artillery and small-arms, his infantry protected by natural and artificial features as long as possible and supported, once their fire had taken effect, by a decisive cavalry action. Napoleon's tactics were faulty in two respects. First, his traditional combination of column and line, *l'ordre mixte*, failed to operate successfully in the narrow confines of this particular battlefield. Second, his various arms were not adequately co-ordinated. Infantry and cavalry did not operate together and each failed because the support of the other was lacking.

N.H.G.

Eire

AUGHRIM (D*); battle of, 12 July 1691; near Ballinasloe; **66**; Irish Campaign of 1689–91. General Ginkel (18,000) routed General St. Just's Irish Jacobites and French troops (25,000) after killing their commander. See Murray, R. H., *Revolutionary Ireland and its Settlement*, London, 1911.

The Boyne (A***)

Date: 11 July 1690*.

Location: On the road from Drogheda to Slane; between Oldbridge and Slane. **65.**

War and campaign: 'The Jacobite War'—part of the War of the League of Augsburg (see p. 195).

Object of the action: William III was attempting to force battle on James II, former King of England, who for his part was trying to retreat back to Dublin.

Opposing sides: (*a*) King William III commanding a multi-national 'Williamite' Army. (*b*) King James II in command of the Franco-Irish 'Jacobite' Army.

Forces engaged: (*a*) Williamites: 26,500 infantry; 8,000 cavalry; 50 guns. *Total:* 35,000. (*b*) Jacobites: 18,000 infantry; 5,000 cavalry; 6 guns. *Total:* 23,000 (exclusive of the garrison of Drogheda).

Casualties: (*a*) Over 2,000 Williamites killed and wounded. (*b*) Over 1,500 Jacobites killed and wounded.

Result: A thorough victory for King William, paving the way for Marlborough's and Ginkel's reconquest of Ireland.

Nearby accommodation: Drogheda.

* *Special Note:* 12 July 1690 is often regarded as the date of the battle. The actual 'Old Style' date was 1 July (thus 11 July 'New Style'). The reason for this discrepancy is that Aughrim was fought on

12 July (N.S.) the following year, and this date was chosen for the commemoration of both battles.

Suggested reading: General Work: Macaulay, Lord, *The History of England from the Accession of James II*, London, 1861. On the Campaign: Belloc, H., *James the Second*, London, 1928. On the Battle: Boulger, D., *The Battle of the Boyne*, London, 1911. Article: Simms, J. G., 'Eyewitness of the Boyne', in *The Irish Sword*, Vol VI, No. 22, Dublin, 1963.

The Boyne is a very difficult battle to describe. The fighting was brief and movements rapid. The historians are for the most part prejudiced, Belloc on one side and Macaulay on the other especially so. Few authorities agree about the casualties. One has therefore to make the nearest possible estimate of these and also of the numbers engaged.

When James reached Dublin on 3 April after landing at Kinsale, time had been wasted and his adherents had incurred heavy loss in men and prestige in the abortive siege of Londonderry. His Viceroy, the Duke of Tyrconnell, had proved a good organiser, but had few trained troops and fewer arms. On the Williamite side Schomberg had landed in the north with over 10,000 men at Bangor in August 1689 and drawn in numbers of Irish Protestants, but still lacked strength for an offensive. He lost some 8,000 during the winter, chiefly from sickness. James, who had lost about the same number before Derry, obtained over 6,000 infantry from France, but only a handful of muskets, because he sent in return an Irish brigade, by agreement unarmed, and it did not occur to the French that this had been without arms at home.

The new campaign opened with the arrival in mid-June of William with reinforcements. His army was mainly foreign, its cream being perhaps the Dutch Brigade of Blue Guards. James marched to Dundalk, but had second thoughts on learning of his enemy's numerical superiority and fell back behind the Boyne, missing a better chance of resistance in the Moyry Pass, between Newry and Dundalk. All he was now ready to undertake was a rearguard action. He was so set on retreat that he sent back his baggage and even six of his guns to Dublin.

William's problem was not simple. He could not cross at Dundalk because it was too strongly held. At Oldbridge, despite its name, there was no bridge, but several fords passable at half flood between it and Drybridge. That at Donore was available at low water only. There was another at Rosnaree and at Slane a bridge cut by the Jacobites. William, slightly wounded the day before by a cannon-ball grazing his shoulder, determined to pass the river at three points: on the right, where Schomberg's son Meinhart was in command, at Rosnaree; in the centre, under Schomberg himself, at Oldbridge; on the left, under his own command, at Drybridge. James had posted only one regiment, Neill O'Neill's Dragoons, opposite Rosnaree, and in Oldbridge Antrim's and Clanrickarde's infantry regiments. He deployed his main body on slightly rising ground from half a mile to a mile from the Boyne. Later on Tyrconnell, still a fair soldier despite hard living, moved 5 more infantry regiments into the village and drew up 3 cavalry regiments and 2 troops of the first-class bodyguard under James's bastard son Berwick in their rear. It is curious that, of the two most celebrated commanders engaged, Schomberg was 72 and Berwick barely 20.

THE BOYNE
11th July 1690

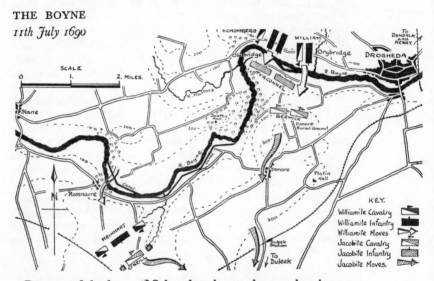

Reports of the hour of Schomberg's attack vary, but it was probably before noon. He had picked infantry: Dutch Blue Guards, Huguenots, Ulster and English regiments. The Dutch were charged by Tyrconnell and Irish cavalry broke the ranks of the Huguenots as they climbed out of the water. Schomberg galloped down to rally the troops and was instantly shot dead. Then followed calamity for the Jacobites. William, despite the fact that the tide was now so high that horses had to swim and infantry to cross in single file, gradually got his wing over. James had meanwhile ridden forward with the intention of transferring troops from the neighbourhood of Oldbridge to his left, from which he feared the hostile cavalry would cut him off at Duleek, where the Dublin road ran through a defile. He found, however, that Tyrconnell needed all the force he had and that none could be spared.

He was awaiting fresh cavalry when he learnt that his right

flank was already beaten, on which, as he writes, 'the King, whispering in Lauzun's ear, told him that there was now nothing to be done but to charge the enemy forthwith before his troops knew what had happened'. But nothing would go right for him. Sarsfield, who had reconnoitred the ground, came up and said a charge was impossible because straight in front were two high-banked double ditches and a brook. Meanwhile a heroic defence by O'Neill with his original regiment and a handful of reinforcements had broken down and the Williamites were moving on Duleek. The dauntless Berwick charged again and again—he says twelve times—and on one occasion broke the Inniskillingers, but concludes that the Jacobites might well not have got through the defile but for the death of Schomberg. As it was they escaped with trifling further loss. James rode to Dublin, finding many raw Irish troops in a panic but the French regiments in good order. He finally embarked for France at Kinsale. It must be added that he is, all through his memoirs, reliable as regards events seen, but has unwittingly deceived later historians by believing reports that young Schomberg crossed at Slane.

The Battle of the Boyne was in the main a fighting retreat. In the brief conflicts at close quarters the odds against the Jacobites in artillery were over eight to one. The Williamite superiority in infantry was far greater than it looks because a large proportion of the Irish were largely untrained and miserably armed. James's venture was a gamble, which might have come off if the French fleet had shown more activity after Beachy Head or William had had to withdraw troops—even to return himself, which was a possibility. As things were, the campaign broke the Jacobite menace for the time being, though for complete success England had to await Ginkel's victory at Aughrim in 1691.

C.F.

DROGHEDA (C**); storm of, 10 September 1649; 30 miles north of Dublin on the T.1; **64**; Cromwell's Campaign in Ireland. Cromwell (12,000) stormed the town defended by Sir Arthur Aston (3,000 Royalists) and put every living soul to the sword. See Curtis, E., *History of Ireland*, London, 1936.

Kinsale (C***)

Date: 26 December 1601.

Location: Two miles east of Kinsale, just south of the Bandon. **68**.

War and campaign: Tyrone's Rebellion (see p. 194).

Object of the action: The rebel Tyrone was attempting to relieve a Spanish force besieged in Kinsale by English forces.

Opposing sides: (a) The Lord Deputy, Lord Mountjoy, commanding the English army. (b) The Earl of Tyrone in command of the Irish army.

Forces engaged: (a) English: 1,100 infantry; 400 cavalry. *Total*: 1,500. (b) Irish: 6,300 Irish; 200 Spaniards; (horse unknown). *Total*: 6,500.

Casualties: (a) One officer and a few English rank and file killed. (b) Approx. 2,500 Irish and Spaniards killed and wounded.

Result: An overwhelming English victory, leading to the abandonment of Kinsale by the Spaniards and the eventual collapse of Tyrone's rebellion.

Nearby accommodation: Cork.

Suggested reading: General Work: Bagwell, R., *Ireland under the Tudors*, Vol III, London, 1890. On the Campaign: Stafford, F., *Pacata Hibernia*, London, 1810. On the Battle: Falls, C., *Mountjoy, Elizabethan General*, London, 1955. Article: Hayes-McCoy, G. A., 'The Battle of Kinsale', in *Irish Historical Studies*, Dublin, September 1949.

The Battle of Kinsale was the result of a siege that had lasted 2 months, of a Spanish expeditionary force which had occupied the walled town. The Earl of Tyrone and Hugh O'Donnell marched south to relieve it. On 3 January the Irish advanced from the west, but at the last moment Tyrone changed his mind and withdrew. Mountjoy, rating the Spanish infantry high and expecting a sally, left the bulk of his forces to watch them and himself led the remainder in pursuit over two boggy causeways, and finally, a mile and a half away, caught sight of the enemy drawn up in three heavy 'battles'.

The fight began with a cavalry attack on Tyrone's centre, commanded by himself, but, seeing the pikemen stand fast, Sir Richard Wingfield wheeled and rode back. Then, his strength raised to some 500, he charged again. This time the Irish horse and Tyrone's infantry broke, and Wingfield's cavalry hurtled into the mass. Panic spread to O'Donnell's troops on the right and they disappeared in wild flight. On the left Richard Tyrrell's Munstermen and 200 or more Spaniards withdrew to a hill near by. Mountjoy ordered one of his 3 infantry regiments to attack them in flank, whereupon the Irish began to break and join the flight. The Spaniards resisted gallantly till half their number had been killed. Finally 48 surrendered and about 60 returned to Castlehaven, occupied by reinforcements which had been unable to reach Kinsale.

Had not the English cavalry horses been in miserable condition for lack of fodder, the slaughter of the vanquished would have been appalling. As things were, the English claimed to have found 1,200 dead. The unarmed mob which escaped suffered more loss on the way north, many being slain —sometimes trodden into bogholes—by fellow-countrymen whose lands Tyrone had ravaged. The Spaniards had made no sortie, apparently not having heard the slight musketry fire, muffled by hills.

Eventually the Spanish commander, Don Juan del Aquila, asked for a parley, as a result of which his troops were shipped home on honourable terms. It was the end of Spain's menace to the Kingdoms of England and Ireland and, for the Irish, a rout all the more extraordinary in view of Tyrone's success at the Yellow Ford and elsewhere. O'Donnell died in Spain, but Mountjoy did not receive Tyrone's surrender till March 1603. The siege and battle stamped Mountjoy as the ablest Elizabethan soldier.

C.F.

LIMERICK (D*); siege of, September to October 1691; at the mouth of the river Shannon; **67**; Irish Campaign of 1689–91. General Ginkel (c. 16,000) induced Patrick Sarsfield (c. 12,000) to surrender the town on terms shortly before the arrival of a French relieving fleet. See Murray, R. H., *Revolutionary Ireland and its Settlement*, London, 1911.

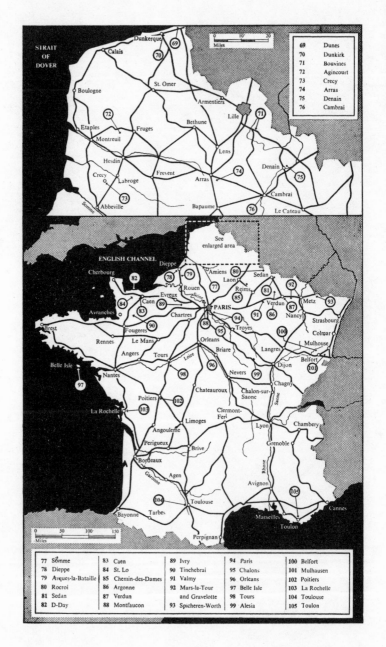

France

Agincourt (A****)

Date: 25 October 1415.

Location: The village of Azincourt lies to the east of the Hesdin-Fruges-Calais road (N.28), about 8 miles north of Hesdin. **72.**

War and campaign: The Hundred Years' War; the invasion of France 1415 (see p. 194).

Object of the action: The Constable of France was attempting to cut off and destroy Henry V's army before it could reach Calais and safety.

Opposing sides: (a) King Henry V, the Duke of York, and Lord Camoys leading the English. (b) Charles d'Albret, Constable of France, commanding the French.

Forces engaged: (a) English: 4,950 archers; 750 knights and men-at-arms. *Total:* 5,700 English. (b) French: 3,000 cross-bowmen; 7,000 mounted and 15,000 dismounted knights and men-at-arms; a few 'bombards'. *Estimated total:* 25,000 French.

Casualties: (a) Perhaps 400 English, including the Duke of York. (b) Probably 8,000 Frenchmen killed, including the Constable; and 2,000 captives.

Result: The complete rout of the French enabled the English to reach Calais safely.

Nearby accommodation: St. Omer or Hesdin.

Suggested reading: General Works: Perroy, E., *The Hundred Years' War*, London, 1951. Oman, C. W. C., *The Art of War in the Middle Ages*, (2nd Edn.), London, 1924. Jacob, E. F., *Henry V and the Invasion of France*, London, 1947. On the Campaign and Battle: Burne, A., *The Agincourt War*, London, 1956. Play: Shakespeare, W., *Henry V*.

The Battle of Agincourt formed the climax of Henry V's invasion of France in 1415, and was practically the last great

English martial achievment of the Hundred Years' War. Henry's army landed near Harfleur on 15 August, and slightly over a month later the town fell into English hands. The siege had been longer than anticipated and this made an immediate advance towards Paris out of the question; instead, Henry decided to march defiantly through French territory to the English-held fortress of Calais, where the army could spend the winter preparing for the next campaign.

This venture involved considerable risks: by early October the French Constable had already collected some 14,000 men at Rouen, and to reach Calais the English would have to cross the broad River Somme. Everything depended on a free passage over the 'Blanchetaque' ford below Abbeville.

The 6,000-strong English army left Harfleur on 8 October, each man carrying 8 days' rations—sufficient, it was hoped, for a fast 160-mile march; all the heavy impedimenta was left with the Harfleur garrison, including the 'bombards'. Everything went well until the 13th, when Henry's scouts reported that the vital ford was strongly held by the enemy. Constable d'Albret had devined Henry's intention and sent his advance guard to hold the crossing while the main French army advanced from Rouen and crossed the Somme at Amiens.

For the next 5 days Henry marched up the river vainly searching for another ford, and by the 16th rations were running low and the army was becoming increasingly dispirited. Two days later an undefended crossing was at last discovered near Nesle, and by the end of the next day the English army was safely over the Somme. But now the French army was only 7 miles distant near Peronne, and although d'Albret played 'cat and mouse' with the English army for 6 more days, it was evident that Henry would have to fight his way through to Calais against great odds. On the 24th the English came upon the encampments of the 'terrific multitude' in the Fernoise valley, and halted for the night in the neighbouring village of Maisoncelles. The men were understandably weary: they had covered 260 miles in the last 17 days.

The morning of St. Crispin's Day found the two unequal armies facing one another across the narrow and gently undulating plain bounded by the forests of Agincourt and Tramcourt. The French were gay and confident—laying wagers on the prisoners they would take—but King Hal had whipped up his army's morale to fever-pitch, and knight and archer shared a feeling of kinship: 'We few, we happy few, we band of brothers' was how Shakespeare immortally described the mood of the English army. Determined to show that his army was not afraid of its vast opponent, Henry ordered 'Advance Banner!' at 11 am and moved his men forward to the narrowest neck of the plain, hardly 400 yards from the

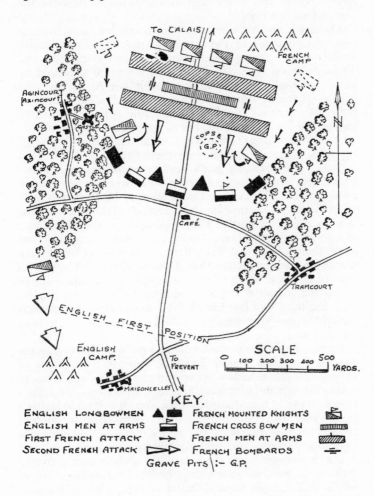

KEY.

ENGLISH LONGBOWMEN	FRENCH MOUNTED KNIGHTS
ENGLISH MEN AT ARMS	FRENCH CROSS BOW MEN
FIRST FRENCH ATTACK	FRENCH MEN AT ARMS
SECOND FRENCH ATTACK	FRENCH BOMBARDS
GRAVE PITS :- G.P.	

serried French ranks. The archers were massed on the flanks and in two 'wedges' covering the centre, their positions protected by a fence of sharpened stakes driven into the rainsodden earth; the men-at-arms were stationed to hold the intervals, but there were insufficient men to form a reserve and so the camp had to be entrusted to the sick. The front covered 940 yards.

Constable d'Albret deployed his men in three dense lines along a 1,200-yard front, the first two on foot, the third mounted, while two further bodies of mounted knights—each 600 strong—were placed slightly in rear on the flanks. The cross-bowmen and a few cannon were situated between the first and second lines.

The battle opened when the French cavalry flank divisions —stung into action by the long-range shooting of the English archers—made disorganised charges against Henry's flanks. These achieved nothing: 'Their horses were so wounded by the arrows that they were unmanageable' (St. Remy), and the fleeing horsemen trampled through the advancing ranks of their own centre. The French first line rushed forward to engage the English knights, but as they came they inevitably narrowed their front to come at their adversaries and to avoid the hail of arrows poured into their flanks by the English archers. The resulting press became appalling, and many Frenchmen were unable to raise their weapons to strike a blow, and into this confused mass plunged Henry at the head of his knights. Meanwhile, 'the English archers, perceiving this disorder . . . quitted their stakes, threw their bows and arrows on the ground, and seizing their swords . . . sallied out upon them.' The first French line was soon reduced to a shambles, and the second shared the same fate. Only half an hour after the opening of the battle the French attack lay in ruins, and a wall of bodies separated the victorious English from the third and last line of the French army. The archers busied themselves seizing prostrate French noblemen to hold for ransom.

Despite appearances the battle was not quite over: disturbing news reached Henry from the rear. A detachment of French marauders had surprised and looted the English camp, killing the sick and capturing, amongst other items, the King's crown and seals. Simultaneously, the French knights to Henry's front—who still outnumbered the entire English force—showed signs of renewing the attack. It appeared probable that Henry's army was about to be assailed from front and rear at a moment when the bulk of the archers were scattered seeking for loot, while the large body of prisoners—many of whom had not yet been divested of their armour—already constituted a menace in the very midst of his position. Faced with the prospect of losing the battle, Henry gave the order to kill the prisoners—and with long faces the soldiers turned to the gory task which deprived them of many a rich ransom. This 'cruel butchery' has been widely criticised, but in Henry's defence it is hard to see what else he could have done in the face of an impending attack. In the event, however, this did not materialise, and the slaughter was stopped.

The Battle of Agincourt cost France at least half the nobility, including the Constable, 3 Dukes, 90 Lords and 1,560 knights besides a host of men-at-arms and cross-bowmen. The English losses were astonishingly light—but included in their number the stout Duke of York, commander of the left wing, who was stifled in his armour beneath a pile of slain—a fate that befell many more on the field. Shortly afterwards the English army with its remaining 2,000 prisoners resumed the march to Calais. Had it turned in its tracks and marched on Paris, peace might have been won that same year, but Henry considered the season too far advanced for further operations. The French were consequently awarded a breathing-space, and the effects of Henry V's great victory failed to come up to the most optimistic expectations.

D.G.C.

Alesia (D***)

Date: 52 B.C.

Location: Alesia, now called Alise-Sainte-Reine is in the Côte d'Or Department, not far from Dijon. The site lies east of the town. **99.**

War and campaign: Caesar's Gallic War. (see p.193).

Object of the action: Caesar was attempting to force the Gallic leader, Vercingetorix, to capitulate, despite unfavourable circumstances.

Opposing sides: (a) Julius Caesar at the head of a Roman Army. (b) Vercingetorix at the head of the Gauls.

Forces engaged: (a) Romans: several Legions supported by cavalry detachments. *Total*: approx. 70,000. (b) Gauls: besieged force, 80,000 foot and 15,000 cavalry; relieving army, perhaps 250,000 foot and 8,000 cavalry. *Total*: 353,000 Gauls.

Casualties: Unrecorded.

Result: Vercingetorix's enforced surrender and the defeat of the Gallic armies completed the Roman conquest of Gaul, and founded modern France.

Nearby accommodation: Dijon.

Suggested reading: General Works: Mommsen, T., *The History of Rome*, Vol. IV (Everyman's Library Edn.), 1920. Rice Holmes, T., *The Roman Republic*, Vol. II, Oxford, 1923. On the Campaign and Battle: Caesar, J., *The Gallic War*, Book VII. Biography: Dodge, T. A., *Caesar*, New York, 1891. Work of Fiction: Warner, R., *Imperial Caesar*, London, 1960.

After nearly 7 years of campaigning, Caesar's conquest of Gaul culminated in a general rising of the Gallic tribes under a young chieftain of outstanding ability, by name Vercingetorix. After an abortive attempt to ambush Caesar's army, as Hannibal had trapped Flaminius' at Lake Trasimene (q.v.) he withdrew to his mountain stronghold of Alesia.

There Caesar laid siege to him. First, he encompassed the mountain with a line of contravallation; it consisted of a series of entrenchments 11 miles in circuit. But before it was completed, shortage of forage compelled Vercingetorix to send his cavalry away and appeal to the Gallic tribes to come to his relief. According to Caesar, they mustered an army of 250,000 infantry and 8,000 cavalry.

When Caesar learnt of this, his problem became, not only how to prevent Vercingetorix from breaking out of his stronghold, but also how to prevent the relieving army from breaking into it. He solved it by encompassing his line of contravallation with a line of circumvallation 14 miles in circuit, which faced outwards; he prepared to be himself besieged.

When the relieving army arrived, a desperate series of engagements, in which Vercingetorix attempted to break out, followed. In the last one the relieving army was decisively beaten, and Vercingetorix, whose army was now starving, capitulated.

Thus this remarkable siege was brought to an end by the simultaneous defeat of two armies by a single army, no greater than the one and incomparably smaller than the other. An army which not only was the besieger but itself was besieged, and which had to hold 25 miles of entrenchments in order, at one and the same time, to achieve its aim and secure itself against defeat.

J.F.C.F.

The Argonne (B***)

Date: 26 September–11 November 1918.

Location: Between Verdun, the western edge of the Argonne Forest, Veuziers and Brieulles. Near Route Nationale 48. **86.**

War and campaign: The First World War; the Meuse-Argonne Offensive of 1918 (see p. 197).

Object of the action: The Americans and French wished to cut the strategic German railway running through Mezières and Sedan.

Opposing sides: (a) General Pershing in command of the American Expeditionary Force. (b) The Crown Prince commanding a German Army Group.

Forces engaged (outset of battle): (a) 15 U.S. divisions, later supplemented by a few French. (b) 11 German divisions.

Casualties: (a) 122,000 Americans. (b) 16,000 German prisoners; other casualties not revealed.

Result: A successful break-through towards the Meuse was achieved at high cost.

Nearby accommodation: Sedan.

Suggested reading: General Works: Falls, C., *The First World War*, London, 1960. Pershing, *My Experiences in the World War*, New York, 1931. Hunter Liggett, *Commanding an American Army*, New York, 1925. Work of Fiction: Remarque, E. M., *All Quiet on the Western Front* (English Edn.), London, 1929.

The battle of the Argonne was America's most important contribution to the Allied effort on the Western Front and her most notable victory of the First World War. The Argonne is an area of broken hills and forest, between the Meuse and the Champagne, whose natural defences had been so improved by the Germans that it formed, by 1918, perhaps the most formidable position on the Western Front. The French had made no progress against it in four years of bitter if intermittent fighting, but its proximity to the German strategic railway, which ran through Mezières and Sedan, made its capture essential to the Allied strategy in the autumn of 1918. Marshal Foch entrusted the task to the American army, whose inexperience was outweighed by its strength and enthusiasm.

The front selected for attack was bounded by two river valleys, the Aire and the Meuse. German strength stood at 11 divisions, against which General Pershing's 1st Army could deploy 9, with 6 in reserve, 2,800 guns and 180 tanks. He took over the sector from the French on 22 September, in almost complete secrecy, and began his attack with a short and violent bombardment on 26 September. The French 4th Army on his left attacked at the same time. His immediate objective was the clearing of the forest to the line Montfaucon–Romagne, an ambitious project which stout German resistance obstructed. His inexperienced troops exposed themselves recklessly and suffered heavily. By 3 October they had advanced 10 miles at most and only 5 in the Argonne itself. The arrival of battle-hardened divisions from St. Mihiel on 4 October kept the advance going slowly, gradually freeing the Americans' flanks from enfilade fire and allowing the French to advance to the upper Aisne. On 1 November the 1st Army, further reinforced and now commanded by General Hunter Liggett, launched its final assault against the last German line (Vouziers–Brieulles). With massive air and artillery support and strong French activity on the left, it quickly broke through; by 6 November the enemy were in full retreat. At the Armistice the Americans stood everywhere on or beyond the Meuse.

J.D.P.K.

ARQUES (B**); battle of, 21 September 1589; near Dieppe; **79**; the French Wars of Religion. King Henri IV (8,000 Huguenots and Royalists) repulsed the Duke of Mayenne's attempt to crush his army with 24,000 Leaguers by holding a narrow defile. See Oman, Sir C., *A History of the Art of War in the 16th Century* (Revised Edn.), London, 1954.

Arras (C**)

Date: 21 May 1940.

Location: Arras stands on the River Scarpe, about 50 miles from the Belgian frontier. **74.**

War and campaign: The Second World War; the Battle of France, May 1940 (see p. 197).

Object of the action: An improvised attempt by the B.E.F. to check the German advance towards the Channel coast.

Opposing sides: (*a*) Major-General Franklyn commanding the British 5th Division. (*b*) General Rommel in command of 7th Panzer Division.

Forces engaged: (*a*) British: 2 infantry battalions; 2 regiments of the R.T.R.; light French units. (*b*) Germans: 2 rifle regiments; the S.S. Totenkopf Division; 25th Panzer Regiment.

Casualties: (*a*) 57 British tanks out of 83 engaged. (*b*) About 20 German tanks and a considerable number of motor vehicles.

Result: Tactically a failure, but psychologically it instilled caution into the German High Command and thus contributed to the successful evacuation from Dunkirk (q.v.).

Nearby accommodation: Arras.

Suggested reading: General Works: Churchill, W. S., *The Second World War*, Vol II, London, 1949. On the Campaign: Draper, T., *The Six Weeks' War*, London, 1946. Liddell Hart, B. H., *The Rommel Papers*, New York, 1953. Liddell Hart, B. H., *The Tanks*, Vol. II, London, 1959.

On 21 May 1940 Rommel's 7th Panzer Division, leading the inner flank of the thrust from the Meuse, was temporarily checked south of Arras by an improvised British formation, 'Frankforce'. Due to hurried assembly the counter-attack was initiated by two columns of tanks only (4th and 7th Royal Tank Regiments), followed closely by two infantry battalions, but without artillery or air support. At 1330 hours the columns moved (from Vimy) to the west of Arras and then swung eastward across the Arras–Baumetz railway, striking 6th and 7th Rifle Regiments and the unblooded S.S. Totenkopf Division just as they were beginning a disorderly advance through the villages of Wailly, Ficheux and Agny. Impervious to German anti-tank fire the British tanks wrought havoc among the chaos of troops, guns and transport.

Although daily anticipating a counter-attack, Rommel was so shaken that he thought five British divisions were defending Arras.

Only on the arrival of 25th Panzer Regiment at dusk, and after twelve hours' fighting, did the few surviving British tanks and infantrymen withdraw north of Arras. The town was finally abandoned on the night of 23 May.

B.J.B.

Belfort (B***)

Date: 19–22 November 1944.

Location: Between Saverne, Strasbourg and Mulhouse. **100.**

War and campaign: The Second World War; the North-west European Campaign, 1944–5 (see p. 197).

Object of the action: An Allied attempt to break through the Upper Vosges Mountains to the Upper Rhine.

Opposing sides: (*a*) General Devers commanding the 6th U.S. Army Group. (*b*) General Balck (later Himmler) commanding German Army Group 'G'.

Forces engaged: (*a*) Allies: 10 infantry divisions; 5 armoured divisions (750 tanks). (*b*) Germans: 7 or 8 infantry divisions; 4 Panzer divisions (350 tanks).

Casualties: (*a*) approximately 35,000. (*b*) approximately 70,000.

Result: The isolation of the German 19th Army in the Colmar Pocket and the reaching of the Upper Rhine.

Nearby accommodation: Belfort.

Suggested reading: General Works: Wilmot, C., *The Struggle for Europe*, London, 1952. Eisenhower, D., *Crusade in Europe*, London, 1948. On the Campaign: Liddell Hart, B. H., *The Other Side of the Hill*, London, 1952. Tassigny, Laltre de, *History of the French First Army*, London, 1952. Memoirs: Butcher, H. C., *Three Years with Eisenhower*, London and Toronto, 1946.

Throughout October and November, Patton's 3rd Army continued its offensive towards the Saar, taking Metz on 18 November. To the south, Devers's 6th Army Group, consisting of the 7th U.S. Army on the left and the 1st French Army on the right, faced the formidable barrier of the Vosges held by the German 1st and 19th Armies with the 5th Panzer Army in reserve. On 19 November the 1st French Army, brilliantly led by de Tassigny, broke through the Belfort Gap and reached the Upper Rhine and the outskirts of Mulhouse in a single day. Two days later the U.S. 7th Army forced the Saverne Gap and on the 23rd, with the 2nd French Armoured Division in the van, swept on almost unopposed to liberate

Strasbourg. These attacks isolated the German 19th Army in the Colmar Pocket from which Hitler forbade them to withdraw. Instead of ordering the double envelopment of this pocket, Eisenhower switched the U.S. 7th Army to aid Patton on the Saar, leaving the French to deal with the German 19th Army alone. Weakened by detachments to south-west France and exhausted by their recent efforts, this proved beyond their power.

H.E.

Belle Isle (B***)

Date: 7 April–8 June 1761.

Location: Island off Quiberon Point, west coast of France. **97.**

War and campaign: The Seven Years' War; Campaign of 1761 (see p. 196).

Object of the action: The Earl of Chatham hoped to extract better peace terms from the French by seizing a piece of their national territory.

Opposing sides: (*a*) Admiral Keppel and General Hodgson commanding the British forces. (*b*) General Sainte Croix, commander of the French garrison.

Forces engaged: (*a*) British. *Total*: 8,000. (*b*) French. *Total*: 3,000.

Casualties: (*a*) 700 British killed and wounded. (*b*) Very few; the majority capitulated on terms and were repatriated.

Result: The capture of the Island, soon to be restored to the French by treaty.

Nearby accommodation: Quiberon.

Suggested reading: General Work: Corbett, J. S., *England in the Seven Years' War*, London, 1907. On the Battle: Fortescue, J. W., *A History of the British Army*, Vol II, London, 1910.

Pitt thought out this enterprise as a diversion to cover the Mauritius expedition. He saw the country at this time committed to negotiations for peace but wanted to press on with the war with utmost energy to get better terms. He therefore decided to deliver the attack on Martinique the moment the hurricane months were past and send off the Belle Isle expedition at once.

On 7 April the fleet anchored off the island of Belle Isle with their troops shifted to flat-bottomed boats, and an attempt was made to storm the French entrenchments at Port St. André at the eastern end of the island. But owing to the steepness of the ground only 60 men reached the summit, and these were overpowered, so the rest of the troops were re-embarked after having lost about 500 men killed, wounded and prisoners. However, the commanders, a fortnight later, decided on several attacks along the north and east coasts, and although the main assault was held, Brigadier Lambart developed a feint attack east of St. Foy successfully and reached the summit unobserved in a sector which the French had thought unscaleable. When charged he drove back the enemy, and after being reinforced compelled the French to retire into the fortress of Palais. Hodgson, the British commander, had to wait two weeks to land his heavy artillery owing to continual gales; but at length, on 13 May, the enemy entrenchments were carried by storm. Next the French retired to the citadel which, after a gallant defence, was compelled to surrender on 7 June. The French commander, Sainte Croix, had fought bravely and was, therefore, on 8 June, allowed to march out through the breach with all the honours of war, and was conveyed to L'Orient with all that was left of his force.

J.M.S.

Bouvines (A***)

Date: 27 July 1214.

Location: South-east from Lille, best reached by Route Nationale 35; the battlefield lies on the road from Bouvines to Gruson near the railway crossing. **71.**

War and campaign: The Anglo-Imperial invasion of France, 1214 (see p. 194).

Object of the action: The Imperial army was trying to force its way through to Paris.

Opposing sides: (*a*) The Emperor Otto IV commanding the Imperial army. (*b*) King Philip Augustus in command of the French army.

Forces engaged: (*a*) Imperialists: approx. 6,000 cavalry; 18,000 foot. *Total*: 24,000. (*b*) French: approx. 7,000 cavalry; 15,000 foot. *Total*: 22,000.

Casualties: (*a*) 170 knights killed; 140 nobles and 1,000 rank and file prisoners. (*b*) French: details unknown, but very slight.

Result: A complete victory for the French, securing the ruling dynasty, dashing King John of England's hopes of regaining his French possessions, and ending the Imperial rule of Otto IV.

Nearby accommodation: Lille or Tournai.

Suggested reading: General Work: Poole, A. L., *From Domesday Book to Magna Carta*, Oxford, 1954. On the Battle: Oman, C. W. C., *A History of the Art of War in the Middle Ages*, Vol. I (2nd Edn.), London, 1924. Colin, *Les Grandes Batailles de l'Histoire*, Paris, 1915.

On 15 February 1214 King John of England landed in France determined to win back the lands of the Angevin empire lost to the French. In alliance with Emperor Otto IV of the Holy Roman Empire and various disaffected French vassals he planned a double invasion of France. By ravaging southern France the King hoped to attract the French field army towards him; meanwhile Otto would enter France from the north and capture Paris.

This plan was marred by the delays of the German emperor. King John's operations in Poitou and Anjou drew Philip Augustus south in March, but Otto failed to march on Paris. Leaving an army under Prince Louis to watch the English, the French king hurried northwards. Otto did not leave his base in the Netherlands, where he had been supplementing his meagre German forces with the tenants of his allies, the Dukes of Brabant, Limburg and Lorraine, and the Counts of Flanders, Holland and Namur. In addition a large force of mercenaries, paid by English gold, swelled his ranks. At last on 12 July he entered Nivelles in Brabant and then moved southwards into Hainault in the right direction for Paris.

In the meantime Philip had summoned the feudal array of east, central and north France. He mustered his forces in the middle of July at Péronne, in Vermandois, 70 miles north of Paris. He then moved into Flemish territory and captured Tournai on 26 July. Here he learnt that the invaders had left Flanders and were in fact at Valenciennes, in his rear. At once the French king decided to march southwards with all haste, making a detour to the west to pass round the Germans. Accordingly he marched westwards towards Bouvines, where there was a bridge over the River Marque. But Otto had resolved to seek battle. He led his army north-westwards. On the morning of 27 July the Imperialists, having by-passed Tournai, caught up with the French before they had crossed the Marque. Already the French rearguard cavalry under the Viscount of Melun had fought an action against the Flemish cavalry, and although Philip had sent the Duke of Burgundy to stiffen this resistance it had become clear that the army would not be able to cross the bridge at Bouvines in time. Therefore Philip ordered his army to face about, and take up positions on the slight rise east of the river astride the Roman road to Tournai. The French soldiers were drawn up in 3 lines —cross-bowmen, cavalry and foot soldiers. These in turn were divided into 3 divisions. On the left stood the men of the Counts of Ponthieu, Dreux, Auxerre and many other companies from northern France. The king commanded the centre, composed of baronial tenants including 70 Norman knights. On the right wing, under the Duke of Burgundy, were mustered many more feudal contingents from all over France.

The Imperialists deployed a long line of pikemen first, and

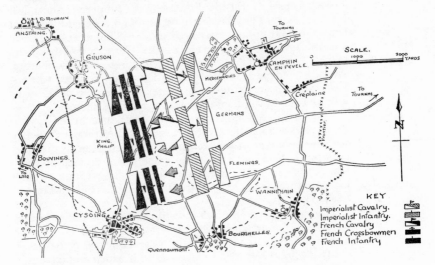

supported these with their cavalry. The left division consisted mainly of Flemings; the centre of Germans supported by men from Brabant, Namur and Limburg; and the right wing of mercenaries under the Earl of Salisbury and the cavalry of the Count of Boulogne.

A squadron of 300 men-at-arms from the French right charged first, hoping to break the Imperial line, but they were repulsed by the Flemish, who advanced upon the French. Soon the whole Imperial left wing was in action against the French opposite them, and a confused cavalry fight ensued. In the centre the Imperialist pikemen soon routed the French infantry and continued to advance. King Philip then led the heavy cavalry under his command, charging into their disordered ranks. Soon each French knight was hacking about him at a cluster of German pikemen, and the King himself almost lost his life when he was pulled off his horse. Mounting again he directed his cavalry in repeated charges among the disorganised Imperial infantry, who fell back rapidly behind their own cavalry.

On the French left the battle had also gone well for King Philip. After the capture of Salisbury by the Bishop of Beauvais his mercenary soldiers fled. The Count of Boulogne and his feudal array stood their ground valiantly against the Count of Dreux, but as a fighting unity the Imperial left wing was no more. The Flemings on the right of Otto had by now lost most of their leaders, and gradually they also gave ground and scattered for safety.

In the centre a furious battle raged between the unwearied

German chivalry and the tired knights of King Philip. A French knight, Gerard la True, slew the Emperor's horse, but his loyal Saxons gathered around him and covered his retreat from the field upon a borrowed mount. The absence of their general lowered the morale of the German nobility who engaged the French cavalry with desperate counter-charges As more soldiers from the French left wing gathered to reinforce their fellows in the centre, increasing numbers of Germans followed the example of their leader and fled the field.

The Count of Boulogne, however, continued to resist, with some 700 pikemen formed in a circle protecting his cavalry whenever they returned from their charges. He was defeated only by the combined efforts of 3,000 mounted men-at-arms, who cut their way past the spearmen. The Count himself became a prisoner of the martial Guérin, the Bishop-Elect of Senlis.

The triumphant French king signed a truce on 18 September with King John, which was to last until Easter, 1220. The Emperor Otto lost his throne as a consequence of the battle and King John returned to face the crisis which culminated in the signing of Magna Carta.

J.E.A.

Caen Area (A***)

Date: 6 June–25 July 1944.

Location: The road-triangle Caen-Villers Bocage-Bayeux (best approach Route Nationale 13). **83.**

War and campaign: The Second World War; the North-west European Campaign of 1944–5 (see p. 197).

Object of the action: Montgomery intended to tie down as many German Panzer divisions as possible, and thus facilitate the American 1st Army's breakout through St. Lo (q.v.).

Opposing sides: (a) Field-Marshal Montgomery in command of the Allied 21st Army Group. (b) Field-Marshal Rommel commanding Army Group 'B'; later, General Hausser.

Forces engaged: (a) British 2nd Army: 10 infantry, 3 armoured, 1 airborne divisions, and 6 armoured brigades (1,350 tanks).
(b) German 7th Army and Panzer Group West: 6 infantry divisions and 7 Panzer divisions (670 tanks).

Casualties: (a) British (to 19 July): 6,010 killed; 28,690 wounded.
(b) German (to 23 July): 116,863 killed and wounded (Normandy Front).

Result: The bulk of the German armour was attracted to the British front; this enabled Bradley to break out on 25 July.

Nearby accommodation: Caen.

Suggested reading: General Works: Wilmot C., *The Struggle for Europe*, London, 1952. Essame and Belfield, *The North-west Europe Campaign*, Aldershot, 1962. On the Campaign: Speidel, H., *We defended Normandy*, London, 1951. Stacey, *The Victory Campaign*, Ottawa, 1960. Carell, P., *Invasion—They're Coming*, London, 1962. Essame and Belfield, *The Battle of Normandy*, London, 1965.

A glance at the map suffices to explain the immense strategic importance of Caen in the Battle of Normandy. At the outset, the bulk of the German mobile reserves were sited north of the Seine. They must therefore approach the bridgehead from the east and thus converge on Caen. The city was also the sally port offering the invaders the shortest route to Paris and the Seine ports and to the best country for the establishment of airfields.

Montgomery accordingly planned to threaten to break out here, thus drawing the German armoured divisions on to the British and Canadians and wearing them down. He then proposed to pivot the whole front on Caen and break out on the west flank with the American armies under Bradley. Despite pressure from American and, regrettably, British sources he never once deviated from this aim.

Bayeux and Caen were included in the D-Day objectives of the British 2nd Army. Bayeux fell on 7 June. Partly owing to the intervention of the 21st Panzer Division and partly through failure to exploit fully initial surprise, the chance of taking Caen on D-Day was missed. The Germans quickly endeavoured to concentrate 4 very good Panzer divisions in the area. The theme of British operations for the next month thus became the capture of Caen. Three battles resulted. The first, an attempt between 10 and 15 June to outflank and encircle the city with the 30th Corps from the Bayeux area towards Villers Bocage and Evrécy, 8 miles south-west of Caen, and with the 1st Corps east of the Orne. This drew all the available German armour on to the British front. The storm from 18 to 21 June delayed the start of the next offensive to 25 June. This involved a thrust by the 8th Corps from the north between Caen and Tilly across the River Odon and aimed at placing the British armour astride the Caen–Falaise road. By 29 June it had forestalled the last effective German attempt to break the Allied front. His strategic aim achieved, Montgomery suspended the battle.

At 2100 hours on 7 July, 467 Lancasters of Bomber Command dropped 2,560 tons of bombs on Caen causing immense damage and much civilian suffering. The city, but not the Faubourg de Vaucelles south of the Orne, fell to the British 2nd Army on the following day.

For the next 20 days Montgomery continued to pull the weight of the enemy's armour on to the British front, attacking both east and west of the Orne, with the result that on 25 July, when the Americans were at last ready to break out at St. Lo, he was holding 7 Panzer divisions, 6 infantry divisions and 3 Nebelwerfer brigades (over 600 tanks) in the Caen area, whereas the Americans were faced only by 9 divisions of sorts and not more than 100 tanks. As the American breakout proceeded, the 1st Canadian Army, supported by Bomber Command, relentlessly continued the attack down the road towards Falaise.

H.E.

Cambrai (A****)

Date: 20 November–5 December 1917.

Location: Follow Route Nationale 17 or 29 from Gouzeaucourt or Boursies to Cambrai. **76.**

War and campaign: The First World War; the Western Front, 1917 (see p. 197).

Object of the action: An Allied large-scale raid on the Somme front, where the terrain was favourable for the employment of the tank.

Opposing sides: (a) General Byng commanding the British 3rd Army. (b) General von der Marwitz in command of the German 2nd Army.

Forces engaged (on 20 November): (a) British: 19 divisions; 3 tank brigades; 5 French divisions in reserve. (b) Germans: 6 divisions (ultimately strengthened to 20).

Casualties: (a) 44,000 British (approx.). (b) 53,000 German.

Result: A brilliant initial success was nullified by a lack of reserves to resist German counter-attacks.

Nearby accommodation: Cambrai.

Suggested reading: General Works: Cruttwell, C. M. F., *History of the Great War*, Oxford, 1936. Liddell Hart, B. H., *The Tanks*, Vol. I, London, 1959. Fuller, J. F. C., *Tanks in the Great War*, London, 1920. On the Campaign and Battle: Miles, W. and Edmonds, J., *Military Operations. France and Flanders. Cambrai 1917*, London, 1948.

The Royal Tank Regiment, the direct descendant of the Tank Corps of 1917, annually and rightly celebrate 20 November as their regimental day, for Cambrai was the first great tank offensive in history, an indication of the work of the tank pioneers and the nearest approach to a quick and cheap breakthrough which any army had hitherto achieved on the Western Front since the construction of the continuous trench system in November 1914.

The main efforts of the British Army in the summer and autumn of 1917 were engaged in Flanders where Haig's obsession with the scene of his first major command was worked out in a series of dreadful and fruitless frontal assaults on the ridges before Ypres. By the middle of October it was clear even to him that the battle could not be prolonged with any profit in the worsening autumn weather and, anxious for a success and a diversion elsewhere, he turned again to a plan which he had briefly considered earlier. The tanks at Ypres had, as the experts forecast, bogged in the autumn quagmire. Farther south, the rolling chalk downs of the Somme provided the 'going' which they needed and offered a good chance of exploitation if the tanks could secure the preliminary break-through which the tank staff confidently predicted. On 13 October Haig gave his approval to the withdrawal of tanks from Ypres and the inception of detailed planning.

The front chosen for attack was bounded on the east and west by the Canal du Nord and the St. Quentin canal, about 7 miles apart. The gap was blocked by the main Hindenburg position, a belt of wire, trenches and interlocking strong points some 4,000 yards deep, behind which ran a second position (the Masnières–Beaurevoir line). Supporting the main position and narrowing the gap was a westward loop of the St. Quentin canal which turned north again to Cambrai before it reached the dominating spur of the Bourlon ridge on the left. Behind Cambrai the upper Sensée river ran at right angles across the axis of advance. The British would thus attack into a narrow-ing pocket and would have to seize both the ridge and the canal to break across the flanks and secure crossings over the Sensée to break through in depth. The open country in the centre, however, offered the chance of a quick advance for it was largely free of the shell craters which had trapped the tanks at Ypres and was weakly garrisoned.

Fuller, the Tank Corps staff officer who had selected Cambrai as a profitable tank zone, had advocated no more than a raid on an enormous scale, designed to humiliate and confuse the enemy by a short and dramatic *coup de main*. Byng, commanding the 3rd Army, which was to strike the blow, prepared a more ambitious project whose objects were, firstly to break through the Hindenburg line, next to capture Cambrai, Bourlon wood and the Sensée crossings, thirdly to cut off the Germans between the Sensée and the Canal du Nord and, lastly to push north-west towards Valenciennes. These objectives were approved but Haig, who knew only too well how few were the reserves available, set a time limit of 48 hours for the seizure of the flanks and the crossings. Unless the original force could keep to schedule the operation would fail for lack of support and must be abandoned.

By 19 November the 3rd Army had 19 divisions on the front.

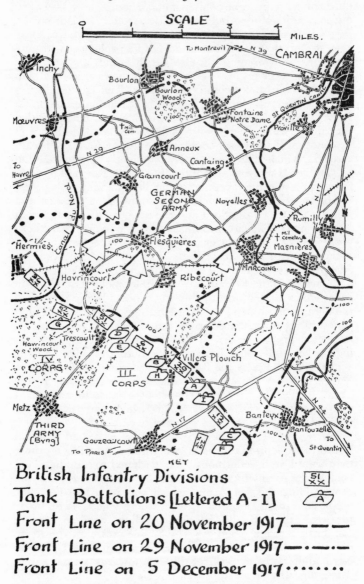

KEY

British Infantry Divisions

Tank Battalions [Lettered A - I]

Front Line on 20 November 1917 — — —

Front Line on 29 November 1917 —·—·—

Front Line on 5 December 1917 ········

Six of these were to make the break-in which the Cavalry Corps (5 divisions) was to exploit. The artillery numbered 1,000 guns, secretly assembled and masked from discovery by dependence on a new and most difficult technique: shooting from the map without preliminary registration. There was to be no preparatory bombardment, a departure from convention which lulled enemy suspicion. Finally, 3 brigades of tanks stood ready to move off, 476 in all, of which 378 were fighting tanks and the rest supply or gun-carriers. The assaulting infantry and tanks had practised the techniques of co-operation thoroughly in back areas, and the tanks had been brought forward by train, completing their approach under cover of noise from low-flying aeroplanes. During the night of 19 November they leaguered in the ruined villages and the dense thickets of Havrincourt wood.

There were also 3 French infantry and 2 cavalry divisions behind the British, disposed there at the insistence of Pétain to help in enlarging the expected success. Although the Germans had received rumours of an impending attack they were quite unaware of the nature of the blow about to fall. They had only 2 divisions in the line, with 4 in support, and only 150 guns. Paschendaele had worn down their army to a dangerously weak level and it could not be made up until the Russian armistice released troops from the east. But some were already on their way, while Haig had almost nothing on hand.

At 6.20 am on 20 November the bombardment opened and the infantry and tanks moved forward. This unprecedented simultaneity carried the British quickly and easily through the German first positions. Within 4 hours the whole of the Hindenburg line was in British hands, except around the fortified village of Flesquières in the centre which was stubbornly defended. The commander of the 51st (Highland) Division distrusted the new arm and had kept his infantry too far behind the tanks. Thus the infantry were exposed to German machine guns undestroyed by the tanks, who were themselves subjected, as they moved onward, to intense fire from 3 field batteries in the orchards around the village. The village might have been taken at any time by a flank attack from right or left, but the other divisions were intent upon securing their own objectives and the notorious weakness of communications prevented a clear picture of the situation percolating to 3rd Army H.Q. By evening, although the situation looked promising on the map, less had been achieved than was necessary. The 'cavalry gap' had not appeared, Bourlon was unattacked, the troops were tiring and 179 of the tanks were out of action. The church bells were rung next morning in London, for the first and last time before the armistice, to salute a victory, but if dramatic it was not complete. The well-known 'diminishing power of the attack' had set in and the Germans were hurrying troops to the area. Haig had nothing in hand to reinforce his effort, but the exposed advance must be extended if the attackers were themselves to escape harm.

Flesquières was, in fact, evacuated during the night, but this came too late for a quick success at Bourlon against which Haig was now forced to concentrate. After an initial advance of a mile and a half, which seemed to promise a continuation of the previous day's progress, the infantry met tenacious resistance in Bourlon wood and the advance ceased. For the next week bitter fighting raged around this little spur. Although his time limit had been exceeded, Haig was unable to disengage or, for lack of troops, to divert the enemy by attacks on the right where he held crossings over the St. Quentin canal. As his casualties mounted the Germans were assembling divisions from east and west for the counter-stroke.

On 29 November they repaid the surprise. In Russia and Italy they had recently experimented with a technique of hurricane bombardment and infantry infiltration which had proved enormously successful. Against the more resolute British defence the effect was minimised but, with 20 divisions in hand, their attacks drove in the sides of the salient and regained much of the ground lost. They also broke through the original British line south of Villers Plouich. It was clear that the British posture was unbalanced and, on the night of 4/5 December Haig ordered a withdrawal to a line from Flesquières to Gonnelieu, almost exactly the area captured in the first day's fighting, although German gains to the south had turned it into an uncomfortable salient.

Thus, in material terms, Cambrai was a disappointment, but this is no fair measure of its importance. The success of the Allied armies in late 1918 and the later development of all armoured forces stem from the surprise and triumph of 20 November 1917.

J.D.P.K.

Châlons-sur-Marne (Méry-sur-Seine) (B***)

Date: A.D. 451.

Location: Follow Route Nationale 19 from Paris for 139 km. to Méry-sur-Seine, 29 km. from Troyes. 95.

War and campaign: The Hun Invasion of Gaul (see p. 193).

Object of the action: The Romans were attempting to repulse the Huns from northern Gaul.

Opposing sides: (a) The Roman Master of the Soldiers, Aetius, and the Visigoth king, Theoderic. (b) Attila the Hun commanding his barbarian army.

Forces engaged: Uncertain.

Casualties: Not known.

Result: Neither side gained a clear victory, but the Hun impetus was checked for the first time.

Nearby accommodation: Méry-sur-Seine or Troyes.

Suggested reading: General Works: Gibbon, E., *The Decline and Fall of the Roman Empire* (Edn. J. B. Bury), London, 1900. Hodgkin, T., *Italy and her Invaders* (2nd Edn.), London, 1892. On the Battle: Creasy, E., *Fifteen Decisive Battles of the Western World* (Oxford Edn.), 1915. Fuller, J. F. C., *Decisive Battles of the Western World*, Vol. I, London, 1954. Article: Grant, M., 'Attila the Hun', in *History Today*, Vol. IV, 1954.

In A.D. 451 Attila, the King of the Huns, was still the terror of the entire Roman Empire after eighteen years of rule over his barbaric horde of nomads based to the north of the Danube. The Huns, who, centuries before, had ravaged the Chinese Empire, although not large in numbers or physique, appeared to be militarily invincible: living in the saddle, their horsemanship and mobility in the field were incredible, and their powers were yet further enhanced by the acquisition of Roman horses of superior size and endurance. Worse still for Rome, the attractions of civilised life meant nothing to them, in contrast to the Germanic invaders who had preceded them into the Empire. They were destroyers, pure and simple, living as devouring parasites in every society at which they struck. For long Attila had been content to exact a tribute in gold, but in 450 the new eastern Emperor Marcian suspended payment. Surprisingly, Attila decided to attack in the west first. His reasons were twofold. First, he conveniently had a pretext, for the Emperor Valentinian's repressed and half-crazed sister Honoria had secretly sent him her ring and a request for marriage. Attila, who already had numerous wives, took up the offer, demanded his bride and half Valentinian's Empire as her dowry. The request was refused. At the same time, the Ripuarian Franks who were settled in north-west Gaul were without a king, and the rival candidates appealed to Attila and to Rome. This in particular directed Attila to Gaul rather than Italy, though it is possible that concerted action was planned with Geiseric the Vandal king, now dominating North Africa, who may have been supposed to attack Italy. At any rate, Attila must have known that his most formidable opponents were not the Romans themselves, but the powerful Visigothic kingdom of Theoderic in Aquitaine.

The Visigoths, who a generation before had captured and sacked Rome, under Alaric, were still a danger to the Empire, and Rome had in fact employed Huns as mercenaries against them to defend Provence. But the Visigoths were now in conflict with Attila's Vandal allies, and would certainly oppose Attila himself. They were by now relatively civilised, their nobles at least were educated men, and they were Christians.

The native peasantry of Gaul looked on Roman and Visigoth armies alike as oppressors, and had been in a state of rebellion for many years, under the name of Bagaudae. From them Attila might expect welcome as a deliverer.

He entered Gaul in early summer of 451, in three columns, striking at Arras, Metz and Strasbourg. Over a dozen cities, including Trier, Cologne, Mainz and Strasbourg, were sacked and burned. From Paris, which was miraculously saved, he moved towards the south and besieged Orléans, strategically controlling an important crossing of the Loire. Meanwhile the Roman forces had been gathering in the south. The Roman commander-in-chief was Aetius the Patrician, Master of the Soldiers, and for the past twenty years virtual ruler of the Western Empire. As a young man he had lived as a hostage among the Huns, had spent a period of exile with them, had on several occasions employed them as mercenaries, and knew Attila personally. Aetius had crossed the Alps with a token force only. Through the mediation of the powerful Gallic senator Avitus, living in retirement on his estates at Clermont, the Visigoth king Theoderic at Toulouse was given eloquent warning of the common danger, and mustered his forces. The united army advanced on Orléans, and Attila raised the siege which had lasted five weeks. On 14 June he began his retreat towards the Seine, clearly planning to give battle in the wide plains of Champagne, where his cavalry could be used to full advantage. Aetius pursued his rearguard and inflicted severe casualties on the motley forces of the Huns and their allies. The Roman and Visigoth army had now been strengthened by the adhesion of Sangibanus, King of the Alans, another barbarian people settled in Gaul, but he was suspected of being ready to change sides.

Attila moved back on the Seine and halted at Méry. It was an ideal position for him. When the Romano-Gothic force arrived Attila realised that he was outnumbered, and decided to wait till the early afternoon before giving battle. In the meantime a small Visigoth force under Thorismond, son of King Theoderic, managed to occupy a small prominence overlooking the plain, the only hill of any size and thus a tactical position of immense importance, overlooking the Hun left flank.

Aetius and Theoderic put the suspect Alans in the centre, and took the left and right wings respectively for their own forces. Attila put the Huns in his centre, the Ostrogoths facing their Visigoth kinsmen on the left wing, and the Gepidae and other contingents on the right. After the initial exchange of missiles Attila's cavalry charged the centre, the allied weak spot, broke through and wheeled round to take the Visigoths in the rear. In the clash King Theoderic was struck by a missile and trampled to death in the mêlée. Attila took this as a sign

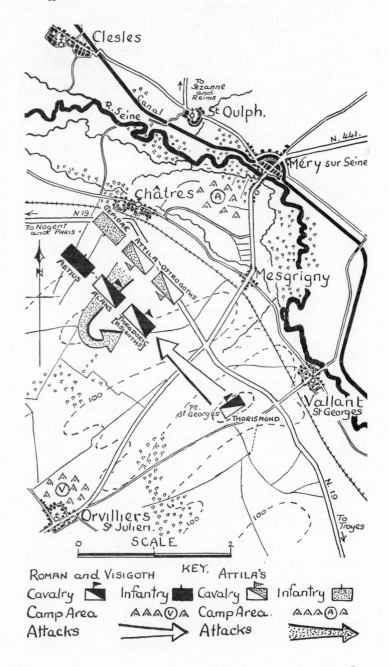

Clesles

To Sezanne and Reims

R. Seine
Canal
St Qulph.

N. 441.

Méry sur Seine

Châtres (A)

N 19
GERIDAE
To Nogent and PARIS

ATTILA
OSTROGOTHS

Mesgrigny

AETIUS

ALANS

THEODORIC (VISIGOTHS)

100

pt. St Georges
THORISMOND

Vallant
St Georges

N 19

100

(V)

Orvilliers
St Julien.

100

100

To Troyes

0 SCALE 2

KEY.

ROMAN and VISIGOTH   ATTILA'S
Cavalry ◣ Infantry ▰ Cavalry ◺ Infantry ▦
Camp Area ᴧᴧᴧ(V)ᴧ Camp Area. ᴧᴧᴧ(A)ᴧ
Attacks ⟹ Attacks ⟹

of victory, but the result was to bring on a furious charge from the dead king's son Thorismond from his position above the plain. The rest of the battle had been indecisive so far, but Attila and the Huns were now forced to retreat and were pursued right up to their encampment. Here Thorismond was thrown from his horse and narrowly escaped, causing the pursuit to lose its impetus. It was now dusk and he rode back with his men to the Goth camp, to which Aetius also had come, after managing to hold out on the Roman left wing. Here Thorismond was formally elected king by the army in succession to Theoderic and swore revenge against the killers of his father.

Attila, in the safety of his camp, was prepared for the worst, barricaded by wagons. He had even prepared his own funeral pyre. It was the first time that his invincibility had been shaken in pitched battle. The Visigoths were breathing fire and slaughter, and were prepared either to fight him again or to starve him out. But the next morning the Visigoth and Roman contingents dispersed and went their separate ways. Attila remained in his camp for several days, sullenly suspecting a trap. Eventually he came out, retired north across the Rhine and went back to his primitive cantonments on the Danube.

What had happened was the work of the diplomatic Aetius, who had feared that the Visigoths, if completely victorious over Attila, would present an intolerable menace to Rome once more. He had preyed on Thorismond's fears that if he did not return at once to Toulouse he might be ousted from the throne. So the Visigoths left. Aetius preferred to maintain a balance of terror. The next year Attila descended on Italy itself, destroying numerous cities, including Aquileia, Padua and Verona, and occupied Milan. Here a deputation led by Pope Leo somehow persuaded him, perhaps by preying on his superstitions, to leave Italy. The next year, after a barbarous revel to celebrate yet another marriage, this chieftain who still claimed the Emperor's sister and her dowry, died from a haemorrhage on the marriage bed. After his death his ill-disciplined and motley armies disintegrated, and the Huns were never again a serious threat to Rome.

Although the battle in Champagne in June 451 did not completely finish off Attila, its importance cannot be underestimated. It was the first time that he had not conquered, and he suffered serious casualties, a matter of vital importance to him as the number of actual Huns was always small, and the number of subject allies he could compel to serve him depended largely on the myth of his invincibility. The battle showed that the Germanic barbarians—the Visigoths—could choose civilisation rather than barbarism. The co-operation of Roman and Visigoth was a promising augury for the future, and saved Europe from becoming a desert, like those which the Huns had created in central Asia and which took centuries to recover from the effects of a few years of domination, if they did recover at all.

A.R.B.

CHEMIN DES DAMES (B***); battle of, 16–30 April 1917; near Laffaux; **85**; Western Front, 1917. Much fighting centred along this natural line of resistance between Laon and Rheims; the terrible casualties inflicted on the French during the Nivelle offensive of April 1917 (187,000) led directly to the 'military strike' of May 1917. See Spears, *Prelude to Victory*, London, 1939.

Crécy (A****)

Date: 26 August 1346.

Location: From Abbeville follow the Hesdin-St. Omer road north for 11 miles; turn left 3 miles south of Labroye for Crécy-en-Ponthieu. The battle site lies in the triangle Crécy–Wadicourt–Estrées. **73**.

War and campaign: The Normandy–Calais Campaign of 1346; the Hundred Years' War (see p. 194).

Object of the action: Edward III, moving towards Flanders, turned to face his French pursuers.

Opposing sides: (*a*) King Edward III commanding an army of Englishmen and Welshmen. (*b*) King Philip VI commanding the French forces, with some Genoese and Italian troops.

Forces engaged: (*a*) English: 5,500 archers; 1,000 Welshmen; 2,500 men-at-arms. *Total*: approx. 9,000. (*b*) French: 6,000 foot (including Genoese cross-bowmen); large numbers of communal militia; 10,000 men-at-arms. *Total*: approx. 30,000.

Casualties: (*a*) The English lost about 100 all ranks. (*b*) The French lost 1,500 knights and squires and perhaps 10,000 other ranks.

Result: An overwhelming English victory which in due course opened the way for the siege and capture of Calais.

Nearby accommodation: Abbeville.

Suggested reading: General Works: Oman, Sir C., *A History of the Art of War in the Middle Ages*, Vol. II (enlarged 2nd Edn.), London, 1924. Perroy, E., *La Guerre de Cent Ans*, 1946 (English Edn., *The Hundred Years' War*, London, 1951). Lot, F., *L'Art Militaire et les Armées au Moyen Age*, Vol. I, 1946. On the Campaign and Battle; Fuller, J. F. C., *The Decisive Battles of the Western World*, Vol. I, London, 1954. Burne, A. H., *The Crécy War*, London, 1955. Work of Fiction: Ellis, K. M., *Guns Forever Echo*, London, 1949.

The Hundred Years' War, of which Crécy was the first major land battle, arose out of the rivalry between Philip VI of

France and Edward III of England. Edward, as Duke of Aquitaine, was a vassal of the French king, and the latter wished to insist on as binding a form of vassalage as possible in order to restrain a dangerous and over-mighty subject. Edward III was anxious not to bind himself too strongly as an obedient subject and, in the end, denied the right of Philip to be King of France at all, claiming his own right—through his mother Isabelle, daughter of Philip IV of France—instead. Thus what began as a feudal quarrel developed into a dynastic conflict. In the ensuing clash each king took advantage of the other's domestic problems, whether in Scotland, Brittany or Guienne, to undermine his rival's power.

Active hostilities broke out in 1337 when, after Philip had declared Edward's province of Guienne forfeit, Edward made his first attack on Philip via Flanders. In the next few years there followed further expeditions to Flanders and to Guienne. In these early years of fighting the one decisive action was the naval battle of Sluys of 24 June 1340, which for a generation at least gave the English command of the Channel and therefore the ability to mount expeditions to invade France with relatively little fear of interference.

Early in July 1346 Edward III mustered an army of about 10,000 men at Portsmouth and, on 11 July, set sail for France. It seems that Edward had originally intended to sail for Gascony but changed his mind and made for the Cotentin peninsula. His general strategic plan is far from clear. It had already become a fairly established strategy to divert the King of France from his attacks on Guienne by, in turn, attacking northern France through Flanders. But in 1346 the approach was entirely different, and it is not clear whether Edward intended simply a diversion or a raid in force; or, if the latter, what the precise objective of the raid was to be. A decision was then enforced on Edward by a mutiny among his own ships' crews who, against his orders, returned to England. Edward, deprived of his line of communication, could either move south towards his own troops in Guienne or north-east towards Flanders. He chose the latter, probably influenced in his choice by the news that his Flemish allies had crossed the French frontier and laid siege to Béthune.

But, to get to Flanders, the Seine and the Somme had to be crossed. The lower Seine was found to be impassable, and Edward was forced to go close to Paris before getting across at Poissy. Knowing that Philip now had a large army in the Paris area, Edward hurried northwards towards the Somme at Abbeville. After several vain attempts he crossed the Somme at Blanchetaque, 10 miles below Abbeville, on 24 August, and proceeded to Crécy, some 12 miles farther north. Meanwhile Philip, still in pursuit, crossed the Somme by the bridge in Abbeville.

CRÉCY
26th August 1346

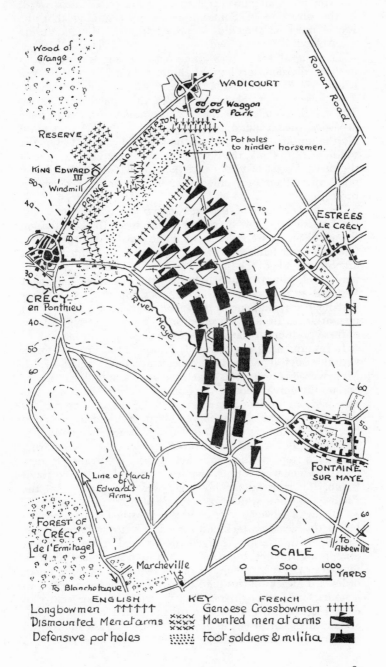

Wood of Grange

WADICOURT

Waggon Park

RESERVE

Pot holes to hinder horsemen.

KING EDWARD III
Windmill

ESTRÉES LE CRÉCY

CRÉCY en Ponthieu

River Maye

Roman Road

FONTAINE SUR MAYE

Line of March of Edward's Army

FOREST OF CRÉCY
[de l'Ermitage]

Marcheville

To Blanchetaque

SCALE
0   500   1000
YARDS

To Abbeville

KEY

ENGLISH
Longbowmen
Dismounted Men at arms
Defensive potholes

FRENCH
Genoese Crossbowmen
Mounted men at arms
Foot soldiers & militia

At Crécy Edward decided to turn and accept battle. He drew up his army in the area between Crécy and Wadicourt, two villages about 3,000 yards apart, and faced south-eastwards in the direction of Fontaine-sur-Maye, assuming that the French must—as they did—approach from this direction using the Abbeville–Hesdin road.

The English army, now about 9,000 strong, was drawn up in three 'divisions' or 'battles', on the forward slope of the rise which lies east of the road between Crécy and Wadicourt. Two divisions were placed forward, a third behind in reserve. The first division, on the right, was commanded by the Prince of Wales; the second, on the left, by the Earls of Arundel and Northampton; the reserve division by Edward III. On the south, or right flank, the position was protected by the edge of the dense Forest of Crécy and the tiny River Maye; on the north the village of Wadicourt itself gave some, though less protection.

The line of battle of the first two divisions was one to which the English were now becoming accustomed. In each division the men-at-arms were dismounted and stationed in the centre. On each outer flank archers, long-bowmen, were drawn up at an obtuse angle to the line and forward of it; on the two inner flanks archers were similarly posted, their positions forming a V-shape at that point. From this position they could pour flanking fire against enemy horsemen attacking the dismounted men-at-arms. In addition many small holes were dug in front of these positions to cause the enemy cavalry to stumble.

In his advance from Abbeville Philip had at first lost touch with the English and had not expected them to turn and fight. Moreover, his army was marching in considerable disorder and totally unready for battle. Contact between the two armies was made in the late afternoon of 26 August and some of his entourage urged Philip to halt and form up his army, delaying battle until the next day. This wise advice was never put into action simply because the advance guard of the French army refused to stop. As they approached the English the Genoese cross-bowmen were thrown forward to begin the attack at about 6 pm. Their weapons, however, were out-ranged by the English long-bow which was capable of being used effectively at ranges of 200–250 yards. As the cross-bowmen gave way before this deadly attack and turned to retire in disorder, the French men-at-arms charged down and through them, attempting to get to grips with the dismounted English men-at-arms. It is calculated that some 12 to 15 quite unco-ordinated attacks of this kind took place during the next 4 to 5 hours, and although some got to grips with the centre of each English division, most were decimated by the English archers firing in from the flanks. On the English side it had been a static battle defending a strong natural position.

By midnight Philip withdrew to the castle of Broye. And on 28 August Edward continued his march via Montreuil to Calais.

Tactically, the battle of Crécy established the supremacy of the long-bow on the battlefields of Europe and gave England the standing of a great military power. Strategically, as we have seen, the whole operation lacked coherent purpose, and its only immediate result was the capture of Calais.

N.H.G.

DENAIN (C***); battle of, 24 July 1712; on the river Scheldt; 75; War of the Spanish Succession. Marshal Villars (24,000) inflicted a sharp defeat on General Albemarle (10,500) and indirectly, on Prince Eugen, thereby regaining Denain, and later St. Amand and Douai from the Allies; this success raised French morale and discouraged the Allies. See Henderson, N., *Prince Eugen of Savoy*, London, 1964.

D-Day (Operation Overlord) (A****)

Date: 6 June 1944.

Location: A 30–mile stretch of the Normandy coast from the river Orne to the base of the Cotentin Peninsula. **82.**

War and campaign: The Second World War; the North-west Europe Campaign, 1944–5 (see p. 197).

Object of the action: The Allies were attempting to establish a bridgehead on the Normandy coast of German-occupied Europe, and thus inaugurate the Second Front in the West.

Opposing sides: (*a*) General Montgomery commanding 21st Army Group (2nd British and 1st U.S. Armies). (*b*) General Hausser's 7th German Army, part of Rommel's Army Group 'B'.

Forces engaged: (*a*) Allies: 3 airborne, 7 infantry divisions; 2 commando and 3 armoured brigades. (*b*) Germans: elements of 3 infantry and 1 Panzer divisions.

Casualties: (*a*) 2,500 Allies killed: 8,500 wounded or missing. (*b*) Germans: no figures known.

Result: Although no final objectives were attained, the Allies achieved a decisive success and thus secured a considerable bridge-head in 'Festung Europa'.

Nearby accommodation: Bayeux or Caen.

Suggested reading: General Works: Montgomery, B. L., *Normandy to the Baltic*, London, 1946. Wilmot, C., *The Struggle for Europe*,

London, 1952. On the Battle: Ryan, C., *The Longest Day*, London, 1960.
American Heritage Junior Library, *D-Day: the Invasion of Europe*, 1962.

D-Day was the breaching of the so-called Atlantic Wall of Hitler's 'Fortress Europe' to enforce the unconditional surrender of Nazi Germany. For the cross-Channel assault Montgomery, under the supreme command of General Eisenhower, had General Bradley's American 1st Army and British 2nd Army under General Dempsey. Field-Marshal Rommel, responsible for defending the whole north-western coast of Europe, planned to fight to a finish on the heavily fortified beaches. But his forces were necessarily widely dispersed, and he could only move up his best armoured reserve divisions with Hitler's direct permission. He was also absent on leave in Germany when the battle began.

D-DAY (OPERATION OVERLORD) *6th June 1944*

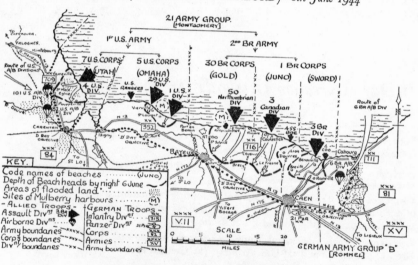

The assault was preceded by a massive, month-long, air offensive against road and rail communications in France and all bridges over the lower Seine. The naval operation to sweep lanes through the minefields, transport two armies across the Channel and support the landings with gunfire involved using over 3,000 ships. Amphibious tanks were to accompany the infantry assault boats; and the British had also a mass of special tanks known as 'Funnies' for gapping minefields and wire, bridging awkward places and blowing up concrete emplacements. Airborne divisions, dropped soon after midnight, had to secure both flanks of the assault, which was to come in at half-tide, from 6.30 in the morning onwards, on five beaches, code-named *Utah* and *Omaha* for the Americans, *Gold*, *Juno* and *Sword* for the British and Canadians. Bradley was to secure a firm base for operations to cut off and capture Cherbourg. Dempsey, by seizing Caen and Bayeux, had to shield the Americans from interference by the German armoured reserve, which was mostly held back in the area between the Seine and the Loire.

Wherever possible, Rommel had strengthened his defences by widespread flooding of the river valleys behind the beaches. The American 101st and 82nd Airborne Divisions had the tasks of securing the five causeways which ran back through the floods behind *Utah* beach and the bridges beyond the floods over the River Merderet. Inexperience and bad navigation led to them being dropped over a widely scattered area, many of them into the floods, where they drowned. But the handful which assembled secured almost all the objectives and caused the maximum bewilderment and confusion among the Germans. The seaborne landing by the American 4th Division on *Utah*, north of the Vire estuary, was also successful. Some assault craft and tanks sank in the heavy seas; and bad navigation brought the whole assault wave in a mile south of the selected beach. By good fortune opposition there was, however, light and two of the five causeways were quickly secured. In spite of confusion on the beaches and some heavy fighting along the dunes, by 1 pm they had linked up with the airborne troops. By midnight they held an area running 9 miles inland, though only 4 miles of coast had been cleared.

At *Omaha*, west of the Vire, the American 1st and 29th. Divisions came very near to disaster. Almost all the tanks launched were swamped. The preliminary air and naval bombardment overshot the target; and the assault companies of infantry, landed at the wrong places and in great disorder under a withering fire from the unsubdued defences, were pinned to the tide-line for hours, while successive waves of troops and vehicles came ashore in mounting confusion. Brilliant leadership and the fighting courage of the troops at last got a few parties moving inland by midday, and the beach defences were gradually worn down. But by midnight they had only penetrated about 1½ miles on a 4-mile front and their situation was still very precarious. On the beach alone they had suffered over 3,000 casualties, whereas at *Utah* there had only been 12 killed and 100 wounded.

Farther to the east the British 2nd Army had three beaches. The 50th Division was to land on *Gold* and capture Arromanches and Bayeux; the 3rd Division, landing on *Sword*, hoped to capture Caen. Linking them were the Canadians on *Juno*, who were to cut the Caen–Bayeux road and threaten Caen from the west. The 6th Airborne Division, dropped at midnight between the rivers Orne and Dives, duly secured the left flank, in spite of some scattering and inevitable losses in the floods; and the landings were made good on all the British beaches, though not without difficulty and confusion. Wind and tide were worse even than at *Omaha*. But the Royal Navy gave them a longer bombardment than the Americans and launched tanks and assault craft nearer the shore. They landed at the right places and with more tanks, as well as the 'Funnies' to support them. Thus, in spite of inevitable mishaps and some bitter fighting on the coast, the British were very little short of their objectives at midnight on 6 June. The 50th Division was in the outskirts of Bayeux and got it without further fighting next morning. The dashing Canadian advance carried them 7 miles inland, to within striking distance of the main road. The 3rd Division, with the 4th Commando, had reinforced the airborne troops and was within sight of Caen; and at dusk a massive glider-borne force had flown in to consolidate the gains.

Things might have gone much worse for the Allies if the Germans had reacted more quickly. Three main factors prevented them: their generals were convinced that Normandy was only a feint and that the real attack was coming in the Calais area; Hitler would not release the precious armoured divisions until too late for them to move under cover of darkness; and air and sea bombardment, paratroopers and French saboteurs so damaged telephone and telegraph communications that the German commanders got little reliable information of what was happening. They only learnt of the sea-borne landings at *Utah* at midday, when their reserves had been dispersed to hunt down the airborne troops. The mobile battalions which might have turned *Omaha* into a total disaster had already been thrown in to save Bayeux from the British; and the efficient 21st Panzer Division—the only armoured reserve available—had been drawn in to the battle to save Caen. There was thus no striking force to take advantage of Allied exhaustion and the confusion on the beaches on the night of D-Day. By the afternoon of 7 June it was too late; and D-Day was left to stand as a clear-cut victory in the most complicated military operation ever planned in human history.

W.L.McE.

Dieppe (A**)

Date: 19 August 1942.
Location: on the coastline of Normandy **78**.
War and campaign: Second World War (see p. 197).

Purpose of the Action: A raid or reconnaissance in force by the Allies, designed to test the strength of Hitler's vaunted coastal defences.

Opposing sides: (*a*) Germans under Colonel-General Haase. (*b*) Allies under Major-General Roberts.

Forces engaged: (*a*) Germans: 302 Division. *Total*: c. 5,000. (*b*) Allies: 2nd Canadian Division and 3 British Commandos; 237 ships and craft. *Total*: c. 6,000.

Casualties: (*a*) Germans: 591 soldiers; 8 guns; 2 ships; 48 planes. (*b*) Allies: 4,617 military personnel; 1 destroyer; 33 landing craft; 28 tanks, 106 planes.

Result: Repulse of the Allies—and the learning of many useful lessons subsequently used in 'Operation Overlord' (see 'D-Day' *q.v.*).

Nearby accommodation: Dieppe or Varengeville.

With the exception of No. 4 Commando, which destroyed the German coast defence battery at Varengeville, no Allied unit captured its objective. The defeat of the raiding force was due to the lack of artillery support, which could have been provided by, say, a 6-in cruiser; lack of a preliminary air bombardment; landing in daylight; lack of a sufficient floating reserve and reinforcing of failure with the reserve that did exist. Poor communications was another factor.

The troops of both sides fought with some skill and much courage. The raid contributed something to the planning for Normandy, for it showed the Allies that they could not count on taking a port on D-Day (q.v.). It may have tended to make the Germans complacent about their defences.

P.Y

The Dunes (B***)

Date: 3 June 1658.

Location: 3 to 4 miles east of Dunkirk, between the Furnes–Bruges canal and the sea. **69.**

War and campaign: The Campaign in Flanders between the French and Spaniards (see p. 195).

Object of the action: The French army wished to take Dunkirk from the Spaniards.

Opposing sides: (*a*) Marshal Turenne in command of an Anglo-French army. (*b*) Don Juan of Austria commanding a Spanish and English Royalist exile army.

Forces engaged: (*a*) Allies: 9,000 foot soldiers; 6,000 horse (including 6 Cromwellian foot regiments). *Total*: 15,000. (*b*) Spaniards: 6,000 foot; 8,000 horse (including a contingent of 2,000 English Royalists). *Total*: 14,000–15,000.

Casualties: (*a*) About 400 killed and wounded. (*b*) 1,000 killed and 5,000 prisoners.

Result: A victory for the French, leading to the capture of Dunkirk, Bergues, Dixmude and Oudenarde.

Nearby accommodation: Dunkirk.

Suggested reading: On the Battle: Spalding, Nickerson and Wright, *Warfare*, New York, 1925. Biography: Ramsay, A. M. de, *Histoire du Vicomte de Turenne*, 2 vols, Paris, 1735.

Turenne invested Dunkirk on 27 May. On 2 June Don Juan of Austria, Condé, the Marquis of Caraçena and James, Duke of York, arrived to relieve the town.

Turenne decided to give battle next day. The brunt of the fighting fell on his English contingent which faced the strongest part of the Spanish line, strongly posted on the sandhills. Led by Lockhart's regiment the Cromwellian soldiers fell on with a joyful shout, and, despite heavy losses and a gallant counter-attack by the Duke of York's troop, broke the Spaniards' flank. When the French cavalry came up in support Don Juan's line began to waver, and though on the extreme left Condé showed a bold front, the Spanish were soon in full retreat. The English (Royalist) Regiment of Guards held their ground, but was eventually compelled to surrender.

Turenne's victory was largely due to the English redcoats. In Lockhart's regiment all but six of the officers and sergeants were hit. With no hope of relief Dunkirk soon fell, and the campaign ended with the assault of Ypres where Morgan's English brigade once more distinguished itself.

P.Y.

Dunkirk (A****)

Date: 26 May–3 June 1940.

Location: On the Channel coast, 20 miles east of Calais by Route Nationale 40. **70.**

War and campaign: The Second World War; the Battle of France, May–June 1940 (see p. 197).

Object of the action: To rescue the men of the British Expeditionary Force from the encircling German forces.

Opposing Sides: (*a*) Lord Gort commanding the B.E.F. aided by French and Belgian units. (*b*) Generals von Runstedt and von Bock commanding Army Groups 'A' and 'B'.

Forces engaged: (*a*) 9 British divisions and supporting units; 5 French divisions. *Totals*: 240,000 British and 80,000 French (approx). (*b*) 10 German Panzer divisions with supporting infantry. *Total*: 200,000 Germans (approx.).

Casualties: (*a*) 68,000 British (whole campaign); 40,000 French prisoners (Dunkirk only). (*b*) Perhaps 156,000 Germans (whole campaign.)

Result: The escape of the men of the B.E.F. but the loss of all their equipment; the success of the evacuation rallied British morale, but that of the French rapidly sank.

Nearby accommodation: Dunkirk or Gravelines.

Suggested reading: General Works: Churchill, W. S., *The Second World War*, Vol. II, London, 1949. Flower, D. and Reeves, J., *The War*, 1939–45, London, 1959. On the Campaign: Divine, D., *The Nine Days of Dunkirk*, London, 1959.   Guderian, H., *Panzer Leader*, London, 1952. Work of Fiction: 'Gun Buster', *Return via Dunkirk*, London, 1940.

The 'miracle' of Dunkirk consisted in the removal of 338,226 Allied troops to England in 848 miscellaneous ships between 26 May and 3 June 1940. The magnitude of the achievement may be judged by Field Marshal Kesselring's admission that at the time the Germans regarded even 100,000 as an excessive claim.

Wars, as Churchill remarked, are not won by evacuations, yet Dunkirk contributed to eventual victory in two respects: it won time, and it preserved the nucleus of Britain's professional army upon which new armies could be built.

Dunkirk was not an isolated battle: it must be seen as the last act in the collapse of northern France and Belgium in face of the German invasion of 10–26 May. When Hitler's forces invaded Belgium on 10 May, the B.E.F. immediately advanced to the river Dyle only to withdraw hastily behind the Scheldt (19 May) while Guderian's southern thrust to Abbeville with his Panzer divisions severed British communications. The Allies were steadily pressed back towards the coast from three sides; hopes of a southward breakout faded; and on 27 May Lord Gort was informed that his sole task was to save as much of the B.E.F. as possible.

Meanwhile the problem facing Admiral Ramsay, the commander at Dover responsible for naval support of the B.E.F., grew increasingly complex owing to the Luftwaffe's predominance in the air, and the rapid, if uneven progress on land of Guderian's Panzer divisions. Evacuation plans had to be refashioned repeatedly as first Boulogne, and then Calais fell. When 'Operation Dynamo' at last began, only Dunkirk and some 25 miles of flat, windswept beaches between Gravelines and Nieuport remained free, and all roads within the perimeter were soon subjected to German artillery fire besides heavy aerial bombardment.

As befitted the third port of France, Dunkirk comprised a vast complex of harbours and docks extending over more than 100 acres. Had these facilities been available the B.E.F.'s weapons and equipment as well as its men might have been saved. Unfortunately, the docks had been bombed into a shambles, so only the two moles could be used. Though extremely long—the East Mole stretched 1,400 yards into the roadstead—neither was intended to provide a berth for ships.

Outside the town the perimeter was taking on the shape— as well as the desperate tactical function—of the classical infantry 'square'. On 29 May the French 16th Corps held a line stretching inland from Gravelines about 10 miles, and the western end of the southern front as far as Bérgues. The rest of the line from Bérgues to the sea by Nieuport was held from right to left by the following British divisions: 46th, 1st, 50th, 3rd and 4th. Thus in the first phase the B.E.F. held roughly two-thirds of a front of some 45 miles.

DUNKIRK

26th May to 3rd June 1940

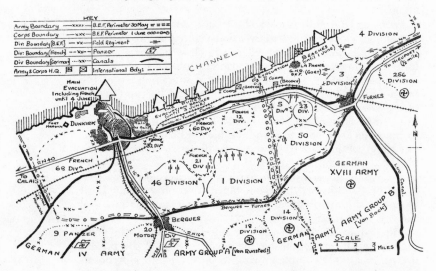

When the first troops embarked at Dunkirk on the afternoon of Sunday, 26 May, the town and harbour were already a blazing inferno. The situation seemed so grave that a 'panic' order from London advised Ramsay that the Germans might put an end to evacuation in two days. Fortunately for the B.E.F. the German advance was not everywhere pressed with Guderian's eagerness. Their naval staff in particular was incredibly slow to realise the purpose and potential of 'Operation Dynamo'.

Again, on 27 and 28 May, the Germans failed to grasp their

opportunities, this time on land. On the eastern front, the collapse and capitulation of the Belgian army opened a gap between the French left flank (3rd Armoured Division) and the sea. General von Bock, admittedly deprived of tanks, was slow and clumsy in exploiting this gap and failed to achieve a breakthrough.

From 29 May the main objective of the Luftwaffe was switched from the perimeter—now becoming a siege against canal lines and flooded land—to Dunkirk, the beaches and the sea approaches. R.A.F. patrols were too few and far between to break up the endless series of raids; most of the damage to shipping was, significantly, suffered in the midday period when the Luftwaffe had the skies to itself.

The confusion, the heroism and the horror of Dunkirk can be imagined. A horrible stench of blood and corpses pervaded the beach. It was like 'a slaughter house on a hot day'. Danger was even greater afloat, since shells lost much of their effect in the sand. A cruel but commonplace fate was for survivors of one sinking to become victims of a second or even third. Hospital ships were attacked indiscriminately, even when, late in the operation, a special plea was wired to the enemy.

The myth of Dunkirk rests on solid foundations. Iron discipline as well as sheer fatigue was responsible for the patient black lines impassively enduring partial submersion, and strafing from the air. There were incidents of hysteria and of small boats being rushed and sunk, but the French '*poilus*' were responsible for the majority of these.

There is a widespread but mistaken belief that the bulk of the evacuation was undertaken by a myriad of small craft under the initiative of heroic individuals. However, the fact that all vessels were under Navy control from start to finish does not diminish their achievement. On 30 May, for example, of 53,823 men landed in England, no less than 30,000 had been taken by small vessels from the open beaches.

By 31 May the operation was nearing its climax. The eastern front was withdrawn 9 miles to the fixed defences of the Franco-Belgian frontier—manned by the French—thus bringing part of the evacuation beaches under German shell fire. On this day, with the bulk of the B.E.F. now safe, Lord Gort embarked according to strict orders, leaving command of the rearguard of the 46th, 1st and 50th Divisions to General Alexander.

The following day losses from air attacks became so heavy that ships were forbidden to sail in daylight, thus postponing yet again the final withdrawal from the shrinking perimeter. Destroyers now performed incredible feats in order to berth alongside the Mole, pack their holds beyond danger point, and pull out stern first into the rough seas strewn with wrecks, debris and mines.

At 11.30 pm on 2 June the Senior Naval Officer, Dunkirk, gave the simple signal: 'B.E.F. evacuated'. The last tragic phase therefore largely concerns the French.

The weakness of French personnel control in Dunkirk was already apparent in the early hours of 2 June when about 10,000 places were left vacant because men were not brought to the right place at the right time. With German guns now less than 3 miles from the Mole it was essential for Admiral Ramsay to know precisely how many men remained in the bridgehead if all the rearguard was to be saved. French estimates were muddled and unhelpful but seemed to suggest a final total of 30,000; and this was the maximum which the Navy undertook to evacuate provided they reached the embarkation area during darkness.

The rearguard disengaged at 10.30 pm and began an orderly withdrawal to the waiting ships. Then, literally at the eleventh hour, thousands of Frenchmen emerged from hiding places in the town and swarmed towards the ships. As a result, although the Navy fulfilled its commitment, about 40,000 men, including many of the luckless rearguard, fell needlessly into German hands.

The British destroyer *Shikari* was the last ship to escape from Dunkirk: at 3.40 am on Tuesday, 4 June. At 9 am Dunkirk surrendered.

B.J.B.

Gravelotte and Mars-la-Tour (A***)

Date: 16 and 18 August 1870.

Location: The first action was fought immediately to the east of Mars-la-Tour; the second battlefield lies to the east of Gravelotte on the N. 3 road from Verdun to Metz, and stretches north to St. Privat. **92.**

War and campaign: Franco-Prussian War of 1870 (see p. 197).

Object of these actions: The Germans intended to intercept the French forces falling back from Metz towards Verdun.

Opposing sides: (a) General H. von Moltke in command of the 1st and 2nd Armies of the North German Confederation.
(b) Marshal Bazaine commanding the French Army of the Rhine.

Forces engaged (Gravelotte only): (a) Germans: 210 battalions; 133 squadrons; 732 guns. *Total:* 187,000. (b) French: 183 battalions; 104 squadrons: 520 guns. *Total:* 113,000.

Casualties: (a) 5,240 Germans killed, 14,460 wounded, 500 missing.
(b) Total losses: 12,800 Frenchmen.

Result: The French were thrown back into the fortress of Metz and played no subsequent part in the campaign. An attempt to relieve them led to the battle of Sedan (q.v.).

Nearby accommodation: Metz.

Suggested reading: On the Campaign: Howard, M., *The Franco-Prussian War*, London, 1961. On the Battle: Hönig, F., *24 Hours of Moltke's Strategy*, Woolwich, 1895. On the Battle: *Der 18 August 1870* (Historical Section of the German General Staff), Berlin, 1906. Memoirs: Vernois, J. von V. du, *With the Royal Headquarters in 1870–71*, London, 1897. Memoirs: Patry, L., *La Guerre telle qu'elle est*, Paris, 1907.

At the end of July 1870 the French Army of the Rhine, under the personal command of Napoleon III, had assembled on the frontiers of Alsace and Lorraine in preparation for an invasion of Germany. But the Germans struck first. The French right wing in Alsace under Marshal MacMahon was driven back to the south-west and rallied only when it reached Châlons-sur-Marne, while the left wing under Marshal Bazaine fell back on the fortress of Metz. The Germans followed cautiously, spread over a wide front. Their right wing, advancing towards Metz and Pont-à-Mousson, consisted of the 1st Army under General von Steinmetz and the 2nd Army under Prince Frederick Charles. Steinmetz made contact with the French outposts before Metz on 14 August, but at that very moment Bazaine was beginning to fall back. Napoleon had decided that the position was untenable, and ordered him to retreat from Metz and link up with MacMahon at Châlons.

On learning of the French withdrawal, General von Moltke ordered Steinmetz to mask the fortress of Metz while the 2nd Army crossed the Moselle farther south and advanced westward towards Verdun to intercept their retreat. The Prussians

GRAVELOTTE AND MARS-LA-TOUR
16th and 18th August 1870

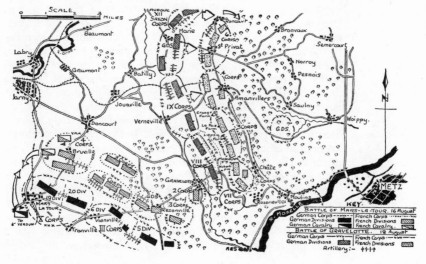

assumed quite wrongly that Bazaine had made good his escape to Verdun. So when early on 16 August General von Alvensleben's 3rd Corps, on the extreme right wing of the 2nd Army, came in contact with the French 2nd Corps south of Vionville, they thought they had to deal only with a rearguard. In fact Alvensleben quickly found that he was at grips with the entire Army of the Rhine. He boldly decided to press his attack in order to cut the French escape-route to the west, which he did by capturing and holding the village of Vionville. His task was made easier by Bazaine, whose main concern was to defend his communications with Metz rather than to press on to Verdun, and who therefore concentrated his forces on his left wing round Rezonville and fought a primarily defensive battle. His right wing however, General Ladmirault's 4th Corps, advancing southward on Tronville, might easily have rolled up the Prussian line and cleared the Verdun road but for the opportune arrival of the Prussian 10th Corps on this part of the front. This unit had turned back from its march to the west on hearing the noise of battle, and reached Mars-la-Tour at about 3.30 pm in time to check Ladmirault's advance and strengthen the Prussian hold on the Verdun road. An attempt by German cavalry to strike at Ladmirault's flank north of Mars-la-Tour was met by French cavalry in a huge mêlée which must rank as the last major cavalry engagement in western Europe. At nightfall the Prussians were thus able to consolidate their positions, and their object was achieved. Bazaine decided that his forces had been so disorganised that he must for the time being abandon his move on Verdun.

On 17 August therefore the French army withdrew, leaving great quantities of stores and wounded, to a strong position on the crests a few miles west of Metz, facing westward towards its own line of retreat. The left wing rested on the main road from Metz to Gravelotte, above the quarries of Rozerieulles, and the right on the village of St. Privat-la-Montagne, 5 miles to the north. Meanwhile Moltke, on learning the result of the previous day's battle, brought up the full strength of the 2nd Army, with two corps of the 1st, in a huge wheel which brought them by the evening of 17 August to a position between Rezonville and Mars-la-Tour facing due north.

On 18 August both sides were ready for battle. While Steinmetz engaged the French left flank before Gravelotte, Frederick Charles ordered the 2nd Army to 'set out . . . towards the north to find the enemy and fight him'. The Prussians did not realise that the entire French force lay immediately on their right flank. When the 9th Corps opened the battle with an attack on the French centre before Amanvillers, it was on the assumption that they had found an open flank. They were totally repulsed, and no further attack could be developed until the German left wing, the Guard

Corps and the Royal Saxon Corps, could be brought up, wheeling eastward through 90 degrees, to attack, respectively, St. Privat and Roncourt. The Guards attack on St. Privat was brought to a dead stop by the fire of Marshal Canrobert's 6th Corps in the village, in one of the most terrible slaughters of nineteenth-century European warfare. At Roncourt, however, the Saxons had found the French open flank, and at nightfall Canrobert, caught between two fires, abandoned St. Privat and fell back towards Metz.

Meanwhile the French left wing had held firm all day against repeated Prussian assaults. Their front was covered by the deep Mance ravine, and their infantry, ensconced in trenches and stout farmhouses, were unshaken even by heavy and accurate artillery fire. Towards evening Steinmetz's troops, crowded helplessly in the Mance ravine, collapsed in wild panic, and for a while it appeared that the whole German right wing had given way. A more enterprising commander than Bazaine might have seized the chance to counter-attack. A success on this part of the front would not only have reopened the Verdun road, but have cut the German lines of communication, with incalculable consequences. As it was, Bazaine remained passive throughout the battle, leaving his corps commanders to conduct purely defensive operations. His decision that night to fall back again under the guns of the fortress of Metz was prompted, not by the collapse of his right wing at St. Privat, but by a desire to rest and re-equip his force. Some historians have attributed to him more devious political calculations.

The French withdrawal took the Germans by surprise. Their terrible casualties, and the total failure of all their attacks before Gravelotte, had left them still in doubt on the evening of 18 August as to the outcome of the battle. Only on the 19th did it become clear that it had been a victory for them. Tactically it was a limited as well as an expensive one. The German losses were over 20,000 to the French 12,800, and the French army was still intact. But Bazaine was now isolated from the rest of France, and Moltke was able to detach enough forces to invest him in Metz and still have enough strength to advance against the remaining French army forming at Châlons and destroy it at Sedan.

M.E.H.

Ivry (A**)

Date: 14 March 1590.
Location: Near Ivry-la-Bataille, 10 miles south of Pacy-sur-Eure. **89.**
War and campaign: The French Wars of Religion (see p. 194).

Object of the action: A pitched battle between the French Royalists and the Catholic Leaguers during the long fight for religious and political supremacy.

Opposing sides: (a) King Henri IV commanding the French Royalists. (b) The Duke de Mayenne in command of the army of the Catholic League.

Forces engaged: (a) Royalists: 8,000 foot soldiers; 3,000 horse; 5 guns. *Total*: 11,000. (b) Leaguers: 15,000 foot soldiers; c. 4,000 horse. *Total*: 19,000.

Casualties: (a) About 500 Royalists killed. (b) 3,800 Leaguer casualties.

Result: A victory for Henry IV and the destruction of the Leaguer field army.

Nearby accommodation: Moulin.

Suggested reading: General Work: Levis Mirepoix, Duc de, *Les Guerres de Religion*, Paris, 1950. Biography: Reinhard, M., *Henri IV*, Paris, 1943. On the Campaign: Oman, C. W. C., *A History of the Art of War in the XVI Century*, London, 1937. Poetry: Macaulay, T. B., 'The Battle of Ivry', included in the *Lays*, London, 1842.

Ivry was a deliberate pitched battle on open ground. Mayenne outnumbered Henri IV, but neither had any advantage of position.

The King drew up his front line in six bodies of horse and foot. He himself commanded the biggest, a picked band, the second from the right. His plan, obviously, was to smash Mayenne's left. In second line he had a very small reserve under Marshal Biron. Before the charge Henri inspired his men with a short speech: 'Comrades, God is with us; there are his enemies and ours; here is your King—have at them! If you miss my standard, rally round my white plume; there lies the way to victory and honour!'

Mayenne's army outflanked the Royalists at both ends and was drawn up in much the same way, bodies of horse, winged with foot. Jean de Tavannes, Mayenne's *maître de camp*, placed the various bodies too close together so that they did not have enough room to manoeuvre.

The armies slowly advanced towards each other. De Guiche who commanded Henri's artillery made long lanes in the enemy cavalry, and was ineffectively answered. A cavalry charge then followed, the various bodies meeting with mixed success. The King's impetuous onset was the vital blow routing Mayenne's main body of horse, who came on too slowly, because they were trying to avoid the flight of some German cavalry.

Mayenne's Swiss foot stood their ground and were granted quarter, as were most of the Leaguers' French infantry. Great slaughter was done among the broken *landsknechts* and Walloons.

Ivry saw the end of the League's field army, but Henri IV, though a gallant warrior, was no general, and though but 50 miles from Paris only exploited his success by marching off to besiege Sens.

P.Y.

LA ROCHELLE (B***); the siege of, November 1626–8 October 1627; Charente–Maritime; **103**; Huguenot Rebellion. Cardinal Richelieu's Royalist army eventually forced the Huguenot garrison to surrender after a siege of 11 months' duration; the collapse of English assistance following the murder of the Duke of Buckingham was a contributory factor. See Romain, C., *Louis XIII*, Paris, 1934.

MONTFAUCON (D*); battle of, A.D. 887; near Paris; **88**; invasion of the Norsemen. Count Eudes with a French force successfully fought off 40,000 Norsemen, thus ending the siege of Paris. See Kendrick, T. B., *A History of the Vikings*, London, 1930.

Mülhausen (B***)

Date: 58 B.C.

Location: Between Belfort and Mülhausen in Haut Rhin, France. **101.**

War and campaign: Caesar's Gallic War (see p. 193).

Object of the action: Caesar intended to repulse Ariovistus' Germanic host from Gaul.

Opposing sides: (a) Julius Caesar in command of the Romans. (b) Ariovistus at the head of the Germanic tribes.

Forces engaged: (a) Romans: 6 legions and Gallic cavalry. *Total*: possibly 35,000. (b) Germans: details unknown, but undoubtedly large.

Casualties: (a) Unknown. (b) Details unknown, but immense.

Result: The Roman victory saved Gaul from a Germanic invasion and finally established Caesar's reputation as a general.

Nearby accommodation: Mülhausen.

Suggested reading: General Works: Dio, *Roman History*, ch. xxxviii, pp. 34–50. Rice Holmes, T., *The Roman Republic*, Vol. II, Oxford, 1923. On the Campaign and Battle: Caesar, J., *The Gallic War*, Book I, 30–53. Work of Fiction: Warner, R., *Imperial Caesar*, London, 1960.

After Caesar's victory over the Helvetii, which initiated his conquest of Gaul, the Gallic tribes appealed to him to save them from Ariovistus, a Germanic chieftain who at the head of an immense horde of warriors had crossed the lower Rhine with the intention of founding a kingdom in Gaul. Caesar agreed to do so, and with 6 legions marched to Besançon. There he established his base, and then pushed on toward Mülhausen. When he learnt of Ariovistus' approach, he fortified a camp at some unidentified spot east of Belfort, and a few days later Ariovistus encamped 2 miles distant from him.

After a week's skirmishing, Ariovistus drew up his army in 7 tribal formations to face Caesar's 6 legions, and when Caesar noticed that his enemy's left wing appeared less steady than his centre and right, he took command of his own right wing.

The battle opened by both sides simultaneously charging each other so rapidly that the legionaries dropped their javelins and closed with their swords. Ariovistus' left wing was routed; but meanwhile the Roman left wing was also pressed back. When young Publius Crassus, who commanded the cavalry in rear, noticed this, he galloped forward and on his own initiative brought up the third line of cohorts to reinforce the struggling troops. This decisive act restored the situation, and soon after the whole of Ariovistus' army took to its heels, and did not stay its flight until the Rhine was reached. Some succeeded in swimming it, others were drowned, and Ariovistus was fortunate enough to find a boat in which he escaped. The rest were caught on the western bank and slaughtered. The victory was decisive, and other Germanic tribes, who were awaiting the issue before joining Ariovistus, turned homeward.

J.F.C.F.

Orléans (A**)

Date: 12 October 1428–8 May 1429.

Location: On the banks of the river Loire; reached from Paris by Route Nationale 20. **96.**

War and campaign: The Hundred Years' War; the Campaign of 1428–9 (see p. 194)

Object of the action: The English forces were attempting to take this important city, but Joan of Arc was equally determined to raise the siege.

Opposing sides: (a) The Earl of Salisbury, succeeded by the Earl of Suffolk. (b) Dunois and Joan of Arc commanding the relief force; de Goncourt leading the garrison.

Forces engaged: (a) 4,000 English; 1,500 Burgundians; approx. 50 cannon. *Total:* 5,500. (b) 2,400 French; 3,000 armed citizens; 72 cannon. *Total* (prior to relief): 5,400.

Casualties: Not known.

Result: The English were compelled to raise the siege; in consequence, French morale greatly improved.

Nearby accommodation: Orléans.

Suggested reading: General Work: Perroy, E., *The Hundred Years' War*, London, 1951. On the Campaign: Burne, A. H., *The Agincourt War*, London, 1956. Villaret, *Campagnes des Anglais dans l'Orléanais*. On the Siege: Creasy, E., *Fifteen Decisive Battles of the Western World*, London, 1851. Biography: Lang, A., *The Maid of France*, London, 1908.

The successful defence of the city of Orléans was the turning point in the long struggle between England and France which dominated the fourteenth and fifteenth centuries. General Weygand once described the great siege as 'the Verdun of the Hundred Years' War', and its progress was watched with the greatest contemporary concern for it was widely considered that the ultimate fate of the city would reveal that of France.

Following their long series of successes dating from Agincourt (q.v.) in 1415, the English were confident of their ability to capture Orléans. After occupying Paris in July 1428, it was logical that they should next move against the great city on the north bank of the Loire, some 60 mi'es away, for it lay midway between Paris and the French Dauphin's temporary capital at Bourges, and the river marked the boundary dividing the two armies' spheres of influence.

In the weeks preceding the opening of the siege, the Earl of Salisbury took considerable pains to capture Beaugency and Meung to the west and Jargeau to the east of the city, thus precluding any possibility of relief by water. Then, in the words of the historian Villaret, 'Salisbury, with the audacity that proclaims assurance of success, attacked the ancient city, the final hope of the poor King of Bourges and the last rampart of his power.'

The citizens of Orléans had long anticipated such an emergency. Under the guidance of the Governor, the Sire de Goncourt, they had improved the defences of the 5 gates and the many towers and long curtain walls, besides mounting no less than 72 'bombards' along the fortifications, some allegedly capable of firing stone cannon-balls weighing 190 lb. The great bridge of 19 arches spanning the river was guarded at its southern end by a fort with two towers called '*Les Tourelles*', further strengthened by an earthen barbican or outwork. The garrison was large and well supported by the citizens.

On 12 October 1428 the English army—initially some 4,000 strong—appeared at the southern end of the bridge after marching from Jargeau, and pitched camp in the suburb of Olivet. There they were joined by 1,500 Burgundians to complete their array. For several days the English bombarded the *Tourelles* and the town beyond—the first time that artillery was extensively used in a major siege—and induced the forward garrison to abandon both the barbican and the fort and to retire within the city on 23 October after destroying two arches of the bridge behind them. The English jubilation at this success was, however, short-lived. The Earl of Salisbury, looking out from the top of one of the captured towers towards the main French defences, was mortally wounded by a chance shot—fired, according to contemporary accounts, by a young boy trespassing on a battery while the gunners were away at dinner. Eight days later the English general died at Meung.

ORLÉANS
12th October 1428 to 8th May 1429

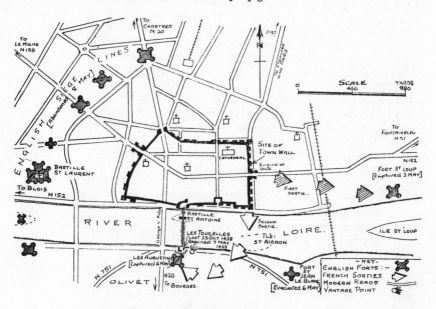

The new commander-in-chief was the Earl of Suffolk—a cautious soldier—who constructed a fort called '*Les Augustins*' to the south of '*Les Tourelles*' and then ordered his troops away into winter quarters. Anxious, no doubt, for the men's health in the razed suburbs of the city which offered little shelter, he left only a small garrison of 500 to hold the forward positions. Orléans, meanwhile, was reinforced by the arrival of Dunois, the 'Bastard of Orléans', who assumed command of the garrison, but nothing was done for three weeks to harass the outnumbered besiegers. Indeed it was the English who unexpectedly returned to the attack in December, the reason for this unwonted and unseasonal burst of energy being the arrival of the fire-eater John, Lord Talbot to share the command with the wary Suffolk and Lord Scales.

It was decided to open regular siege lines against Orléans—but as it was clearly impracticable to cover the whole 2,000-yard perimeter of the walls with the resources available, the besiegers concentrated their efforts on the western side of the city, for it was from this direction that any attempted relief from Chinon could be expected. A large base-camp called *'Bastille St. Laurent'* was constructed on the north bank of the river, supported by a string of 4 forts, while several miles away on the eastern side of the city, a single fort—*'St. Loup'*—was established to watch the Burgundian Gate. However, the townsfolk and garrison remained free to move about in the woods to the north-east of the city, and even to receive limited supplies from that direction.

In the meantime a relief army under the Count of Clermont was approaching from Blois, but on 12 February 1429 this force ran into an English convoy of 300 wagons escorted by Sir John Falstolf and 1,000 mounted archers or 'hobelars' near the village of Janville. The carts contained salted fish, intended for the use of the besieging army during Lent, and this fact gave the action that followed its name—'The Battle of the Herrings'. The doughty Sir John formed his wagons into a laager, and eventually routed the vastly superior French forces. The Count of Clermont abandoned his attempt to reach Orléans, and Falstolf successfully brought his convoy into the English lines. This success vastly encouraged the besiegers, and the spirits of the beleagured city reached their nadir.

By early April the western forts and *'Bastille St. Loup'* were complete, but the intention of the English generals to extend their works to block the eastern approaches to Orléans was frustrated by the sudden departure of the Burgundian mercenaries. Meanwhile a new French army of relief was being collected. The peasant girl Joan of Arc visited the Dauphin's court and persuaded him to produce another force, and on 27 April the Duc d'Alençon marched from Blois at the head of 4,000 men accompanied by the Maid. Her effect on the morale of this army was immediate and startling, and by the last day of the month a convoy of food barges had successfully run the gauntlet of Forts *'St. Jean'* and *'St. Loup'* and Joan herself was within the city. The rest of the army and a further column of food wagons reached Orléans on 4 May. That very day the Maid inspired an attack on Fort *'St. Loup'* which proved completely successful, for Talbot, stationed at his headquarters in Fort *'St. Laurent'*, was too far away to intervene in time to save the post. This French success was the turning point of the siege.

Two days later, accompanied by the Maid, 4,000 troops sallied out of the city and crossed the river to the south bank by way of Ile St. Aignan. The English abandoned Fort St. Jean and fell back on 'Les Augustins' and 'Les Tourelles'. The battle for the forts continued throughout the 6th and 7th; during the bitter struggle Joan was wounded in the shoulder by an arrow, and the English joyfully called out, 'The witch is dead'. However, she soon recovered and returned to the fray, to the dismay of her superstitious opponents. On the evening of the second day the English garrison was forced to surrender after losing more than two-thirds of its strength and after being taken in rear by a body of armed citizens who repaired the gap in the bridge with planks. The Maid rode triumphantly back into the city to receive a rapturous welcome.

Now it was the turn of English morale to plumb the depths. The ordinary soldiers were convinced that Joan of Arc was supernatural, and their generals had to admit that they had lost half of their laboriously constructed forts and that they were seriously outnumbered and outgunned by the reinforced garrison. Simple prudence dictated the abandonment of the siege, and on 8 May Suffolk and Talbot gave the order. The English burnt their forts and stores, but before they marched away they offered battle in No Man's Land. For all their numbers, however, the French were not eager to risk an open conflict against the victors of Agincourt, and so the sullen English army retired unhindered towards Paris. Orléans was saved, and in the Maid a weary France found new strength and a portent of future victory. To this day the anniversary of the city's deliverance is fittingly commemorated.

D.G.C.

Paris (B****)

Date: 20 September 1870–28 January 1871.

Location: Within easy reach of the Paris metro; the unspoilt sites are Buzenval and Bougival. 94

War and campaign: The Franco-Prussian War of 1870 (see p. 197)

Object of the action: The Germans wished to crown their achievements at Metz and Sedan by capturing the French capital, in which the Government of National Defence had its seat, on the assumption that this would end the war.

Opposing sides: (a) General H. von Moltke in command of the North German Confederation's armies. (b) General Trochu commanding miscellaneous French regular and auxiliary troops.

Forces engaged: (a) Prussians: 206,000 infantry; 34,000 cavalry;

898 field and 240 siege guns. *Total*: 240,000. (*b*) French: 355,000
infantry; 5,000 cavalry; 1,964 guns; together with naval and auxiliary
detachments. *Total*: 400,000

Casualties: (*a*) 10,000 killed and wounded; 2,000 missing.
(*b*) 16,000 killed and wounded; 8,000 missing.

Result: The city capitulated on 28 January, and the war was brought
to an end.

Nearby accommodation: Paris.

Suggested reading: On the Campaign: Howard, M., *The Franco-
Prussian War*, London, 1961. On the Siege: Ducrot, A. A., *La
Défense de Paris*, 4 vols, Paris 1874–8. Baldrick, R., *The Siege of Paris*,
London, 1964. Memoirs: *The War Diary of the Emperor Frederick III,
1870–71*, London, 1927. Work of Fiction: Bennett, A., *The Old Wives,
Tale*, London, 1908.

Having incarcerated one French army in Metz, and annihilated the other at Sedan (q.v.), the German armies were able,
in September 1870, to advance on Paris undisturbed, and on
20 September their investment of the city was complete. The
Army of the Meuse lay to the north of the Seine and the 3rd
Army to the south, about 235,000 men in a circle whose
circumference stretched over 50 miles. The King of Prussia
established his headquarters and temporary capital at Versailles. The supply of this great force, as well as of the other
German armies in France, over a single stretch of railway,
created difficulties which the French were surprisingly slow
to exploit.

An immediate assault on the city was rendered out of the
question by the strong fortifications erected some 40 years
earlier, which included 15 detached forts manned by men of
the French Navy. Moltke relied instead on starving the city
out, and made only leisurely preparations for a bombardment
and a siege *en règle*. Bismarck, anxious for political reasons to
end the war as quickly as possible, considered them too
leisurely, and the conflict between the two over this and other
questions created mounting tension at Versailles. The bombardment, when it began on 5 January 1871, effectively
neutralised the forts against which it was directed, but its effect
on the population of the city was negligible and that on neutral
opinion extremely bad.

The forces inside Paris totalled over 400,000. But they consisted largely of poorly trained National Guardsmen. General
Trochu, the Military Governor of the city, and General Ducrot,
his army commander, considered them politically dangerous
and militarily useless, and were reluctant to test them in battle.
Such sorties as were attempted took place mainly to satisfy
civilian impatience at what was regarded, with some reason,
as military defeatism. The main attempt occurred on
30 November–2 December, when Ducrot led 80,000 men in

an attack to the south-east through Champigny, to join hands with a northward advance by the French Army of the Loire to relieve the city. Both attacks were repelled with little difficulty. The city held out for two more months, and a final major break-out was attempted to the west at Buzenval on 19 January. Then, menaced by starvation and riot, the French sued for terms. The armistice which was signed on 28 January brought both the siege and the war to an end.

M.E.H.

Poitiers (B***)

Date: 19 September 1356.

Location: Four miles south of Poitiers near Nouaille and Maupertius, on the north bank of the River Miosson. **102.**

War and campaign: The Hundred Years' War; the Black Prince's *'Chevauchée'* of 1356 (see p. 194).

Object of the action: The French army intended to cut off the English from their base, Bordeaux, and then destroy them.

Opposing sides: (a) Edward the Black Prince with an Anglo-Gascon army. (b) King John II of France with the main French army.

Forces engaged: (a) English: 2,000 archers; 1,000 *sergeants*;* 3,000 men-at-arms. *Total*: 6,000. (b) French: 3,000 cross-bowmen; 17,000 dismounted and 500 mounted men-at-arms. *Total*: 20,500.

Casualties: (a) Details unknown, but only moderate. (b) 2,500 killed; 2,000 captured, including the King of France.

Result: A devastating defeat for the French, its immediate effect being to allow the English to complete their retreat to Bordeaux unmolested. Eventually, it led to the Truce of Bordeaux.

Nearby accommodation: Poitiers.

Suggested reading: On the Period: Perroy, E., *The Hundred Years' War*, London, 1951. On the Campaign and Battle: Hewitt, H. J., *The Black Prince's Expedition of 1355–1357*, London, 1958. Burne, A. H., *The Crécy War*, London, 1955. Novel: Conan Doyle, A., *Sir Nigel*, (New Edn.), London, 1917.

* *Special Note*: See glossary, p. 192.

In the summer of 1356 the Black Prince set out from Bordeaux to carry fire and the sword into the heart of France. His broader intention was to meet the forces of King Edward III and the Duke of Lancaster north of the River Loire. After securing the frontiers of Acquitaine he marched north through Bourges, Vierzon and Romorantin. By 8 September the army was before Tours, but the city was too strongly fortified to allow an attack; even more frustrating, the Loire was in spate, and no crossing-place could be found. For three days the Prince rested his weary troops (who had covered 320 miles in little over a month), but on the 11th he learnt that King John had crossed the Loire in force at Blois and Amboise and was marching to intercept him.

The Black Prince ordered an immediate retreat towards Bordeaux, but his followers—encumbered with booty and very foot-sore—were outmarched by the fresher French forces and King John was soon in a position to threaten the Anglo-Gascon lines of communication. Threatened with disaster the Black Prince offered to release his captives in return for a free passage to Bordeaux, but negotiations foundered when John insisted on hostages being handed over. On 19 September the Black Prince decided to risk all by forcing a battle on his numerically superior opponent.

The selected battle-site favoured the defence: much of the front of the Anglo-Gascon line was protected by two sunken lanes and a hedge of vine-stakes; the southern flank lay on the banks of the Miosson, and the northern was strengthened by a laager of wagons. Apart from a small reserve of mounted knights held in reserve to the right rear, the rest of the army formed up in two main divisions of dismounted men-at-arms, under Warwick and Salisbury respectively, with archers on each flank.

The French advanced in four bodies: the first comprised their archers, javelin-throwers and two parties of mounted knights; the remaining three were made up of dismounted men-at-arms and knights: on this occasion King John was clearly determined to avoid the losses inflicted on the mounted French troops at Crécy (q.v.).

About 9 am the leading French division reached the hedge, and a hard struggle ensued until Salisbury advanced some archers into the marshes to take the attackers in flank. Next the Dauphin led up his array, and a bitter battle raged along the front, forcing the Black Prince to commit almost all his reserves before the French gave ground. The outlook was grim for the Anglo-Gascon army which was already wearying, but fortunately the Dauphin's retreat panicked the next French division (under Orléans) and half the army fled the field. Nevertheless King John still retained his fourth force, perhaps 8,000 strong. A lull ensued (about 10 am) whilst this imposing array marched up over the distance of a mile—the dismounted knights being gravely encumbered by their armour—to reach the line of their weary opponents. The low morale of his men led the Black Prince to make a bold decision; instead of awaiting the new onslaught, he ordered the whole line to advance. Very soon a desperate struggle was in progress on the plain, but Captal de Buch led a party of 200 mounted knights through dead-ground to fall on the left flank and rear of the embattled French host. This event proved decisive: the French cohesion broke, the King was taken captive, and the survivors fled in disorder for Poitiers.

D.G.C.

Rocroi (A***)

Date: 19 May 1643.

Location: Near the Franco-Belgian frontier, 55 miles north-east of Rheims (Routes Nationales 38 and 385). **8o.**

War and campaign: The Thirty Years' War; the Campaign of 1643 in France and Belgium (see p. 195).

Object of the action: The French army was attempting to relieve the siege of Rocroi.

Opposing sides: (*a*) The Duc d'Enghien commanding the French army. (*b*) Don Francisco de Melo in command of the Spanish army.

Forces engaged: (*a*) French: 18 battalions; 32 squadrons; 12 guns. *Total*: 23,000. (*b*) Spaniards: 20 *tercios* * (infantry); 7,000 horse; 28 guns. *Total*: 27,000.

Casualties: (*a*) 2,000 killed and 2,000 wounded. (*b*) 7,500 killed; 7,000 prisoners; 6,500 missing; 200 colours.

Result: A victory for the French presaging the eclipse of Spanish military power.

Nearby accommodation: Rocroi.

Suggested reading: General Work: Wedgwood, C. V., *The Thirty Years' War*, London, 1938. On the Battle: Colin, Lt.-Col., *Les Grandes Batailles de l'Histoire*, Paris, 1915. On the Battle: Spaulding, Nickerson and Wright, *Warfare*, New York, 1925. Biography: Mahon, Lord, *Life of Louis, Prince of Condé*, London, 1872.

* *Special Note*: See glossary, p. 192.

At the beginning of 1643 two armies faced the Spaniards along the northern frontier of France. They were the armies of Picardy and of Champagne—both of indifferent quality and poor discipline. At that time the frontier between the territory of France and that of Spain ran, roughly speaking, from Dunkirk to Metz.

King Louis XIII confided the command of the Army of Picardy to the 21-year-old Louis de Bourbon, Duc d'Enghien (later Prince de Condé), albeit with instructions to take no risks, and with the aged Maréchal de l'Hôpital to act as his mentor. D'Enghien, whose authority as a prince of the blood was increased by his real professional ability, lost no time in re-establishing discipline and sound training, a task in which he was well seconded by the fiery Gassion and the stout-hearted Sirot, both of whom had served under Gustavus Adolphus.

The French soldiery, if turbulent, were not lacking in ardour and responded well.

Meanwhile Don Francisco de Melo, the Spanish governor of the Low Countries, was menacing Rocroi, Landrecies and Arras, with a veteran, if polyglot, army, which had won three victories over the French in the last four campaigns and undoubtedly possessed the moral ascendancy.

Active operations began in mid-May. On the 14th the two French armies concentrated between Saint-Quentin and Guise, and learned that the Spaniards had advanced on Avesnes via Le Quesnoy. Croats were ravaging the country around Hirson and La Capelle. Pushing forward by forced marches a Spanish corps had arrived on the 13th before the little fortress of Rocroi, which was held by a French garrison no more than 400 strong—although at daybreak on the 17th a detachment of 150 men broke through to reinforce the defenders.

ROCROI *19th May 1643*

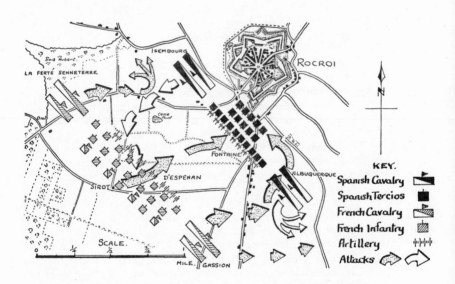

That day d'Enghien encamped at Aubenton, where he was reinforced by such troops as could be spared from his various garrisons. Even so he was outnumbered by the Spaniards, who had 27,000 men to his 23,000, and were expecting the arrival of a corps under Beck.

The two armies arrayed themselves on 18 May as if for battle, the Spaniards having their backs to the fortress. The two armies drew up as was the fashion of the age with the main body of infantry in the centre flanked by two wings of cavalry. The Spaniards, though more numerous than the French, occupied a shorter front; their solid infantry were massed with very small intervals between the *tercios*, so that their array was not unlike one huge square.

The two armies, drawn up about 1,000 yards apart, gazed at one another. The artillery began to play. The more numerous Spanish guns were better served than those of the French, who suffered some 300 casualties.

Since the Spanish line was more than 500 yards shorter than that of the French, there was an empty space opposite the latter's left wing. Into this L'Hôpital, who wished to avoid the bloody solution of a battle, thrust La Ferté-Senneterre's cavalry, pushing them forward to relieve Rocroi. The Spaniards could have cut off Senneterre, but contented themselves with simply repulsing him. Nothing more was done on the 18th. The two armies spent the night facing each other, the only incident being the destruction of a Spanish ambush party by part of the Regiment of Picardy.

Next morning D'Enghien, with considerable skill and originality, changed his tactical dispositions. He divided his right wing into two nearly equal parts, sending Gassion away to the right so that he threatened to outflank the Duke of Albuquerque's horse. The Spaniard reacted as expected by forming front to his flank, whereupon d'Enghien with the rest of the cavalry of his right fell on d'Albuquerque's right flank and routed him. Although the latter endeavoured with his reserves to restore the fortunes of the day, the French charged him again from two different directions and the end of an hour's hard fighting saw d'Enghien triumphant.

Meanwhile upon the other wing La Ferté-Senneterre, who had learned nothing from his misfortunes of the previous day, instead of remaining at the post assigned to him, advanced against Isembourg, only to be defeated and badly wounded. The Spanish cavalry now fell upon D'Eprenan's foot and took their cannon. L'Hôpital counter-attacked with a few squadrons of cavalry that he had managed to rally and some battalions of infantry. He succeeded in retaking the guns, but a second Spanish onslaught overran them once more and this time the Italian infantry in the Spanish service turned the French artillery against its owners. For a time the French centre, especially the Regiment of Piedmont, stood firm, but the fire of 30 guns was too much of an ordeal. The French general La Vallière lost his nerve and ordered a retreat. Fortunately for the French their reserve was intact, and the stout-hearted Sirot not only halted the withdrawal, but led forward his reserve and the remnants of the centre against the Italian *tercios*.

D'Enghien meanwhile had left Gassion with several squadrons to ensure that d'Albuquerque's followers should play no further part in the battle. Returning to the centre with the remainder of the cavalry of his right he fell upon the third line of the Spanish centre, the German *tercios*, and thrust them rudely upon the Walloons who formed the second line. In a matter of minutes the whole of this infantry was broken and put to flight.

This brilliant action had its effect on Isembourg's Spanish cavalry. They charged the French reserve, but it was feebly done, and Sirot, seeing d'Enghien's white plume in the distance, pointed it out to his men, who hurled themselves upon the Spaniards with enthusiasm. Slowly and in good order the Comte de Fontaine's surviving infantry began to fall back towards the north-east.

D'Enghien lost no time in rallying his tired soldiers and re-forming his battle line. Gassion was detailed to watch for Beck, who was expected to appear from the north-east at any moment.

As soon as their ranks had been dressed once more, the French, with small detachments of musketeers—*les enfants perdus*—leading the way, began to advance. Fontaine held his fire and, on his signal, a terrible salvo decimated the French. Three times they recoiled, but their musketeers were taking a toll, and Fontaine himself was struck down.

D'Enghien, with a tactical skill uncommon in his day, massed his cannon against an angle of the Spanish square, and was bringing up his squadrons, when some Spanish officers were seen waving their hats. D'Enghien, riding forward to receive their surrender, was welcomed by a volley which he was fortunate to survive. The angry French then fell on with furious impetus, and the battle was won. Before 10 o'clock all was over; the flower of the veteran Spanish infantry was no more. It was only then that Beck arrived within 5 miles of the field.

Rocroi was a brilliant opening to the reign of King Louis XIV who had succeeded his father on 14 May. For 100 years the *tercios* had made Spain the leading military power. Now it was France's turn. The century that lay ahead was to see many glorious victories won by such men as Turenne, Luxembourg, Villars and Maurice de Saxe. Not least among that talented company was Louis de Bourbon, *le Grand Condé*.

P.Y.

St. Lô (B***)

Date: 24–28 July 1944.
Location: On the river Vire; 20 miles south-west of Bayeux on Route Nationale 172. **84.**
War and campaign: The Second World War; the North-West

Europe Campaign of 1944–5 (see p. 197).

Object of the action: The U.S. 1st Army was attempting to break out from the Normandy battlefield to the west and south.

Opposing sides: (a) General Montgomery commanding 21st Army Group (Bradley (1st U.S.) and Dempsey (2nd British)). (b) Field-Marshal von Kluge commanding Army Group 'B' (Eberbach's Panzer Group West and Hausser's 7th Army).

Forces engaged: (a) 11 U.S. infantry divisions; 4 armoured divisions. (b) 9 German 'composite' divisions; 2 Panzer divisions.

Casualties: (a) Figures not accurately known, but heavy.
(b) Figures not accurately known, but heavy; certain units ceased to exist.

Result: The success of 'Operation Cobra' marked the final defeat of the German attempt to confine the Allied bridgehead in Normandy.

Nearby accommodation: St. Lô.

Suggested reading: General Works: Wilmot, C., *The Struggle for Europe*, London, 1952. Ellis, L. F., *Victory in the West*, Vol. I, London, 1962. Liddell Hart, B. H., *The Tanks*, Vol. II, London, 1959. On the Campaign and Battle: Blumenson, M., *U.S. Army in World War II—Breakout and Pursuit*, Washington, 1961.

By mid-July the Allies had won the battle of supplies and the American 1st Army was ready to break out from its bridge-head. St. Lô itself was captured on 18 July after 12 days' fighting. Meanwhile, the British thrust, centred on Caen, successfully attracted the bulk of von Kluge's armour (7 out of 9 Panzer divisions), and of the newly arrived reinforcements. Thus on the eve of 'Operation Cobra' the British (General Dempsey) with 14 divisions were holding down an equal number of enemy divisions, while to General Bradley with 15 divisions there was opposed only a hotch-potch of battle-weary units, nominally forming 9 divisions of General Hausser's 7th Army.

General Bradley had recently experienced the disadvantages of attacking on a wide front, and now planned a concentrated 'punch' on a 4-mile stretch of the St. Lô–Périers road 5 miles west of St. Lô. The infantry would open a breach after intense air bombardment through which armoured and motorised divisions could exploit westward.

Cobra started inauspiciously on 24 July when premature air bombardment caused 156 American casualties. Early on 25 July the attack began in earnest with 90 minutes' bombing of the forward infantry area, so intense that it virtually obliterated Bayerlein's Panzer Lehr Division. At midday the 7th Corps (Collins) went into action with close air support. By dark only 2 miles had been gained, due as much to the results of bombing as to German resistance.

Although the infantry's objectives had not been reached on the first day Collins decided to unleash his armoured columns early on the 26th. On the American right Marigny was held against the 1st Armoured Division all day, but on the left the 2nd Armoured Division advanced 3 miles to take St. Gilles by dusk, and a further 4 to Le Mesnil Herman by dawn on the 27th. Bayerlein had only 14 tanks left.

The decisive day was 27 July. Thrusting south and south-west the 2nd Armoured Division made for the Bréhal–Tessy road, and the 1st Infantry and 3rd Armoured Divisions made for Coutances. Though the Germans fought stubbornly, the Americans now had the advantage in the *'bocage'* country due to special training and the 'Rhinoceros' device which enabled tanks to slice through hedgerow banks.

By dusk on the 28th the Bréhal–Tessy road 15 miles south of the start line had been reached, and no co-ordinated German front existed west of the river Vire. Bradley therefore dispensed with consolidation and dispatched the 7th Corps south-east to Mortain and the 8th Corps (under Patton) west into Brittany. The success of the break-out was assured.

B.J.B.

Sedan (C***)

Date: 1 September 1870.

Location: Sedan lies at the junction of the N. 77 from Châlons-sur-Marne and the N. 64 from Verdun. The battlefield lies to the north of the town. 81.

War and campaign: The Franco-Prussian War, 1870 (see p. 197).

Object of the action: Marshal MacMahon was attempting to relieve the French forces besieged in Metz. Moltke was determined to thwart this move.

Opposing sides: (*a*) General H. von Moltke commanding the 3rd Army and the Army of the Meuse of the North German Confederation and allied states. (*b*) Marshal MacMahon in command of the Army of Châlons.

Forces engaged: (*a*) Prussians: 222 battalions; 186 squadrons; 774 guns. *Total*: 200,000. (*b*) French: 202 battalions; 80 squadrons; 564 guns. *Total*: 120,000.

Casualties: (*a*) 2,320 Prussians killed; 5,980 wounded; 700 missing. *Total*: 9,000. (*b*) 17,000 French killed and wounded; 21,000 missing. *Total*: 38,000.

Result: Destruction of the French army, the capture of the Emperor Napoleon III, and the fall of the Second French Empire.

Nearby accommodation: Sedan.

Suggested reading: On the Campaign: Howard, M., *The Franco-*

Prussian War, London, 1961. On the Battle: Bastard, G., *Armée de Châlons: un jour de bataille*, Paris, 1872. Ducrot, A. A., *La Journée de Sedan*, Paris, 1871. Work of Fiction: Zola, E., *La Débâcle*, Paris, 1892. Memoirs: Bibesco, Prince G., *Campagne de 1870. Belfort, Rheims, Sedan*, Paris, 1872.

The battles of Vionville and Gravelotte (q.v.) on 16–18 August had cut the line of retreat of the French Army of the Rhine under Marshal Bazaine, and isolated this force around the fortress of Metz. Meanwhile Marshal MacMahon was forming a relief force at Châlons-sur-Marne. On 23 August, having received a report that Bazaine was about to attempt a break-out to the north, MacMahon set out to the north-east to try to join forces with him. General von Moltke, who was directing the German westward advance from Metz, was at first unsure of the direction of MacMahon's march. But on 24 August he discovered the French plans from newspaper reports, and swung his entire force northward to intercept the Army of Châlons. He ran it to earth next day north of the Argonne forest, and on 30 August, at the battle of Beaumont, he destroyed de Failly's 5th Corps and blocked MacMahon's further advance up the Meuse valley.

MacMahon, with 100,000 men, now fell back on the fortress of Sedan to consider his next move: whether to renew his attempt to break through to the east, or whether to withdraw to the west and fall back on Paris. While he pondered, on 31 August, Moltke encircled him with two armies totalling 250,000 men. The Army of the Meuse advanced down the Meuse valley, its right flank on the Belgian frontier; while the 3rd Army advanced to the river from the south, seized the crossings west of Sedan at Donchéry, and pushed two corps across the river to cut the last lines of escape. Since this latter movement was completed only during the morning of 1 September, after the battle had begun, some of the French forces might still have escaped. But a fatal confusion of command followed the wounding of MacMahon early that day. His successor, General de Wimpffen, was ill-informed of the situation, and by cancelling all orders for retreat enabled the Germans to complete their encirclement undisturbed.

The following operations scarcely deserve the name of battle. The German artillery simply battered the French forces to pieces, and all the sporadic attempts at break-out—including the spectacular charges of General Margueritte's cavalry—were easily repelled. Napoleon III, who had accompanied his last army, demanded an armistice to end the carnage, and next morning the French army delivered itself into the German hands. Napoleon accompanied it into captivity, and his Empire fell with him.

M.E.H.

The Somme (A***)

Date: 1 July–18 November 1916.

Location: The battlefield extends from Beaumont Hamel to Chaulnes (north–south) and to Bapaume and Peronne to the eastwards. **77.**

War and campaign: The First World War; the Western Front, 1916 (see p. 197).

Object of the action: The new B.E.F. was attempting to solve the impasse of the trench war by achieving a large breakthrough.

Opposing sides: (*a*) General Haig commanding the British army, assisted by some French divisions. (*b*) General Falkenhayn commanding the German army.

Forces engaged: (*a*) Initially 18 British divisions 5 French. (*b*) Initially 6 German divisions in the line; 5 in reserve.

Casualties: (*a*) 418,000 British; 194,451 French. (*b*) 650,000 Germans.

Result: Uncertain. The Allies made small territorial gains and claimed that the battle forced the German withdrawal to the Hindenburg Line in February 1917.

Nearby accommodation: Bapaume, Albert, Amiens.

Suggested reading: General Work: Cruttwell, C. M. F., *A History of the Great War*, Oxford, 1936. On the Campaign: Edmonds (ed.), *Military Operations, France—1916*. Farrall-Hockley, A.H., *The Somme*, London, 1964. Memoirs: Masefield, J., *The Old Front Line*, London, 1917.

The battlefield of the Somme extends between Arras and St. Quentin where the river winds westwards through the low, rolling downs on which the Germans entrenched themselves after their retreat from the Marne in 1914. An 18-mile portion of this front was chosen to be the scene of the great Franco-British offensive of 1916 in which the Kitchener armies were to intervene for the first time in strength and, it was hoped, with decisive effect. A week's preparatory bombardment preceded the assault, the heaviest yet mounted by the British army; but it proved less than was required to subdue the German defenders who emerged relatively unscathed at zero hour on 1 July and caught the rigid lines of British infantry in a storm of fire, inflicting 60,000 casualties on that first day, most of them on the 140,000 infantry engaged. The 5 French divisions which attacked south of the Somme adopted more supple tactics, suffered less and achieved more, for at the end of the first day the British had advanced nowhere more than 1,000 yards. The battle thereafter proceeded in fits and starts. On 14 July the British made a quick advance towards Bazentin but the attack of 23 July was unsuccessful and the further advance of the French was blocked by the line of the river.

Haig had by now abandoned his hopes of breakthrough and settled for a battle of attrition which was to last until 18 November. The most notable event of the closing stages was the first appearance of the tank, a few specimens surviving the approach march, one to lead a successful if very minor attack on the village of Flèrs.

The material gain to the Allies was a strip of territory 20 miles long and 7 deep at most, between Beaumont Hamel and Chaulnes. The cost in casualties was 613,000, the Germans suffering perhaps as many. The real value of the offensive remains a matter of heated debate.

J.D.P.K.

Spicheren-Wörth (B**)

Date: 6 August 1870.

Location: Three miles south of Saarbrücken on Route Nationale 3 from Forbach to Metz. **93.**

War and campaign: The Franco-Prussian War of 1870 (see p. 197).

Object of the action: The Prussians wished to lure the French army into fighting a battle on the frontiers, but the trap was sprung prematurely—hence these actions.

Opposing sides: (a) General von Steinmetz commanding 3rd, 7th and 8th Corps of 1st and 2nd Armies of the North German Confederation. (b) General Frossard commanding the 2nd Corps of the French Army of the Rhine.

Forces engaged: (a) Prussians: 33 battalions; 33 squadrons; 108 guns. *Total*: 35,000. (b) French: 39 battalions; 24 squadrons; 90 guns. *Total*: 28,000.

Casualties: (a) 850 Prussian dead; 3,650 wounded; 400 missing. (b) Total French losses 4,100, about half comprising prisoners of war.

Result: The French plans for the invasion of Germany were disrupted, and in its place a withdrawal on Metz was commenced.

Nearby accommodation: St. Avold.

Suggested reading: On the Campaign: Howard, M., *The Franco-Prussian War*, London, 1961. On the Battle: Henderson, G. F. R., *The Battle of Spicheren*, London, 1891. Maistre, P. A., *Spicheren (6 août 1870)*, Paris, 1908. Memoirs: Sarazin, C., *Récits sur la derniére guerre franco-allemande*, Paris, 1887. Memoirs: Klein, P., *La Chronique de Froeschwiller*, Paris, 1911.

It was generally expected that the Franco-Prussian War of 1870 would begin with a French invasion of south Germany. But when Napoleon III joined his army at Metz on 28 July he found it too disorganised to take the offensive. So after an initial lunge at the German outposts at Saarbrücken on

2 August, he disposed his forces in a cordon along the frontier. His left wing under Marshal Bazaine (2nd, 3rd, 4th and 5th Corps) stretched from Saarlouis to Saarguemines, separated by the Vosges from the right wing under Marshal MacMahon (1st, 7th Corps) which lay between Strasbourg and Wörth. The German armies were also divided in two. The right wing, consisting of the 1st and 2nd Armies (General Steinmetz and Prince Frederick Charles) was advancing from the Rhine between Coblenz and Mainz towards the Lorraine frontier, while on the left wing the 3rd Army under the Crown Prince of Prussia concentrated round Landau and Speyer, threatening Alsace.

General Helmuth von Moltke, Chief of Staff to the King of Prussia who commanded the German armies, had contemplated a convergent movement of his two wings to trap the French in a battle on the frontier, which he hoped would prove as decisive as had the battle of Sadowa in 1866. His trap was sprung prematurely by the impetuosity of Steinmetz, whose forward units made contact with the French 2nd Corps (General Frossard) on the heights of Spicheren on the morning of 6 August, and who allowed his forces to be drawn into a premature and inconclusive battle, in which the 3rd Corps of the 2nd Army also became involved. The Germans drove the French from their outpost on the Rotherberg, but otherwise their piecemeal and unco-ordinated attacks were successfully repelled. Frossard fell back at nightfall only because his left flank was menaced; having fought successfully all day with no support from his colleagues or superiors.

Simultaneously, and equally unexpectedly, the German 3rd Army stumbled on the French 1st Corps, in a superb defensive position on the slopes above Wörth, and a piecemeal battle developed against the Army Commander's intentions. MacMahon also held out all day without help, and was at length driven back only by overwhelming numbers lapping round his flanks. In both battles the superiority of the French rifle over the German was evident, but it was nullified by the far greater effectiveness of the Prussian artillery fire.

M.E.H.

Tinchebrai (B***)

Date: 28 September 1106.
Location: 35 miles east of Avranches and 10 miles north of Domfront. 90.
War and campaign: The English Conquest of Normandy (see p. 194).
Object of the action: The Norman army was attempting to relieve the siege of Tinchebrai castle.

Opposing sides: (*a*) King Henry I leading an Anglo-Norman army. (*b*) Duke Robert commanding a Norman army.

Forces engaged: (*a*) Anglo-Normans: 5,000 infantry; 2,400 cavalry. *Total*: 7,400. (*b*) Normans: 5,000 infantry; 700 cavalry. *Total*: 5,700.

Casualties: (*a*) 2 Anglo-Norman knights and perhaps 60 foot soldiers killed. (*b*) 60 Norman knights and 250–300 foot soldiers killed; 400 knights captured.

Result: Henry I captured and imprisoned Duke Robert, annexing Normandy to his English possessions.

Nearby accommodation: Domfront or Avranches.

Suggested reading: General Work: Poole, A. I., *Domesday Book to Magna Carta, 1087–1216*, Oxford, 1954. On the Battle: Oman, C. W. C., *The Art of War in the Middle Ages*, London, 1924. David, C. W., *Robert Curthose* (Appendix F), London. Article: Davis, H. W. C., 'Tinchebrai', in *English Historical Review*, Vol. XXIV, 1909.

Henry I's 1106 campaign in Normandy began with the siege of the castle at Tinchebrai. Duke Robert of Normandy with a small army of experienced soldiers attempted to raise the siege. King Henry drew up his own much larger army in two lines. Three divisions of Norman infantry loyal to King Henry from Avranches, Bayeux and Coutances stood in this line supported by 700 mounted men-at-arms. The second line consisted of dismounted knights and infantry from England and Normandy with the King himself at their head. A force of 700 cavalry were arrayed behind them. The counts of Maine and Brittany commanded their feudal vassals in an ambush position somewhat to the left of the expected approach line of the Norman army.

The Norman formation is doubtful, but it is likely that it was composed of 2 cavalry squadrons on either wing of a division of infantry. The Norman left-wing squadron under the Count of Mortain opened the battle by breaking the much larger corps of the Count of Bayeux, but the Normans were checked by King Henry's second line. William of Warrenne on the English right succeeded in holding the Norman left wing under Robert of Belesme. Suddenly the Bretons and men of Maine, 1,000 strong, charged upon the Norman left flank from their place of concealment. Belesme and many of his men made good their escape, as the Norman army collapsed under this unexpected attack. Duke Robert was taken prisoner after a bitter struggle.

The whole fight lasted little more than one hour. Besides giving the English possession of Normandy the battle demonstrated the value of co-operation between infantry and cavalry, a lesson probably learnt from the Crusades.

J.E.A.

Toulon (B***)

Date: 6 September–19 December 1793.

Location: South of France. The sites of some forts still exist. **105.**

War and campaign: The French Revolutionary Wars (see p. 196).

Object of the action: The French army was endeavouring to regain the defected naval arsenal of Toulon from the Allies.

Opposing sides: (*a* A succession of undistinguished Revolutionary generals commanding a French army. (*b*) Admiral Lord Hood in command of an Allied military and naval force.

Forces engaged: (*a*) French: 2 divisions 6 heavy guns (later increased). *Total*: 11,500. (*b*) Allies: 2,200 English, 6,900 Spaniards and approx. 8,000 other Allies (including 1,600 French *émigré* Royalists). *Total*: approx. 16,000.

Casualties: Not known.

Result: The Allies were compelled to evacuate the city and arsenal, thereby providing the French government with an important politico-military success; also the emergence of Napoleon Bonaparte.

Nearby accommodation: Toulon.

Suggested reading: General Works: Wilkinson, S., *The Rise of General Bonaparte*, Oxford, 1930. Colin, Lt.-Col., *L'Education Militaire de Napoléon*, Paris, 1900. On the Siege: Rose, J. H., *Lord Hood and the Defence of Toulon*, Cambridge, 1922. Fortescue, J., *History of the British Army*, Vol. IV Pt. 1, London, 1906.

Toulon was the most important naval arsenal of France, and when the disaffected citizens admitted a British and Spanish fleet into the Inner Harbour (28 August 1793) this represented a heavy blow against the Revolutionary Government in Paris.

At first the Revolutionary forces that laid siege to Toulon were both small in number and badly equipped—being especially short of artillery; nevertheless, General Carteaux succeeded in capturing the western approaches to the port (7 September), and 9 days later a certain captain of artillery, Napoleon Bonaparte, was summarily attached to the army to replace its wounded senior gunner.

Despite his lowly rank, Bonaparte soon became the inspiration of the besiegers. He realised that the vital task was to capture Mt. Caire and its extremity, the peninsula called '*l'Eguillette*', from which guns could command the Inner Harbour and make it untenable for the Allied fleet. Carteaux thought the young artillery officer mad, but Bonaparte was supported by the all-powerful political Deputies attached to the army, and was soon in virtual charge of operations. In accordance with his conviction that 'It is for artillery to take fortresses and for the infantry to support it', by superhuman efforts he cajoled more guns and munitions from the troops stationed at Marseilles, along the Rhone and in Provence, training up infantry soldiers to serve the pieces.

As a preliminary step to the capture of *l'Eguillette*, on 20 September the French guns opened up on the Allied fleet and drove it closer to Toulon. However, the following day the Allied troops forestalled the French and established Fort Mulgrave (*'le petit Gibraltar'*) on the key promontory, mounting 20 guns there. Thus, although the French successfully captured most of Mt. Caire on the 22nd, a major effort was still required to make the port untenable. Friction between the newly promoted Colonel Bonaparte and his superiors caused a lull in operations, but after the arrival of the retired artillery expert Du Teil, and the replacement of two successive incompetent Generals-in-Chief by the abler Dugommier, the young genius won his way. To bring fire on Fort Mulgrave from several directions Bonaparte constructed 11 batteries, and by the end of November all were ready. A series of Allied sorties were repulsed, and on 16 December Fort Mulgrave was taken by storm. Within 48 hours Bonaparte had set up a powerful battery on *l'Eguillette*, and on 18 December Lord Hood ordered the evacuation of both the city and harbour. The following day the Revolutionary troops entered Toulon to wreak a bloody vengeance on the citizens.

The recapture of Toulon represented a great military achievement fraught with political significance of European importance. The credit was justly given to Bonaparte, who was promoted Brigadier-General, and thus started upon the road to fame.   D.G.C.

TOULOUSE (B***); battle of, 10 April 1814; south-west France; **104**; the Campaign of 1814. The Duke of Wellington (49,000 Allies including 10,000 Spaniards) defeated the French Marshal Soult (42,000) and captured the city, unaware that the war had already ended. See Bryant, A., *The Age of Elegance*, London, 1950.

Tours (C****)

Date: 10 October A.D. 732

Location: The exact location is uncertain; one possible site is at La Carte off the Route Nationale 751 south-west of Tours; a second is at Cenon, 18 miles north-east of Poitiers. **98**.

War and campaign: The Saracen Invasions of western Europe (see p. 193).

Object of the action: Charles Martel was attempting to check the Saracen invasion.

Opposing sides: (*a*) Charles 'Martel' ('Hammer') at the head of a Frankish army. (*b*) Abd-er-Rahman, Governor of Spain, leading a Saracen army.

Forces engaged: (*a*) Perhaps 30,000 Franks. (*b*) Probably about 80,000 Saracens, although some Christian sources put the figure as high as 400,000.

Casualties: (*a*) No reliable information: possibly 1,500. (*b*) No reliable information: some sources mention 350,000 Muslims.

Result: Charles's victory decisively checked the tide of Arab conquest in western Europe and delivered Christendom there from the threat of Islam.

Nearby accommodation: Poitiers or Tours.

Suggested reading: General Work: Gibbon, E., *The Decline and Fall of the Roman Empire*, Vol. VII, 1783. On the Battle: Lot, F., *L'Art Militaire et les Armées au Moyen Age . . .*, Paris, 1946. On the Battle: Creasy, E., *The Fifteen Decisive Battles of the World*, London, 1851. Fuller, J. F. C., *The Decisive Battles of the Western World*, Vol. I, London, 1954.

The Saracens, having overrun Syria, Egypt and North Africa, invaded Spain in 711 and as early as the following year began raiding over the Pyrenees into Aquitania. They later secured Narbonne before being repulsed outside Toulouse by Eudo, Duke of Aquitania. He was, however, unable to prevent them from taking Carcassonne and Nîmes as a preliminary to pushing up the Rhone into Burgundy. Disliking the precarious position of his territories, Duke Eudo thought that he had brought off a master-stroke when he married his daughter to an emir from northern Spain, Othman by name, who had recently rebelled against the Governor there, Abd-er-Rahman. This alliance made Eudo so confident of dealing with any more incursions from the south that he unwisely broke with Charles, Duke of Austrasia, with whom he had already, in 719, been in disadvantageous conflict. Charles, who had been waging war along the Danube and in Saxony, crossed the Loire with an army and in 731 put his rival to flight.

Next year Abd-er-Rahman, having determined upon a punitive expedition against Aquitania, assembled his troops, set off from Pamplona, crossed the Pyrenees and laid siege to Bordeaux. Eudo, after vainly trying to halt the Arab advance on the Garonne, retreated farther north-east and was defeated, losing most of his men. Othman perished when he leapt over a precipice to evade capture. As for his widow, Eudo's beautiful daughter, she was sent to a Damascus harem.

Eudo now called upon Charles for help, and this was readily promised, despite their previous antagonism, because the Saracens' light cavalry had meantime been ravaging the countryside, storming towns, taking captives and collecting plunder. Attracted by the famed treasures of St.-Hilaire near Poitiers and St.-Martin at Tours, Abd-er-Rahman had continued his campaign northwards, leaving in his wake a trail of murder and looting. Having seized and destroyed the monastery of St.-Hilaire, he bypassed Poitiers, set off along the Roman road towards Tours, and somewhere along this route encountered Charles Martel.

According to one Spanish chronicler, the two armies faced each other for a week, Charles awaiting the arrival of levies, Abd-er-Rahman endeavouring to get his plunder away beyond Poitiers. The Franks took up defensive positions. Their army, composed largely of foot soldiers armed with shields, swords, axes, javelins and daggers, was well trained but ill-disciplined. So were the levies, and ill-armed too. The Saracen army, its great strength lying in cavalry equipped with lance and sword, was encumbered by its loot-laden baggage mules and, as a result, seriously reduced in mobility. When Abd-er-Rahman ordered his cavalry to attack, the reiterated and headlong charges failed to shake the Franks drawn up in phalanx, and losses were severe. If we are to believe one chronicler, 'The men of the North stood as motionless as a wall; they were like a belt of ice frozen together, and not to be dissolved, as they slew the Arab with the sword. The Austrasians, vast of limb, and iron of hand, hewed on bravely in the thick of the fight; it was they who found and cut down the Saracen King.' A counter-attack by Eudo and his Aquitanian troops turned the enemy's flank, and Abd-er-Rahman was killed while trying to rally his followers. Nightfall brought the fighting to a close.

Next morning Frankish scouts reported that the Saracen camp was empty. Martel suspected trickery and an ambush, but he was wrong: the Muslim army had withdrawn by night, abandoning much plunder and leaving the battlefield strewn with corpses.

A.B.-J.

Valmy (B***)

Date: 20 September 1792.

Location: At the intersection of Reute Nationale 31 and Route Nationale 33 (Châlons-sur-Marne to Ste. Menehould). **91.**

War and campaign: The French Revolutionary War; the Campaign of North-East France, 1792 (see p. 196).

Object of the action: The Prussian army was intending to crush the weak French army and open the road to Paris.

Opposing sides: (a) Generals Dumouriez and Kellerman commanding the composite Revolutionary forces. (b) King Frederick William IV and the Duke of Brunswick leading the Prussian army.

Forces engaged: (a) French: 35 battalions; 60 squadrons; possibly 40 guns. *Total*: 52,000 (36,000 engaged). (b) Prussians: details uncertain, but including 36 guns. *Total*: Probably 34,000.

Casualties: (a) 300 French killed and wounded. (b) Approx. 180 Prussians killed and wounded.

Result: Brunswick's advance was checked and French morale rapidly rallied.

Nearby accommodation: Châlons-sur-Marne.

Suggested reading: General Work: Madelin, L., *The French Revolution*, (English Edn.) London, 1916. On the Campaign: Phipps, R. W., *The Armies of the First French Republic*, Vols. I and II, London, 1926 and 1929. On the Battle: Creasy, E. S., *The Fifteen Decisive Battles of the World*, London, 1851. Fuller, J. F. C., *The Decisive Battles of the Western World*, Vol. II, London, 1955.

In the summer and autumn of 1792 France was invaded by the Armies of the First Coalition which were determined to destroy the Revolution and reinstate Louis XVIII. At first the French armies, preoccupied with intrigues and purges amongst their senior officers, were unable to offer effective resistance, and Brunswick captured both Longwy and Verdun, thus cutting the link joining the French Northern and Central Armies. Panic gripped Paris, for only a horde of '*fédérés*'* at Châlons stood between the invaders and the capital.

Fortunately General Dumouriez was equal to the occasion, and he at once took the dangerous step of placing himself across the Prussian communications near Ste. Menehould at the cost of abandoning the Argonne passes and his own links with Paris. He was joined near Valmy by General Kellerman on 19 September with part of the French Army of the Centre.

Brunswick turned south and east at King Frederick William's insistence to seize the Châlons road and wipe out the impudent French force. The result was the celebrated 'Cannonade of Valmy'. The French army had eventually taken up a semicircular position, Stengel commanding the right, Kellerman the centre and Chazot the left, with Dumouriez in central reserve. The Prussians approached out of the mists in the early morning of the 20th, drove a French outpost from La Lune, and drew up their battle line between that village and the hamlet of Somme Bionne, 1,300 yards from Kellerman's position on a small hill surmounted by a windmill which still stands today.

About midday the rival batteries opened a heavy cannonade, the Prussians directing all their fire against Kellerman's mixed force of regulars and volunteer *fédérés*. Somewhat unexpectedly the French withstood the ordeal without flinching, the soldiers chanting '*Vive la Nation! Vive la France! Vive notre général!*', and when the first lines of Prussian grenadiers started to advance at 1 pm they were met with such a hail of fire that they halted after only 200 yards. The French cohesion almost broke, however, when a lucky Prussian shot caused three ammunition waggons to explode close behind the windmill, but Kellerman in person rallied his men and Dumouriez sent forward two fresh batteries to reinforce the position. The Prussians failed to seize the opportunity—largely because Brunswick had already left the field. The action dragged on indecisively until 4 pm, when torrential rain put an end to hostilities.

The importance of Valmy was that it marked the end of the period of eighteenth-century 'limited' war, and introduced the concept of 'national' struggles fought by volunteer and conscript armies. Its immediate effect was to check Brunswick's advance on Paris, and within a month the Prussian forces were in full retreat for the Rhine. The Revolution had survived its first great military crisis.

Special Note: See glossary, p. 197.   D.G.C.

Verdun (A****)

Date: 21 February–20 December 1916.

Location: On the river Meuse; several relics are preserved. **87.**

War and campaign: The First World War; the Western Front 1916 (see p. 197).

Object of the action: The Germans were trying to pare down French strength and protect their adjacent strategic railways and the iron basin of Briey by capturing the salient.

Opposing sides: (*a*) General Falkenhayn and the Crown Prince in command of the German forces. (*b*) Generals Joffre and Pétain commanding the French forces.

Forces engaged (on 21 February): (*a*) 6 German divisions—but numbers rose rapidly. (*b*) 3 French divisions—but numbers rose rapidly.

Casualties: (*a*) 336,831 Germans killed and wounded. (*b*) 362,000 French killed and wounded.

Result: A near escape for the French from defeat by exhaustion; it also severely weakened the Germans.

Nearby accommodation: Verdun.

Suggested reading: General Work: Cruttwell, C. M. F., *History of the Great War*, Oxford, 1936. On the Campaign: Zweig, A.,

Education before Verdun, London, 1916. On the Battle: Pétain, H. P., *Verdun*, (trans. by M. MacKeogh), London, 1930. Horne, A., *The Price of Glory*, London, 1962. Work of Fiction: Barbusse, H., *Under Fire*, (English translation) London, 1916.

The city of Verdun, which stands astride the Meuse between Sedan and St. Mihiel is one of the most ancient and important fortresses of France. Its Vauban enceinte was extended by a chain of detached fortresses after 1870 and by the beginning of the century further improvements had transformed it into one of the most formidable defended areas in Europe. The danger it posed to the flank of an attack from Lorraine was material in turning Schlieffen towards his scheme for a wider envelopment through Belgium and it formed the pivot of French resistance to that manoeuvre in 1914. For the next 18 months, however, there was little fighting around Verdun. The circle of subordinate fortresses 5 miles from the city and the line of entrenchments 3 miles farther on held the Germans away in a large salient of great strength and deterred them from any serious assault. This inactivity encouraged a severe reduction of the garrison and the defence was further weakened by the removal of most of the heavy guns from the armoured forts. The German siege artillery had smashed the Liège fortresses so quickly and completely in 1914 that the French High Command, in a disastrous misappreciation, had decided that such positions possessed no further military value and formed, in fact, a danger to their garrisons.

At the beginning of 1916, therefore, Verdun belied its strength. Apparently a rock of resistance, it formed in effect an exposed salient and its inconvenient proximity to the German strategic railway system and the iron basin of Briey seemed bound to attract German attention sooner rather than later.

But when it did so, in January 1916, it was for altogether more ominous reasons. Falkenhayn, the German Commander-in-Chief, anxious to exhaust the French will and ability to resist before the full power of the British army was deployed, settled upon the city as an execution place into which he might tempt France and 'bleed her to death' in a purely symbolic struggle. He was convinced that the French would not yield Verdun. He was sure that the advantageous situation of his troops, their superior communications (14 railways to 1 French narrow-gauge line) and an overwhelming artillery would allow him to win a battle of material at little cost. By 12 February he had assembled in great secrecy a force of 6 divisions, 1,700 guns and 2,500,000 shells and achieved a concentration of more than two to one. Bad weather postponed zero day until 21 February and allowed the French to improve their position marginally, but the odds were heavily against them.

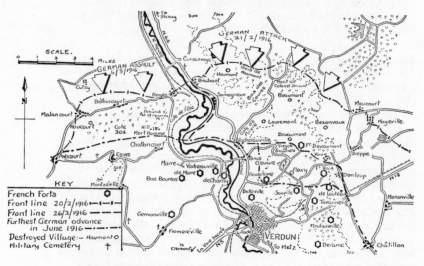

The French forces were disposed in a line of entrenchments
before and between the disarmed forts and along the spurs of
the river heights, from Avocourt in the west via Forges,
Brabant and Ornes to Maucourt, where the line dropped into
the plain of the Woeuvre. Although not high, the ground is
excessively broken, a jumble of well-wooded spurs and
re-entrants which covered the attackers from fire and view.
Falkenhayn's plan was for a limited assault on a 6-mile front
on the right bank, nullifying local resistance with a shattering
artillery bombardment, obliterating the trench system and
sealing it off from reinforcement. Only then would his infantry
move into the devastated zone. This plan was an early exercise
in the doctrine 'Artillery conquers; infantry occupies'. It very
nearly succeeded. When, on the evening of 22 February, after
24 hours' bombardment, the first German patrols began to
infiltrate the French positions they found little initial resistance.
Quickly, however, the survivors, often only the mere shred of
a battalion, rallied and returned fire. Although the Germans
made some progress, it was slower and more costly than
expected. There were, however, no French reserves to sustain
the effort and by 25 February the Germans were in the second
position. On this day the greatest catastrophe of the battle
befell the French. Reinforcements had begun to arrive and
Pétain was on his way to assume his legendary command, but
the front was still desperately weak and the forts not yet
restored to their real rôle as the centres of defence. Counter-
orders were being written but before they arrived a patrol of
10 Germans, arriving miraculously unscathed beneath the

gates of Fort Douaumont, found its moat unmanned and an entry port open, climbed inside and captured it. The military value of the stroke was perhaps less than the dismay which it caused in France, but it was great enough. The Germans had now penetrated some 4 miles into the French position, forced their withdrawal from the Woeuvre and inflicted grievous loss.

Joffre, had, however, as Falkenhayn had anticipated, resolved to retain the city. As it could not be supplied by rail, it must depend upon a train of lorries operating along the only open road (later to become famous as *'la Voie Sacrée'*) and the whole French army would, if necessary, march to its defence. Already by 26 February these decisions were felt in a stiffer resistance, and by 28 February the assault was at a standstill. The Crown Prince had from the first urged Falkenhayn to attack on both banks of the Meuse. As French enfilade fire from the left grew heavier, he got his way and on 6 March a new corps (7th Reserve) began the assault. Again it made quick initial gains but again the French recovered, and the tempo of battle on these more open slopes settled down into a slow and murderous deadlock. The centres of the fighting were two hills *'Cote 304'* and the ominously appropriate *'Mort Homme'*.

On 30 March Falkenhayn proposed to end the offensive. His vision of a 'cheap' battle of attrition had proved to be vain. Although it was devouring French divisions at an enormous rate, it was doing almost as much damage to his own army. It had become an artillery struggle in which the infantry neither advanced nor retreated but merely endured. The Crown Prince, however, held out against him and the battle ground on. On 7 June Fort Vaux, on the right bank, fell to the Germans after a heroic resistance. On 20 June the Germans attacked behind a phosgene-gas barrage and the French broke before this new hazard, allowing the Germans to the gates of Fort Souville. But thereafter the German effort fell away. On 26 June the preparatory bombardment for the Allied offensive on the Somme had begun. It was weaker than planned after the usury of Verdun but it was enough to draw the teeth of the Germans' offensive. By 14 July the Germans had reached their nearest point of approach to the city and been driven from it.

The battle was to drag on at half strength throughout the summer and in the autumn the French were to regain much of what they had lost, but the battle of the 'execution place' ended on 11 July. Between 21 February and 15 July, 70 of the 96 French divisions had passed through Verdun, and 46 German. The Germans had fired some 22,000,000 shells into the salient, the French some 15,000,000 back. The battlefield remains a wilderness to this day.

J.D.P.K.

Gibraltar

Gibraltar (B****)

Date: 24 June 1779–7 February 1783.

Location: The eastern extremity of the peninsula enclosing Algeçiras Bay. **123.**

War and campaign: The War of American Independence; the European Coalition against England (see p. 196).

Object of the action: The French and Spaniards hoped to wrest the fortress from British control.

Opposing sides: (a) General Eliott, Governor and Commander-in-Chief of Gibraltar. (b) Don Alvarez, later joined by the Duc de Crillon and Admiral Morena.

Forces engaged: (a) 5 English and 8 Hanoverian battalions; 412 fortress guns. *Total*: 5,000 (later raised to 7,500). (b) 16 Spanish battalions; 12 squadrons; 150 guns. *Total*: 14,000 (later raised to 40,000 after Crillon's arrival).

Casualties: (a) 333 British killed; 536 died of sickness; 911 wounded. (b) Not known, but probably about 5,000 Allies.

Result: General Eliott defied all Franco-Spanish attacks and held out until finally relieved.

Nearby accommodation: Gibraltar.

Suggested reading: On the Siege: Drinkwater, J., *A History of the Siege of Gibraltar* (Edn.) London, 1905. Hargreaves, R., *The Enemy at the Gate*, London, 1945. Spilsbury, J., *A Journal of the Siege of Gibraltar*, Gibraltar, 1908. Article: McGuffie T. H., in *History Today*, November, 1964.

For more than $3\frac{1}{2}$ years General George Eliott defied Franco-Spanish efforts to wrest control of the 'Key of the Mediterranean' from the British Crown.

The first stage of the siege began in June 1779, and took the form of a loosely co-ordinated Spanish blockade by land and sea, but supplies continued to reach the garrison from Morocco.

In January 1780 the Royal Navy passed in a large convoy of store-ships and a reinforcement of 1,000 men, and 15 months later repeated the performance under the very nose of the Spanish fleet. The same April (1781), however, the Spaniards opened a heavy bombardment which was due to last—on and off—for the next 15 months. Much damage was inflicted on the town, but the fortifications remained strong—thanks to Eliott's improvements carried out between 1777 and 1779—and loss of life was small. Through the long months of continuous siege, the General maintained an iron discipline and gave the finest possible example to his men, earning the nickname of 'old Cock o' the Rock'. On 27 November 1781 he organised a most successful sortie against Fort St. Carlos, destroying the besiegers' forward works and spiking many guns at trifling cost. Morale remained remarkably high.

Events took a turn for the worse, however, in February 1782, when the fall of Minorca released a French army under the Duc de Crillon to reinforce the casual Spanish forces, and a new vigour was soon evident in the prosecution of the siege. By the end of June the investing forces numbered 40,000 men, supported by a fleet of 40 sail, and a grand assault was clearly in preparation. It came on the morning of 13 September. Covered by their fleet, 10 floating batteries were towed over Algeçiras Bay to within 1,000 yards of the King's Bastion, protecting the western side of the Rock. The bombardment that followed reached phenomenal proportions—but the garrison's red-hot shot wrought havoc with the enemy vessels. By one o'clock the following morning 6 floating batteries and 2 warships were ablaze, and into the confusion sallied the 12 gun-boats of Captain Curtis, R.N. The attackers lost 2,000 casualties, and by dawn the assault had been finally beaten off.

The resolution of the besiegers never recovered from this costly failure, and in the following month Admiral Lord Howe had little difficulty in breaking the blockade and further reinforcing the garrison. Although reduced to a sham, the siege dragged on until 5 February 1783. A grateful nation rewarded Eliott with a peerage, and his stout defence of Gibraltar for 3 years, 7 months and 12 days did a great deal to rally national morale after the disasters sustained by British arms in the American Colonies.

D.G.C.

Map of Great Britain and Ireland showing battle sites.

GREAT BRITAIN							
23	Culloden	34	Flodden	46	Worcester	58	Hastings
24	Grampians	35	Ancrum Moor	47	Evesham	59	Lewes
25	Killiecrankie	36	Hadrian's Wall	48	Tewkesbury	60	Lostwithiel
26	Stirling Bridge	37	Marston Moor	49	Colchester	61	Londonderry
27	Bannockburn	38	Stamford Bridge	50	St. Albans (1)	62	Ford of the Biscuits
28	Falkirk (1)	39	Preston	51	St. Albans (2)	63	The Yellow Ford
29	Falkirk (2)	40	Towton	52	Assandune	EIRE	
30	Prestonpans	41	Wakefield	53	Barnet	64	Drogheda
31	Dunbar	42	Bosworth	54	Chalgrove	65	Boyne
32	Pinkie	43	Naseby	55	Newbury (1) (2)	66	Aughrim
33	Philiphaugh	44	Northampton	56	Ethandune	67	Limerick
		45	Edgehill	57	Sedgemoor	68	Kinsale

Great Britain

ANCRUM MOOR (B*); battle of, 17 February 1545; 3½ miles north-west of Jedburgh on the A 68 to Melrose; **35**; Anglo-Scottish Wars. Sir Ralph Evans and Sir Brian Latour (5,000) were defeated by a Scottish army under the Earl of Angus owing to the desertion of their Border troops in search of loot. See Lang, A., *A History of Scotland*, Vol. I, London and Edinburgh, 1870.

Assandune (or Ashingdon) (C**)

Date: 18 October 1016.

Location: Ashingdon lies between the rivers Crouch and Roach, 5 miles north of Southend on Sea. **52**.

War and campaign: The Saxon Campaign against the Danes (see p. 193).

Object of the action: The Anglo-Danish contest to decide the future of the English throne.

Opposing sides: (*a*) King Edmund Ironside leading the Anglo-Saxon forces. (*b*) Cnut (Canute) leading Danish forces.

Forces engaged: No details known.

Casualties: No details known.

Result: A complete victory for Cnut leading to the partition of the kingdom.

Nearby accommodation: Southend-on-Sea.

Suggested reading: General Works: Stenton, F. M., *Anglo-Saxon England*, Oxford, 1943. Green, J. R., *The Conquest of England*, London, 1883. Garmonsway, G. N., *The Anglo-Saxon Chronicle*, London, 1953. Work of Fiction: Bengtsson, F., (trans. Meyer), *The Long Ships*, London, 1954.

Edmund Ironside, who succeeded Ethelred the Unready in April 1016, united the forces of Wessex against the Danes. After this the Danes besieged London and cut off the city completely. During the summer Edmund advanced from Wessex and tried to raise the siege of London but suffered very heavy losses and retired again to Wessex. Cnut was hard pressed for supplies and after a final and unsuccessful attempt to capture the city he withdrew his forces to the mouth of the Orwell from which position he made a plundering raid into East Anglia. The Danes then crossed the Thames and plundered Kent until they were defeated by Edmund at Otford (near Sevenoaks), and withdrew to the Isle of Sheppey. From here after substantial reorganisation Cnut again led a large-scale raid into Essex and Mercia. By this time most of southern England and Mercia had rallied to Edmund. Edmund caught up with Cnut's forces at Ashingdon. There was a bloody, even and hard-fought battle but at the climax of the action Eadric and his Mercians broke and fled and the result was a complete defeat for the English. The chronicle records, 'Among the slain were bishop Eadnoth, abbot Wulfsige, ealdorman Aelfric, ealdorman Eodwine, Ulfcytel from East Anglia and Aethelweard.' Edmund fled to Wessex where shortly after he made peace with Cnut. This gave Wessex to Edmund with London and the eastern part of the country going to Cnut. Edmund died in November 1016 and Wessex then accepted Cnut as King.

D.D.R.

Bannockburn (A***)

Date: 24 June 1314.

Location: One mile south-east of Stirling; reached along the A 905 road at Kerse Mills. **27.**

War and campaign: The Wars between England and Scotland (see p. 194).

(see p. 194).

Object of the action: King Robert the Bruce wished to complete the expulsion of the English from Scotland; the English king to trap the Scots into a decisive battle.

Opposing sides: (a) King Edward II in command of an English army. (b) Robert the Bruce commanding the Scots.

Forces engaged: (a) English: 20,000 foot soldiers; 3,000 mounted men-at-arms. *Total*: 23,000. (b) Scots: 14,500 foot soldiers; 500 mounted men-at-arms. *Total*: 15,000.

Casualties: (a) 22 barons, 68 knights and perhaps 1,000 men. (b) 2 knights and perhaps 500 spearmen.

Result: The Scottish victory at Bannockburn secured the country's independence for the following three centuries.

Nearby accommodation: Stirling.

Suggested reading: General Work: McKisack, M., *The 14th Century*, Oxford, 1959. On the Battle: Hunter, D. M., *The Battle of Bannockburn*, 1962 (available locally). Morris, J. E., *Bannockburn*, Edinburgh, 1914. Young, P. and Adair, J., *Hastings to Culloden*, London, 1964. Article:Mackie, J. D., *Scottish Historical Review*, Vol. 29, Edinburgh, 1950.

In December 1313 Sir Edward Bruce, King Robert's brother, laid siege to one of the few castles in Scotland remaining in English hands. This was Stirling, the key to the Lowlands. It was agreed with Sir Philip Mowbray, the captain of Stirling, that if no English army arrived to relieve the castle by 24 June 1314, Midsummer Day, then the fortress should be surrendered to the Scots.

In spite of baronial dissensions in England King Edward determined to invade Scotland, hoping to use Stirling as a bait to attract the Scots army and then to defeat King Robert in the field. The first part of his plan worked well. At Berwick he assembled a vast army by the standards of the day, composed mainly of foot soldiers, for, as he wrote in the preamble to the 'commissions of array', it had been said that 'a great part of the exploit will come to footmen'. On 12 June 1314 the English marched north, reaching Edinburgh a week later.

As the English advance continued, slowed down by a train of 106 ox-drawn supply wagons, King Robert mustered an army of enthusiastic Scots at Torwood, close to Falkirk. His soldiers, mostly yeoman farmers, numbered over 14,000 and were equipped with 14-foot pikes, the traditional weapon of the Scotsmen of those days. King Robert then moved to a position 2 miles south of Stirling astride the road from the south which King Edward would have to follow to reach the castle. He divided his army into divisions and fortified his position in front with knee-deep potholes covered with bracken, which he hoped would break up any English cavalry charge.

The English army approached Stirling with caution on 23 June. Some miles short of the Scottish defences King Edward dispatched two reconnaissance parties. One, under Sir Humphrey de Bohun, rode directly up the road towards Stirling, until they reached the Bannockburn, a stream which flowed across the road some two score yards south of King Robert's divisions, who were probably hidden in the trees of New Park. De Bohun splashed across the burn and found himself face to face with Bruce, sitting on a grey pony and apparently alone. The young knight charged him, but at the last moment the King stood up in his stirrups, deflected the

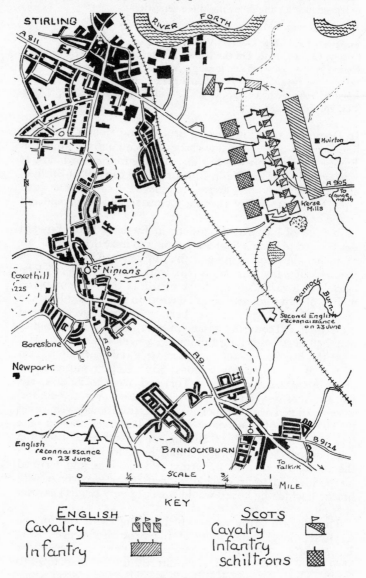

STIRLING

River Forth

Muirton

Kerse Mills

To Grangemouth

St Ninian's

Coxethill
.225

Second English
reconnaissance
on 23 June

Bannock Burn

Borestone

Newpark

English
reconnaissance
on 23 June

BANNOCKBURN

To
Falkirk

SCALE

0   ¼   ¾   1

MILE

KEY

ENGLISH		SCOTS	
Cavalry		Cavalry	
Infantry		Infantry schiltrons	

lance and struck out the Englishman's brains with his battle-
axe. The remaining Englishmen fled.

After the second English squadron had fared equally badly
against a tight phalanx of Scots spearmen near St. Ninian's
Kirk, King Edward's war council decided to move the whole
army over the Bannockburn that night. The crossing points

selected were above the village of Bannockburn, east of the
Scots army. This move was successfully accomplished, and
dawn discovered the English host in the marshy area known
as the 'Kerse'.

After the successes of the previous day Scottish morale was
high. King Robert formed his men into 4 'schiltrons' or
phalanxes of pikemen, commanded by himself, the Earl of
Moray, Sir Edward Bruce and the Earl of Douglas. Sir Robert
Keith and the Scots light horse stood somewhat to the north.
The English leaders, by contrast, had arrayed their cavalry in
9 squadrons in front of their archers and spearmen, with a
larger body of cavalry, known as the 'vanguard', under the
Earls of Hereford and Gloucester, upon their left.

Personal relations among the English commanders had
steadily deteriorated. The 24-year-old Earl of Gloucester, after
a violent quarrel with the Earl of Hereford, and an exchange
of recriminations with the King, opened the battle by hurling
himself against the spears of Sir Edward Bruce's division. His
men rather half-heartedly attempted to rescue him, and the
battle developed all along the line as a series of cavalry charges
against the 4 'schiltrons', which steadily advanced across the
level ground. The English archers, in their efforts to shoot at
the enemy, struck many of their own knights in the back with
clothyard shafts. Some more enterprising bowmen ran to the
right flank of the English cavalry and sent volleys of arrows
towards the Scots. Bruce, however, had planned for this
eventuality, and with a great shout Keith's horsemen charged
down upon the archers, scattering them in all directions.

'On them, on them, they fail!' roared the Scots spearmen,
pressing ever forward. After a bitter hand-to-hand struggle
the English began to give way, and the battle turned into rout
when the English, seeing some Scots camp followers waving
banners on Coxet Hill and imagining that reinforcements had
arrived, turned and fled.

King Edward eventually made his way to Dunbar, but other
fugitives, such as the Earl of Hereford, were not so fortunate.
At Bothwell Castle the Earl, with 600 men-at-arms and 1,000
foot soldiers, was captured by a pursuing Scots force. The
Privy Seal of England, which was with this English party, also
fell into Scots hands, symbolising the completeness of the
Scottish victory. Yet never again did the Scots win a com-
parable battle against the English in the field.

J.E.A.

BARNET (B*); battle of, 14 April 1471; fought on Hadley
Green on Road A 1000; **53**; Wars of the Roses. King Edward
IV (10,000 Yorkists) defeated the Earl of Warwick (15,000

Lancastrians), killing the 'Kingmaker' but failing to destroy the cause of the 'Red Rose'. See Burne, A. H., *The Battlefields of England* (2nd Edn.), London, 1951.

Bosworth (A***)

Date: 22 August 1485.

Location: South of Market Bosworth on the Dadlington road in the vicinity of the Ashby-de-la-Zouche canal. **42.**

War and campaign: The Wars of the Roses (see p. 194).

Object of the action: The Yorkists were attempting to intercept the Lancastrian march on London, and thus secure Richard III's tenure of the throne of England.

Opposing sides: (*a*) Henry Tudor, Earl of Richmond with a mixed force of Lancastrians and mercenaries. (*b*) King Richard III commanding the Yorkist Army.

Forces engaged: (*a*) Lancastrians: 10,000. (*b*) Yorkists: 12,000.

Casualties: (*a*) 100 Lancastrians. (*b*) 900 Yorkists.

Result: A decisive victory for Henry Tudor, winning him the Crown, establishing the Tudor dynasty, and bringing the Wars of the Roses to a conclusion.

Nearby accommodation: Leicester or Market Bosworth.

Suggested reading: Biography: Kendall, P., *Richard III*, London, 1955. On the Battle: Hutton, W., *The Battlefield of Bosworth Field* (2nd Edn.), 1813. Burne, A. H., *The Battlefields of England* (2nd Edn.), London, 1951. Young, P., and Adair, J., *Hastings to Culloden*, London, 1964. Play: Shakespeare, W., *Richard III*.

On 7 August 1485 Henry Tudor, Earl of Richmond, landed at Milford Haven to claim the throne of England. King Richard III heard the news at Nottingham and waited confidently for his captains in Wales to crush the Lancastrians, but instead they deserted to Richmond. By the time Henry had reached Lichfield (17 August) his original force of Flemish mercenaries had swollen to an army of 5,000 men. Moreover, Henry had secured a promise of support from Lord Stanley, his stepfather, a powerful baron of the north. The Lancastrians planned to march south along Watling Street and take London.

King Richard set out from Nottingham as soon as he heard that Henry had reached Lichfield. Moving by way of Leicester he came within sight of Watling Street just north of Hinckley but could see no signs of the enemy on the Roman road. He camped for the night of 20 August south of Stapleton in a place called 'the Bradshaws'.

Meanwhile Henry had reached Atherstone (20 August) and there he persuaded Lord Stanley to give him almost half of his forces, bringing his army up to a strength of 7,000. The remaining Stanley retainers, under the baron's brother, Sir William, camped on their own in between the two armies. The probable reason for this is that King Richard held as a hostage for Lord Stanley's conduct his eldest son, Lord Strange, and therefore there could be no open declaration for Henry by the Stanleys until the battle had begun.

On 21 August Henry's army took a branch road from Watling Street, called Fenn Lane, as if they intended to march to Leicester. Richard accordingly moved camp to 'Dicken's Nook', just east of Sutton Cheney, in order to oppose his advance. According to Tudor historians King Richard spent a terrible night haunted by visions of those he had murdered. Be this as it may, he was up early next morning and arrayed his soldiers for the forthcoming battle. He deployed his 'forward' of archers and billmen in a long thin line in order to deceive the Lancastrians into believing that he had even more troops than they already imagined that he had. Behind this came his main division, under the standard of England, composed of pikemen and billmen, flanked on both sides by two bodies of cavalry under the Earl of Northumberland and Sir Robert Brackenbury, the Constable of the Tower. The King also had a number of field guns but it is uncertain where these were placed.

Henry Tudor's formation corresponded with that of the Yorkists. A long slender 'forward', with Flemish and Cheshire archers intermingled, stood under the command of the same Earl of Oxford who had escaped from Barnetfield. Behind this line came the remaining troops, mostly cavalry. under the

BOSWORTH *22nd August 1485*

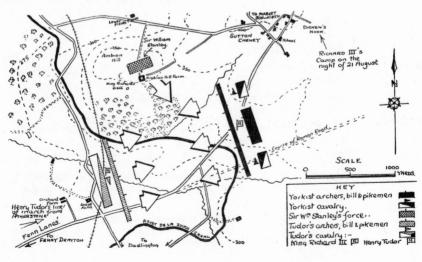

'Red Dragon of Cadwaller' standard. Sir William Stanley's men, displaying Lord Stanley's banner, probably stood on Ambion Hill, like spectators in a grandstand, as the two armies closed together beneath them on the plain of Redmore.

The battle opened with a vigorous discharge of guns and arrows. Then the Earl of Oxford led his men against the Yorkists and engaged them in hand-to-hand combat. The exact details of the mêlée which followed are obscure, but it would appear that King Richard lost his life when he led an impulsive charge with a small band of followers against Henry Tudor's main division. Although he succeeded in cutting down the Lancastrian standard bearer he was slain himself, according to tradition in the marshy area around 'King Richard's Well'. Either before or after this event Sir William Stanley led his men down the side of Ambion Hill in a fierce attack on the Yorkist army, which turned and fled. The battle lasted for scarce two hours, and was decided mainly by the archers under Oxford's command and the intervention of the Stanley force.

The temptations to sack the Yorkist camp proved too strong for Henry's soldiers and therefore there was little pursuit. Some nameless soldier found the crown which Richard had worn in a thornbush and brought it to Lord Stanley, who set it upon Henry Tudor's head. Leicester gave a royal welcome to the Earl of Richmond, and he proceeded on his way to London and the throne. He successfully defeated the serious rising of Lambert Simnel at Stoke in 1487 and during a long reign laid the foundations of the greatness of England in the sixteenth century.

J.E.A.

Camulodunum (or Colchester) D**)

Date: A.D. 61

Location: In and around the modern Colchester, 54 miles from London on the A 12. **49.**

War and campaign: The Rising of the Iceni against the Romans; Boudicca's Revolt (see p. 193).

Object of the action: Revenge for Roman tyranny.

Opposing sides: (a) Queen Boudicca (or Boadicea) at the head of the Iceni tribe. (b) Suetonius, Roman Governor of Britain, at the head of the legions.

Forces engaged: (a) Iceni—Roman estimate (probably exaggerated). *Total:* 100,000. (b) Romans: the IX Legion with auxiliaries and a number of reservists settled around Colchester.

Casualties: (a) Not known. (b) Not known, but the Romans lost almost the entire IX Legion.

Result: A short-lived success for Boudicca, but in the long run a victory for Suetonius, leading to a more disciplined but more tolerant Roman rule for Britain.

Nearby accommodation: Colchester.

Suggested reading: General Works: Oman, C. W. C., *England before the Norman Conquest*, London, 1924. Collingwood and Myres, *Roman Britain*, Oxford, 1936. Dudley, D. R., and Webster, G., *The Rebellion of Boudicca*, London, 1962.

The sack of Camulodunum (or Colchester) resulted from a combination of a harsh military tyranny, extortionate taxation and the unscrupulousness of Roman money-lenders who had got most of the British landowners in their toils. Colchester was a *'colonia'*—a settlement of army veterans who lived in the town and farmed their holdings outside. Their establishment had necessitated the wholesale expropriation of British landowners and was already very unpopular with the local tribe of the Trinovantes. Then in A.D. 61, while Suetonius, the Roman Governor, was away campaigning in north Wales, the powerful East-Anglian tribe of the Iceni was driven to revolt by tyranny and extortion. Their Queen, Boudicca, attempting to resist the confiscation of her property, was flogged. Her daughters were raped and her palace sacked. The simmering discontent came to a head, and all eastern Britain revolted.

Too late the colonists of Colchester tried to organise some defence. But their town was unfortified and only 200 regular troops were available. Boudicca's tribesmen easily stormed and burnt the town, and the next day routed out and massacred the armed garrison, who had taken refuge in the temple of Claudius, the only stone building. Finally when the IX Legion, with some auxiliary cavalry, arrived from Lincoln it was ambushed, surrounded and annihilated. London and Verulamium were taken and burnt and all their inhabitants massacred; and it seemed that Roman rule in Britain would perish altogether. Suetonius, however, kept his nerve and his head, and with forces he brought back from Wales routed Boudicca's army and exacted a fearful revenge from the revolted tribes. But two years later the Emperor Nero dismissed him for excessive harshness, and the whole episode in fact laid the foundations for a juster and more tolerant Roman government in Britain.

W.L.McE.

CHALGROVE (C**); battle of, 18 June 1643; between Thame and Dorchester; **54**; First English Civil War. Prince

Rupert and a Cavalier force (1,850), *en route* for Oxford, fought and defeated Sir Philip Stapleton's Roundheads (approx. 1,000), killing Sir John Hampden. See Burne, A. H., and Young, P., *The Great Civil War*, London, 1959.

Culloden (A***)

Date: 16 April 1746.

Location: Five and a half miles east of Inverness by way of the A 9 and the B 9006. **23.**

War and campaign: The Jacobite Rebellion of 1745 (see p. 195).

Object of the action: Cumberland was determined to defeat the Jacobite army following the failure of its attempted night attack against his camp.

Opposing sides: (*a*) The Duke of Cumberland in command of the Government forces of King George II. (*b*) Prince Charles Edward Stuart leading the Jacobite forces.

Forces engaged: (*a*) Government: 15 battalions; Scottish volunteers; 4 dragoon regiments; 16 guns. *Total*: 9,000. (*b*) Jacobites: 22 infantry regiments; 400 cavalry; 12 guns. *Total*: 5,400.
Special Note: a proportion of both sides were never actively engaged.

Casualties: (*a*) 50 Government troops killed and 259 wounded. (*b*) 1,000 Jacobites killed and 558 taken prisoner.

Result: A complete victory for Cumberland, marking the collapse of the Jacobite Rebellion.

Nearby accommodation: Inverness and Nairn.

Suggested reading: General Work: Tomasson, K. and Buist, F., *Battles of the '45*, London, 1962. On the Period: Taylor, A. and H., *1745 and After*, London, 1935. Tomasson, K., *Jacobite General*, London, 1961. On the Battle: Prebble, J., *Culloden*, London, 1961. Novel: Broster, D. K., *The Gleam in the North*, London, 1934.

After Falkirk (q.v.) the Duke of Cumberland took over Hawley's demoralised command at Edinburgh. Dissension was however already weakening the Jacobites. Charles's reliance upon Irish companions from France was disliked by Lord George Murray and the clan chiefs. Charles himself was inclined to be tactless and lacking in judgment. On 28 January 1746 the clan chiefs had presented an address to Charles pointing out the alarming numbers of desertions (exaggerated in fact) and the unlikelihood of their being able to capture Stirling Castle before Cumberland's arrival. They accordingly advised retreat to the Highlands and renewed activity in the spring. This advice, which was accepted with reluctance by Charles, was basically sound enough but was very damaging to morale, and the withdrawal across the Forth on 1 February was extremely disorderly. The objective was Inverness, a convenient headquarters for the Highlands and accessible by sea. It fell on 20 February. Fort Augustus fell to the French contingent a week later and only Fort William disturbed Charles's grip on the Highlands.

Meanwhile Cumberland, heavily reinforced, followed the withdrawal and the situation of the Highlanders grew increasingly precarious. There was no money in the treasury and dissension between Scots and Irish grew. Cumberland spent March at Aberdeen using the period of inaction to practise a new bayonet drill for use against the targe(t) and broadsword. This halt was further delayed by the swollen river Spey and it was not until 8 April that his last division left the town. Having crossed the Spey on 12 April he made his way by forced marches to Nairn. On the 14th his advance party had a skirmish with the enemy rearguard. Charles stayed the same night in Culloden House while his dispirited and starving army lay on Culloden Moor. The next day he drew up his forces in line of battle, but as the English did not move he decided to surprise them by a night attack on their camp. This never really had much hope of success owing to the exhaustion of the troops. It proved impossible to maintain order, and was finally abandoned on Lord George Murray's orders, serving only to make the Jacobites more despondent. Some of Charles's officers were now in favour of moving back to a stronger position but he refused as he had already done the previous day.

After an 8-mile march from Nairn which he had started as early as possible on the morning of the 16th, having learnt of the failure of the night attack, the Duke of Cumberland soon received news from his advanced parties of the enemy position. He at once formed line of battle, but finding that the Jacobites stayed where they were, he continued his march. The Jacobite forces were deployed in two rather ragged lines, with their right resting on some park walls, huts and a turf dyke and their left extending towards Culloden House and its enclosures. The position was not well chosen, for it was not realised that the ground to the front was boggy while the left was particularly vulnerable to attack in flank and rear owing to some dead ground to the front which had not been occupied. The Duke's force was drawn up in three lines, each of the first two consisting of 6 battalions of infantry and 2 regiments of dragoons on the wings while the third was composed mainly of Highland irregulars. The force had 10 three-pound guns, stationed in pairs between the battalions in the first line while the mortars were placed in 2 batteries of 3 to the left.

The Duke had just posted part of Cobham's dragoons and Kingston's light horse on his right when the rebels opened fire with their artillery which was arranged in 3 four-gun batteries

CULLODEN
16th April 1746

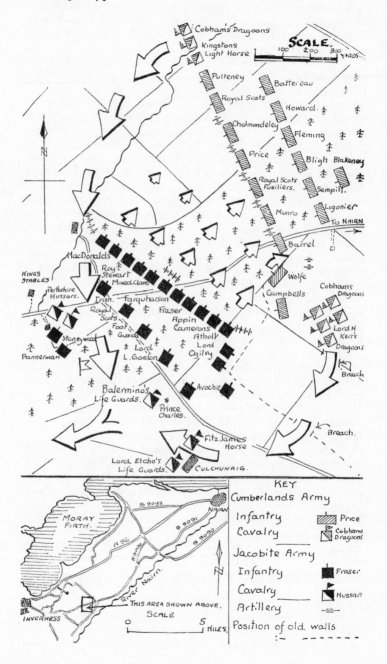

Cobham's Dragoons
Kingstons Light Horse

SCALE
100 200 300 YARDS

Pulteney
Royal Scots
Battereau
Howard
Cholmondeley
Fleming
Price
Bligh Blakeney
Royal Scots Fusiliers.
Sempill.
Munro
Ligonier
TO NAIRN
Barrel

MacDonalds
Roy^l Stewart
Mixed Clans
Wolfe
Campbells
Cobhams Dragoons
KINGS STABLES
Perthshire Hussars.
Irish. Farquharson
Royal Scots
Fraser
Appin
Cameras
Atholl
Lord H Keir's Dragoons
Foot Guards
Stoneywood
Bannerman
Lord L. Gordon
Lord Ogilvy
Breach
Balermino's Life Guards.
Avochie
Prince Charles.
Breach.
Fitz James Horse
Lord Elcho's Life Guards.
CULCHUNAIG.

KEY
Cumberlands Army
Infantry — Price
Cavalry — Cobhams Dragoons
Jacobite Army
Infantry — Fraser
Cavalry — Hussan
Artillery
Position of old walls

MORAY FIRTH.
B 90-92
NAIRN
B 9091
A 96
B 9090
INVERNESS
River Nairn.
THIS AREA SHOWN ABOVE.
SCALE
0 ___ 5 MILES.

sited in the centre and on the wings slightly in front of the main line. This was instantly replied to and the Duke's fire, lasting some 25 to 30 minutes, proved a great deal more effective, tearing holes in the Highland right and centre. Unable to sustain such a bombardment, they surged forward and swept round the left of the British line to attack the flank and rear of the 4th and 27th Regiments, causing them to give ground. Everywhere else they were quickly repulsed, the English having the advantage of the wind blowing away from them, and the 4th and 27th themselves being reinforced, rallied and helped to defeat the enemy with the bayonet. The Highlanders' rage at this reverse was so great that for a few moments they threw stones at the enemy.

On the Jacobite left, meanwhile, the MacDonalds, in part because they were sulking at being refused the place of honour, had refused to move. They were now dangerously isolated owing to the defeat of the centre and were under constant artillery fire. In consequence they had to meet the English attack from both sides. This was followed up by the dragoons who now burst through the Culloden enclosures, and the Macdonalds were quickly routed. The whole Jacobite line was now in full retreat and the defeat was made more certain by an encircling movement by Kerr's dragoons who went through breaches in the East and West Park walls to take up a position near Culchunaig. Only a heroic delaying action by two squadrons of Jacobite cavalry under Elcho and Fitzjames enabled the Jacobite right to escape at all. That this retreat was carried out in good order was due in the main to the efforts of Lord George Murray and was in marked contrast to the rout on the left. The English cavalry finally met in the centre of what had once been the Jacobite second line and pursued the fleeing enemy to within a mile of Inverness. Cumberland followed with his infantry and artillery more slowly.

The victory was a decisive one and marked the end of the rebellion. For this Cumberland, despite his ruthless conduct after the battle, must take the chief credit. On taking over command he had found the British regulars in a demoralised state which easily led to panic, and his reversal of this situation was a key factor in the Government's success.

H.G.M.

Dunbar (B**)

Date: 3 September 1650.

Location: To the south of the town on the Cockburnspath road (A 1087, A 1). **31.**

War and campaign: Cromwell's War against the Scots (see p. 195).

Object of the action: After failing to capture Edinburgh, Cromwell had retired on Dunbar, followed up by Leslie. Instead of evacuating by sea, Cromwell seized the chance of a battle.

Opposing sides: (*a*) Oliver Cromwell in command of the Parliamentary army. (*b*) David Leslie commanding the Covenanter army.

Forces engaged: (*a*) Parliamentarians: 7,500 foot; 3,500 cavalry; some guns. *Total*: 11,000. (*b*) Scots: 16,000 foot; 6,000 cavalry; approx. 30 guns. *Total*: 22,000.

Casualties: (*a*) Cromwell claims only 30 Parliamentarians were killed; undoubtedly an underestimate. (*b*) Perhaps 3,000 Scots killed, 10,000 prisoners and 30 guns.

Result: An English triumph, leading to the capture of Edinburgh and the occupation of the west of Scotland. The Kirk Party sustained a severe blow to its morale.

Nearby accommodation: Dunbar.

Suggested reading: General Work: Abbott, W. C., *Writings and Speeches of Oliver Cromwell*, London, 1937–47. Biography: Young, P., *Cromwell*, London, 1962. On the Battle: Young, P. and Adair, J., *From Hastings to Culloden*, London, 1964. Article: Firth, C. H., published in the *Transactions of the Royal Historical Society*, New Series, Vol. XIV, 1900.

Cromwell's invasion of Scotland had begun badly. for he had found the Scots in an almost impregnable position before Edinburgh and had been compelled to fall back on Dunbar. His army was suffering greatly from sickness and hunger and the road to England was cut at Cockburnspath. Although he had a fleet a re-embarkation could scarcely be effected without the loss of his guns, horses and rearguard.

David Leslie with a superiority of two to one occupied a strong position on Doon Hill, but on the day before the battle he was persuaded by his civilian advisers to move down and destroy the English. Cromwell saw his opportunity and explained his plan to Lambert and Monck who agreed. It was a stormy night and while the less-disciplined Scots sought what comfort they could find the stern Ironsides moved into their attacking positions. As dawn broke the English crossed the Brox Burn and fell on Leslie's right wing, keeping his left in play with their guns. The fight was fierce for a while and at first the English were repulsed, but after a time Cromwell himself led a column to outflank Leslie's right. The move was decisive, and as the sun was rising Cromwell halted his men on Doon Hill. There they sang the 117th Psalm, and by the time it was done he had rallied a good body of horse, who pursued the Scots for nearly 8 miles, with great slaughter. In less than an hour the Scots army had been destroyed. The power of the Kirk was broken.

P.Y.

Edgehill (or Kineton) (A***)

Date: 23 October 1642.

Location: North-west of Banbury and south-west of Warwick on the A 41. **45.**

War and campaign: The First English Civil War (see p. 195).

Object of the action: King Charles was attempting to win through towards London.

Opposing sides: (*a*) King Charles I in command of the Royalist army. (*b*) The Earl of Essex commanding the Parliamentarians.

Forces engaged: (*a*) Royalists: 10,000 foot; 2,500 horse; 1,000 dragoons; 20 guns. *Total*: 13,500. (*b*) Parliamentarians: approx. 10,500 foot and 2,500 cavalry; 15 guns. *Total*: approx. 1300.

Casualties: (*a*) Comparatively light—mostly infantry. (*b*) Uncertain. Possibly a joint-total of 4,000.

Result: A slight advantage for the Royalists, who were enabled to take Oxford and continue their advance towards London.

Nearby accommodation: Banbury.

Suggested reading: General Work: Wedgwood, C. V., *The King's War*, London, 1958. On the Battle: Burne, A. and Young, P., *The Great Civil War*, London, 1959. On the Battle: Young, P. and Adair, J., *Hastings to Culloden*, London, 1964.

On 12 October 1642 King Charles I marched from Shrewsbury intending to take London. His opponent, the Earl of Essex, was then at Worcester, which is not directly between Shrewsbury and the capital which his army was supposed to protect. Both armies were newly levied and inexperienced. They marched through the Midlands ignorant of each other's whereabouts, and when on the evening of 22 October they clashed near Kineton the Royalists were actually nearer London than the Parliamentarians.

Next morning the Cavaliers had their rendezvous on the summit of Edge Hill, but their position was too strong, and since the Parliamentarians made no move they descended to the plain. After a somewhat ineffective cannonade the King's army made a general advance. Prince Rupert with the right wing of horse swept away the opposing cavalry under Sir James Ramsey and a brigade of foot. On the left Lord Wilmot's cavalry routed a regiment of horse and another of foot, but missed the two cavalry regiments under Sir William Balfour and Sir Philip Stapleton.

In the centre the Royalist foot under the veteran Sir Jacob Astley drove back the Parliamentary infantry, but were counter-attacked by Balfour, who broke through and reached the King's guns. The Royalists had no reserve, and with Rupert's cavalry engaged in pursuing the broken enemy and in plundering the baggage train in Kineton, Balfour's horse had nobody to oppose them. A strong attack of horse and foot broke the redcoats of the King's Lifeguard (foot); the Knight Marshal, Sir Edmund Verney, was killed and the Banner Royal fell into the hands of the Roundheads—though it was soon recaptured. With their centre broken the Cavaliers fell back towards Radway, but the King was able to re-form them. Some of his cavalry and dragoons returned and helped to show a bold front. The Parliamentarians advanced, but they were tired and short of ammunition. A few salvoes of caseshot helped to discourage them. Night parted the exhausted armies.

The casualties have been variously reported. They may have numbered as many as 4,000 or as few as 1,000. After the battle Essex retired to Warwick leaving 7 guns in the hands of the Royalists, who were permitted to occupy Oxford and resume the march on London. Some say that Edgehill was a drawn battle. Certainly it was not the decisive victory it might have been had the King kept a proper reserve. Even so the advantage lay with the Cavaliers.

P.Y.

Ethandune (or Edington) (B**)

Date: A.D. 878.

Location: Three miles north-east of Westbury along B 3098 stands the village of Edington. 56.

War and campaign: The Danish Invasions of England (see p. 193).

Object of the action: King Alfred was attempting to wrest Chippenham and parts of occupied Wessex from the Danes.

Opposing sides: (a) King Alfred commanding the forces of Wessex. (b) Guthrum at the head of the Danish forces.

Forces engaged: Not known in any detail.

Casualties: Not known for either side, but clearly more Danes than Anglo-Saxons.

Result: A victory for Alfred which led to the agreed withdrawal of the Danes north of the Thames.

Nearby accommodation: Westbury.

Suggested reading: General Works: Stenton, F. M., *Anglo-Saxon England*, Oxford, 1943. Garmonsway, G. N., *The Anglo-Saxon Chronicle* London, 1953. Biography: Williams, P., *Alfred the King*, London, 1951. Work of Fiction: Bengtsson, F. (trans. Meyer), *The Long Ships*, London, 1954.

During 877 the Danes under Guthrum had advanced from Gloucester, capturing Chippenham and subjugating large areas of the lands of the West Saxon peoples. Alfred fell back to the area of the Somerset marshes at Athelney. From there he was able to elude the main Danish forces but at the same time harry them. Early in 878 the fyrd of Devon attacked and destroyed a Danish army at Countesbury Hill, Lynton; and then in May Alfred gathered men from Hampshire, Wiltshire and Somerset and concentrated them at Ethandune 15 miles south of the Danish stronghold at Chippenham. Alfred won a decisive victory over Guthrum, and the battered Danish army retreated within its fortress. Alfred besieged the town for 14 days, at the end of which the Danes capitulated. The Parker Chronicle, which provides the greatest known detail of this action, describes the battle of Edington thus: '. . . there Alfred fought against the entire host and put it to flight and pursued it up to the fortification, and laid siege there a fort-night; and then the host gave him preliminary hostages and solemn oaths that they would leave his Kingdom and promised him in addition that their King would receive baptism . . . and three weeks later the King Guthrum came to him . . . at Aller which is near Athelney where the King stood sponsor to him at baptism'. This agreement is known as the Treaty of Wedmore. The battle of Edington thus halted and turned back the Danish advance, cleared the Danes from the whole of England south of the Thames and west of Watling Street and led to the concentration of Danish influence in East Anglia.

D.D.R.

Evesham (B***)

Date: 4 August 1265.

Location: The crossroads where the B 4084 meets the A 435, north of Evesham. 47.

War and campaign: The Baronial Wars (see p. 194).

Object of the action: Simon de Montfort was advancing to a rendezvous at Kenilworth, and Prince Edward set out to crush him with a superior force.

Opposing sides: (*a*) Prince Edward leading the Royalist army. (*b*) Simon de Montfort at the head of a Baronial army.

Forces engaged: (*a*) Royalists: 7,000 foot soldiers; 1,000 mounted men-at-arms. *Total*: 8,000. (*b*) Barons: 5,000 foot soldiers; 350 mounted men-at-arms. *Total*: 5,350.

Casualties: (*a*) 20 knights and 2,000 foot killed and wounded. (*b*) 300 barons and knights and 2,000 foot killed or captured.

Result: A victory for Prince Edward and the death of Simon de Montfort, leading to the restoration of King Henry III to sovereign power.

Nearby accommodation: Evesham.

Suggested reading: General Work: Powicke, M., *The Thirteenth Century*, Oxford, 1953. Biography: Bemont, C., *Simon de Montfort* (English Edn.), London, 1930. On the Campaign: Blaauw, W. H., *The Barons' War* (2nd Edn.), London, 1871. On the Battle: Young, P. and Adair, J., *Hastings to Culloden*, London, 1964.

On 28 May Prince Edward escaped from the custody of Simon de Montfort and raised an army. At first he prevented Simon, who was at Hereford, from crossing the Severn, but on 1 August he carried out a successful raid on a Baronial force gathered at Kenilworth Castle. This, however, left the river unguarded, and Simon forded the river on 2 August. He marched as far as Evesham on the following day, intending to join his eldest son at Kenilworth. Meanwhile Prince Edward had left Worcester a second time and advanced upon Evesham from the north with an army much stronger in the all-important cavalry arm than that of the Barons.

It is said that Earl Simon's barber first sighted the banners of the advancing Royalist army from the bell tower of Evesham Abbey, and warned his master. The old Earl realised his plight at once, for the town of Evesham lay in a loop of the Avon, and the one bridge leading out of the town had almost been reached by a Royalist column under Mortimer. On Green Hill to the north of the town Prince Edward and the Earl of Gloucester spread out their divisions in a long line: the door had shut on the trap.

Simon formed up his army like an iron-tipped arrow, with a solid front of heavily armoured knights, his Welsh foot soldiers drawn up behind them, and then charged up the hill. At first the impact of his tight, narrow column drove the Royalist centre back, but it did not break through. The wings of the Royalist army closed like pincers upon the infantry 'shaft' of the arrow: the Welsh turned and fled towards the river. Surrounded, Earl Simon fought on courageously with his family and household knights. No quarter was asked or given, and the battle degenerated into a bloody slaughter. 'Such was the murder of Evesham,' wrote a contemporary chronicler, 'for battle it was none.' The Prince's victory and Earl Simon's death, however, did almost bring the civil wars to an end. At least there were no more pitched battles.

J.E.A.

Falkirk — 1 (B**)

Date: 22 July 1298.

Location: Falkirk is 25 miles west-north-west of Edinburgh on A 9.
28.

War and campaign: The Anglo-Scottish Wars (see p. 194).

Object of the action: King Edward I was in pursuit of Wallace's Scottish army.

Opposing sides: (*a*) King Edward I at the head of the English army. (*b*) Wallace commanding a Scottish army.

Forces engaged: (*a*) English: 16,000 foot soldiers; 2,500 men-at-arms. *Total*: 18,500. (*b*) Scots: 10,000 foot soldiers; 200 men-at-arms. *Total*: 10,200.

Casualties: (*a*) 200 English mounted men-at-arms killed and wounded. (*b*) 40 Scots knights and perhaps 5,000 foot soldiers.

Result: Indecisive politically, but Wallace quitted the field and sustained heavy losses.

Nearby accommodation: Falkirk.

Suggested reading: General Work: Oman, C. W. C., *The Art of War in the Middle Ages*, Vol. 2 (2nd Edn.), London, 1924. Sellman, R. R., *Mediaeval English Warfare*, London, 1960. Biography: Tout, T. F., *Edward I*, London, 1893.

In the years following Stirling Bridge King Edward I personally led a large army into Scotland. Wallace fell back to Torwood forest and enlarged his own army. At length Edward came upon the Scots, positioned on a hillside 2 miles south of Falkirk, with his front covered by a treacherous bog (Darnrig Moss). The Scots chief had arrayed his men, who were armed with 12-foot pikes in 'schiltrons', the customary phalanx of spearmen. The English army, in its traditional 3 divisions, marched up to the marsh and soon found that it was impossible to get across it.

The English right wing, under the Earls of Norfolk and Hereford, marched around to the right flank of the bog and the two other divisions moved past it on the left. The cavalry then charged against the Scots and put their few archers and cavalry men to flight. But they were unable to break the hedgehog of spears presented by Wallace's 'schiltrons'. The stalemate lasted for several hours before King Edward ordered his horsemen to disengage the enemy. Then the English bowmen were ordered to advance, and break the Scots formation with flights of arrows. This stratagem worked effectively as Wallace's pikemen had little protection against the shafts. Once gaps had appeared in the Scots line the English cavalry charged again, smashing through the 'schiltrons' and putting the Scotsmen to the sword.

Wallace made good his escape, but many thousands perished in the ensuing pursuit or were drowned attempting to swim the river Carron. Politically Falkirk was not decisive, but it demonstrated the value of both cavalry and archers in combining together on the battlefield against phalanxes of pikemen.

J.E.A.

FALKIRK—II (B**); battle of, 17 January 1746; near South Bantaskin; **29**; Jacobite Rebellion of '45. General Hawley's Government forces (8,000) were severely mauled by the Young Pretender's clansmen (8,000), losing 400 killed and as many prisoners. The last Jacobite victory of the Rebellion. See Hunter, D. M., *The Second Battle of Falkirk*, Falkirk, 1959.

Flodden (B**)

Date: 9 September 1513.

Location: Three miles south-east of Coldstream; turn off the A 697 for Branxton. **34**.

War and campaign: The Anglo-Scottish War of 1513–14 (see p. 194).

Object of the action: The English troops were seeking to clear the Scots invaders from the Border territories.

Opposing sides: (*a*) The Earl of Surrey commanding King Henry VIII's army. (*b*) King James IV in command of the Scots army.

Forces engaged: (*a*) 20,000 English with 22 light guns. (*b*) 25,000 Scots with 17 guns.

Casualties: (*a*) 4,000 English killed and 120 captured. (*b*) The King of Scotland, 8 earls, 13 barons and 10,000 others slain.

Result: The battle prevented any major Scottish invasion of England and decimated the Scots nobility.

Nearby accommodation: Berwick or Coldstream.

Suggested reading: On the Battle: Mackay Mackenzie, W., *The Secret of Flodden*, Edinburgh, 1931. Young, P., and Adair, J., *Hastings to Culloden*, London, 1964. Article: Mackie, J. D., 'The English Army at Flodden', in *Scottish Historical Miscellany*, Vol. 8, Edinburgh, 1959.

On 22 August 1513 the Scots army crossed the border and besieged three English castles. The Earl of Surrey hastened northwards, gathering a large army as he went, and took the field on 5 September. He secured an agreement with King James IV that a battle would be fought on the following Friday. The English commander then outflanked the Scots army, which was camped in an impregnable position on Flodden Edge, by crossing the River Till on the Twisell Bridge. The Scots moved north to Branxton Hill on 9 September and awaited the English who were advancing southwards upon them. The 5 Scots divisions were armed with 16-foot pikes and were supported by 17 cannon.

The English army was also arrayed in 5 divisions. The Scots

charged down the hill slopes towards them and were greeted by salvoes from 22 English field pieces and hundreds of arrows loosed by the English bowmen from the northern shires. The division of the Earl of Home dispersed Sir Edward Howard's men on the English right, but the Scots did not go to the aid of their fellows in the centre who were unable to break through the English corps commanded by Lord Thomas Howard and the Earl of Surrey. On the English left Sir Edward Stanley succeeded in routing the division of Highland clansmen opposite him, and then attacked the rear of the central Scots phalanxes. Soon King James, his nobles and several thousand spearmen were surrounded and pressed into a circle by the English. The fighting continued until evening, by which time the Scots monarch had been killed.

The English completed their victory next day by securing the Scottish ordnance and plundering the Scottish camp. As a reward for his services the Earl of Surrey was created Duke of Norfolk.

J.E.A.

The Ford of the Biscuits (B***)

Date: 7 August 1594.

Location: The Ford of Drumane over the river Arney, 5 miles south-west of Enniskillen on the Cavan Road. **62.**

War and campaign: Hugh O'Donnell's Revolt (a prelude to Tyrone's Rebellion) (see p. 194).

Object of the action: An English force was attempting to raise the siege of Enniskillen by the Irish.

Opposing sides: (*a*) Hugh Maguire and Tyrone's brother, Cormac, leading the Irish. (*b*) Sir Henry Duke and Sir Edward Herbert commanding the English.

Forces engaged: (*a*) Irish: approx. 1,000 infantry; no known cavalry or guns. *Total*: 1,000. (*b*) English: 600 infantry; 46 cavalry; no guns. *Total*: 646.

Casualties: (*a*) Irish losses unknown, but no more than a handful. (*b*) 56 English killed; 69 wounded.

Result: An Irish victory, but Enniskillen was relieved in August— only to fall into Irish hands the following spring.

Nearby accommodation: Enniskillen.

Suggested reading: Background Source: *The Calendar of State Papers, Ireland*, P.R.O. General Works: Byrne, M. J., *Ireland under Elizabeth*, London, 1909. *The Carew Calendar*, London, P.R.O. General Work: *Annals of the Four Masters*, Dublin, 1851. On the Campaign and Battle: Falls, C., *Elizabeth's Irish Wars*, London, 1950.

Enniskillen, with its castle which in part remains and is still in use, was a place of importance during O'Donnell's revolt against English rule in the late sixteenth century, as it was again to prove in the rebellions of 1641 and 1689. Standing on an island in the River Erne, which links the Upper and Lower Loughs, it afforded the best means of crossing the water for something like 30 miles. When, therefore, it was besieged by the redoubtable Hugh O'Donnell it became necessary to relieve it, and a force, small but adequate for the purpose, set out to do so. The Irish decided to intercept it and chose the ford of Drumane, on the Arney just above where it enters the Erne, a strong situation. The leader, Hugh Maguire, had many Scots mercenaries in his ranks. One can pinpoint features because the modern bridge traverses the old ford, and on the north side the road swings sharply right to pass a hill, which was then thickly wooded.

The English must have been pleased to find the ford undefended. Their little cavalry force moved on round the hill without seeing a sign of the enemy, and it looked as though there would be no engagement until the neighbourhood of Enniskillen was reached. Behind it marched the infantry with a long train of wagons and pack-horses carrying food to revictual the castle. Suddenly there came a typical Irish yell from the hill, followed by a blast of fire. So far as is known, the men in ambush were armed mainly, if not entirely, with the bow, but the Scots mercenaries may well have had some muskets. In any case the English were easy targets at this range, so that the shooting was deadly. Then the Irish charged down to complete their work.

Hampered by the train, Duke's men found themselves in a hopeless plight. To judge by their loss, rather less than a quarter of the force, they must have fought well, but the end was disaster. The Four Masters write:

'They came on without noticing anything till they fell in with Maguire's people . . . The name of the ford at which this great victory was gained was changed to Bel-atha-na-in-Briosgadh (Mouth of the Ford of the Biscuits), from the number of biscuits and small cakes left there to the victors.'

It was a sharp blow, but its effects were mainly of prestige and hardly damaged English power in Ireland.

C.F.

THE GRAMPIANS (D*); battle of, A.D. 84; probably near Coupar Angus or further north; **24**; Roman Conquest of Britain. The Roman Governor, Agricola, with two legions and auxiliaries (16,000), heavily defeated Calgacus (poss. 30,000) and the northern tribes but was not strong enough to conquer and hold the Highlands of Scotland. See Tacitus, *Agricola* (trans. Edn. Mattingley), London, 1948.

HADRIAN'S WALL (A****); fortification built *c*. A.D. 122–128; from Wallsend to Bowness-on-Solway; **36**; Roman Occupation of Britain. The Wall was intended to serve as a defence against the raids of the barbarians from southern Scotland, and held an estimated garrison of some 14,000 troops (including reserves); the best section to visit is Housesteads. See Birley, A.R., *Hadrian's Wall–An Illustrated Guide*, London, 1963.

Hastings (A****)

Date: 14 October 1066.

Location: Astride the A 21 just south of the small town of Battle in East Sussex. **58**.

War and campaign: The Norman Conquest of England (see p. 194).

Object of the action: King Harold was attempting to check the Norman invasion; Duke William was determined to secure the English crown.

Opposing sides: (*a*) Duke William of Normandy commanding a Norman and mercenary army. (*b*) King Harold (Godwinson) in command of the Anglo-Saxon army.

Forces engaged: (*a*) Normans: perhaps 6,000 archers and spearmen; 3,000 mounted troops. *Total*: approx. 9,000. (*b*) Saxons: possibly 2,000 'huscarles' and 8,000 'fyrd'. *Total*: approx. 10,000.

Casualties: (*a*) Unknown. (*b*) Unknown, but probably several thousands, including King Harold.

Result: The Norman victory ensured the Norman Conquest of England and won Duke William the crown.

Nearby accommodation: Hastings or St. Leonards.

Suggested reading: Sources: *English Historical Documents*, Vol. II (1042–1181) Oxford, 1953. Biography: Compton, P., *Harold the King*, London, 1961. On the Battle: Lemmon, C. H., *The Field of Hastings*, London, 1956. Young, P. and Adair, J., *Hastings to Culloden*, London, 1964. Work of Fiction: Muntz, H., *The Golden Warrior*, London, 1949. Pictorial Record: *The Bayeux Tapestry*, Phaidon Books, London, 1957.

On 5 January 1066 King Edward the Confessor died in London. One claimant to the throne, Harold, Earl of Wessex, had himself crowned King of England the following day. At once the King of Norway, Harold Hardrada, who was a kinsman of the Canute family and therefore had a slight claim to the English throne, began to prepare an invasion of England in league with King Harold's disaffected brother, Tostig, sometime Earl of Northumbria. Also Duke William of Normandy, who had extracted some vague oath of allegiance from Harold in 1064 after a shipwreck on the Norman coast, summoned his tenants and made ready to take England by storm.

The first invasion came in September in the north. Hardrada's wild Vikings defeated the northern levies at the battle of Fulford (20 September) near York, only to be themselves crushed at Stamford Bridge (q.v.) 5 days later by King Harold's army of fyrdmen (levies) and housecarls (household professional soldiers). Harold had achieved surprise by hurrying up the Roman roads to the north with his whole army on horseback. On the battlefield his men had fought on foot with a ferocity which surprised even the hardened Norwegian sea warriors.

On 2 October King Harold heard that the Normans had crossed the channel on the night of 27 September and camped near Hastings. At once Harold rode for London with his housecarls. They reached London on 6 October, having ridden 190 miles in 4 days. From his capital Harold sent urgent summons to the sheriffs of the southern counties: they were to raise the shire fyrd and join him at once. On 11 October the King led his army southwards. On 13 October the English host had come to Caldbec Hill, within 7 miles of the Norman camp, and here King Harold halted.

Caldbec Hill itself marked the centre of several roads and tracks: the 'hoar apple tree' which the *Anglo-Saxon Chronicle* mentions as the mustering place of the English army may well have been a well-known landmark at the junction. Whichever way to London he selected, Duke William had to come as far as Caldbec Hill. Therefore on a ridge astride the London road a few hundred yards south of the hill King Harold arrayed his army in one long, compact phalanx facing towards Hastings.

As soon as he heard of the English approach Duke William led out his army in battle array. Unlike the English army, which fought on foot with axe and spear, the Normans believed in combining cavalry, spearmen and bowmen together. Therefore in his front line Duke William placed his archers, armed with the short bow, and behind them the infantry. In the rear, waiting in their troops and squadrons, stood the Norman cavalry, upon whose shock charge Duke William relied for victory.

In the early hours of 14 October the Norman array advanced towards the English position. The archers darted forward and shot at the English, but Harold's housecarls and thegns, who

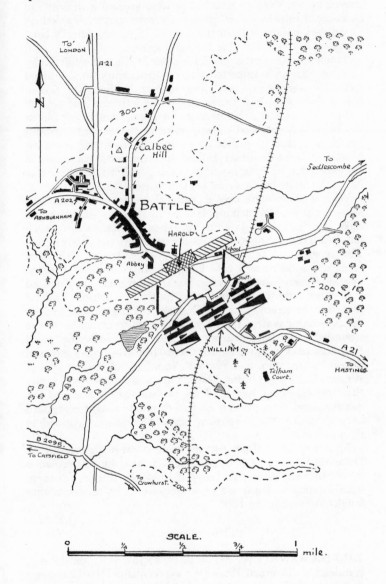

SCALE.

KEY

Norman archers :–

Norman spearmen :–

Norman cavalry :–

Saxon housecarls :–

Saxon fyrdmen :–

lined the foremost ranks, took the volleys of arrows on their hardened limewood shields. When the Norman spearmen moved up the slope to attack they were greeted with a hail of ill-assorted missiles—axes, javelins, arrows and stones tied on to wooden handles—from the English phalanx. After a brief struggle they fled from the English axemen.

This was a moment of crisis for Duke William, for the panic-stricken infantry stampeded some of his cavalry who plunged away into a morass on the left of the Norman line. The Breton foot soldiers who had retreated on the left, and one or two troops of horsemen, therefore found themselves struggling in the mud in a confused crowd. Some of the Saxons, seeing a golden opportunity, rushed down upon them. At this moment, however, Duke William rallied his men and countered a rumour that he was slain by taking off his helmet. The Norman ranks steadied and kept their formation.

With the help of his archers firing their arrows high into the air—one reputedly striking Harold in the eye—the Norman duke and his mailed knights, by repeated charges and much hand-to-hand fighting, began to force gaps in the English line. The struggle lasted through the hours of the October afternoon. 'This was a battle of a new kind,' wrote William of Poitiers, 'one side vigorously attacking, the other resisting as if rooted to the ground.' It was indeed a battle of attrition, and by nightfall the strength of the English had been exhausted by the Norman cavalry. In the gathering darkness many of the wounded and faint-hearted slipped away into the great Andredsweald forest behind them, but the housecarls and thegns battled on under Harold's standards of the 'Dragon of Wessex' and the 'Fighting Man'. Then some nameless Norman slew the wounded English King with a sword. Some of the Saxons stood their ground and died, others fought rearguard actions against the horsemen, but the majority dispersed to their homes.

After the battle there was no more organised resistance to Duke William. On Christmas day that year he was crowned in Westminster Abbey as King of England. Rarely has there been a battle so complete or so decisive in its results as that fought at Hastings in 1066.

J.E.A.

KILLIECRANKIE (C**); battle of, 27 July 1689; on the A 9, 7 miles north-west of Pitlochry; **25**; Willaim III's Campaign in Scotland. Dundee with a Jacobite army (2,800) routed General Mackay's Williamite army (3,400) in an evening attack; however, the death of 'Bonny Dundee' outweighed the effects of the victory, proving fatal to the Jacobite cause. See Wood, E., *British Battles on Land and Sea*, London, 1915.

LEWES (B**); battle of, 14 May 1264; north-west of the town; **59**; Baronial Wars. Simon de Montfort with a Baronial army (5,000) routed the left and centre of King Henry III's Royal army (7,000) below Offham Hill. See Young, P. and Adair, J., *Hastings to Culloden*, London, 1964.

Londonderry (A***)

Date: 17 April to 30 July 1689.

Location: Near the mouth of the river Foyle. **61**.

War and campaign: 'The Jacobite War'—part of the War of the League of Augsburg (see p. 195).

Object of the action: The capture of Derry was vital to the Roman Catholic cause of James II: its defence as important to the Protestants.

Opposing sides: (*a*) Colonel Baker commanding the Protestant garrison. (*b*) Richard Hamilton in command of the Jacobite forces.

Forces engaged: (*a*) Protestants. *Total*: 7,000. (*b*) Jacobites. *Total*: 20,000.

Casualties: (*a*) Estimated at 4,000 Protestants. (*b*) Estimated at 5,000 Jacobites.

Result: The raising of the siege saved the Protestant cause in Ireland.

Nearby accommodation: Londonderry.

Suggested reading: General Work: Curtis, E., *A History of Ireland*, London, 1936. On the Campaign: Murray, R. H., *The Revolutionary Settlement in Ireland*, London, 1911. On the Campaign: Macaulay, T. B., *History of England*, London, 1914.

After the defeat of the Jacobites in Scotland, James II's one hope of regaining his throne lay in Ireland, where the Lord Deputy Tyrconnell commanded a predominantly Roman Catholic army. Derry, a strongly Protestant city, had sparked off civil war in Ireland when the 'Apprentice Boys', affectionately remembered in many Orange songs, closed the gates of Derry against the Catholic troops of the Earl of Antrim, December 1688.

Derry, standing on the River Foyle, fortified by formidable walls, which still stand, was besieged from 17 April to 30 July 1689. The garrison of 7,500 was vigorously supported by the people. The Governor of the city, Lundy, who is frequently burned in effigy during the Twelfth of July celebrations, treacherously fled, and the leaders during the siege were Colonel Baker and a remarkable and militant clergyman,

Reverend George Walker. After failing to carry the city by storm the attackers under General Richard Hamilton and the French General Rosen mounted an effective blockade, a vital part of which was a wooden boom over the river. The besieged suffered extreme privations but their resolution was unshaken either by promises of pardon or by the barbarous threats of Rosen. Kirke's relieving forces on Lough Foyle did little, but eventually on 28 July 1689 three small ships including the *Mountjoy* and H.M.S. *Dartmouth*, laden with provisions, sailed up the river Foyle and, in spite of heavy fire from the besiegers, crashed into the boom and after one failure broke through and safely reached the quayside in the city. Almost immediately the Jacobite forces gave up the siege and rejoined Tyrconnell's army.

The successful resistance in Derry did much to preserve the Protestant cause until the arrival of Schomberg and 14,000 reinforcements (August 1689). Many details of the siege and interesting relics are preserved in the Protestant cathedral of Derry.

D.D.R.

LOSTWITHIEL (C**); battles of, 21 August and 2 September 1644; **60**; First Civil War. In the first battle, King Charles's Royalist army (16,000) took Beacon Hill, the key to Lostwithiel; although the Earl of Essex escaped by sea, the remnants of the Roundhead army (originally 10,000) were forced to surrender (2 Sept.) at Castle Dore near Fowey. See Burne, A. H., and Young, P., *The Great Civil War*, London, 1959.

Marston Moor (A**)

Date: 2 July 1644.

Location: Six miles west of York on the A 59. **37**.

War and campaign: The First Civil War (see p. 195).

Object of the action: Prince Rupert and a Parliamentary army were contending for control of the north of England.

Opposing sides: (*a*) A Parliamentary Council-of-War commanding the Scottish, Eastern Association and West Yorksnire armies.
(*b*) Prince Rupert in command of his own and Newcastle's armies.

Forces engaged: (*a*) Roundheads: approx. 18,000 foot; 9,000 horse; 25 guns. *Total*: approx. 27,000. (*b*) Royalists: approx. 11,000 foot; 6,500 horse; 16 guns. *Total*: approx. 17,500.

Casualties: (*a*) Not known. (*b*) No accurate figures known, but probably heavy.

Result: The total eclipse of the Royalists in the north followed this Parliamentarian victory.

Nearby accommodation: York.

Suggested reading: General Work: Wedgwood, C. V., *The King's War*, London, 1958. Biography: Young, P., *Oliver Cromwell*, London, 1962. On the Battle: Burne, A. H. and Young, P., *The Great Civil War*, London, 1959. Woolrych, A., *Battles of the Civil War*, London, 1961. Young, P., and Adair, J., *Hastings to Culloden*, London, 1964.

The biggest battle of the English Civil War was Marston Moor, in which 5 armies were engaged.

Two Parliamentarian armies and the Scots had laid siege to York, which was bravely defended by Newcastle and the northern Cavaliers. Prince Rupert crossed the Pennines from Lancashire and relieved the city. Then, although outnumbered, he somewhat unwisely offered battle.

The fight began during a thunderstorm late in the evening. Cromwell shattered the Royalist right under Lord Byron, but Goring routed the Parliamentarian right and much of their centre, though some of the Scots infantry stood firm. Rupert successfully counter-attacked Cromwell, but the Scots cavalry under David Leslie finally turned the scales.

Sir Thomas Fairfax and Cromwell next fell upon Goring's horse, and beat him. Then the surviving Parliamentarian foot advanced. Newcastle's infantry, the famous Whitecoats, made a desperate stand in White Syke Close and were practically annihilated.

After the battle Rupert rallied much of his cavalry, but Newcastle fled abroad, York fell and, though the Scots and Parliamentarians failed to prosecute their victory, the north was lost to the Crown.

P.Y.

Naseby (A****)

Date: 14 June 1645.

Location: Eight miles south-west of Market Harborough; north of the village, reached by the B 4036 road. **43.**

War and campaign: The First Civil War (see p. 195).

Object of the action: The Parliamentarians were determined to seek out and defeat the King after the Royalist storm of Leicester.

Opposing sides: (*a*) Sir Thomas Fairfax and Oliver Cromwell commanding the Parliamentarian 'New Model Army'. (*b*) King Charles I and Prince Rupert commanding the Royalist army.

Forces engaged: (*a*) Roundheads: 7,000 foot; 6,000 horse; perhaps 13 guns. *Total*: 13,000. (*b*) Cavaliers: 4,000 foot; 5,000 horse; 12 cannon. *Total*: 9,000.

Casualties: (*a*) Probably 6,000 Cavaliers, mostly infantry, and 12 guns lost. (*b*) Not accurately known, but probably less than 1,000 Roundheads.

Result: A complete victory for the New Model Army which doomed King Charles's cause and made the ultimate triumph of Parliament virtually inevitable.

Nearby accommodation: Rugby or Market Harborough.

Suggested reading: General Work: Wedgwood, C. V., *The King's War*, London, 1958. Biography: Young, P., *Cromwell*, London, 1962. On the Battle: Burne, A. H., *The Battlefields of England* (2nd Edn.), London, 1951. Burne, A. H. and Young, P., *The Great Civil War*, London, 1959. Poetry: Macaulay, T. B., 'The Battle of Naseby', in the *Lays*, London, 1842. Young, P. and Adair, J., *Hastings to Culloden*, London, 1964.

Naseby was the decisive battle of the Great Civil War. When the campaign began in May the King had about 11,000 men, but he unwisely permitted Lord Goring to return with his forces into the west, while he himself marched northwards hoping to undo the harm done to his cause at Marston Moor (q.v.). On 30 May the Cavaliers stormed Leicester, which further weakened their army for they left a garrison there. This event galvanised the Parliamentarians. The New Model Army, which had been blockading Oxford, now marched to seek out the King. Oliver Cromwell was made second-in-command to Fairfax and hastened to join him. Meanwhile Charles, unable to make up his mind as to his aim, hovered about Daventry.

On 13 June some Roundheads surprised a party of Cavaliers carousing in the village of Naseby. The news of this incident was an unpleasant surprise to the King who had not appreciated that his enemies were so close. Nevertheless a Council of War held in the early hours of 14 June determined to fight.

After some preliminary manoeuvring the two armies came in view of each other between Sibbertoft and Naseby. The map shows how they were drawn up, but, since the Royalists advanced without delay, it represents but a short space of time.

The Royalists drew up in four main bodies. In the centre the veteran Lord Astley commanded 3 brigades of foot. They were but few in numbers, perhaps not more than 3,000, but they had the close support of a brigade of horse under Colonel Thomas Howard. Astley was flanked by 2 wings of horse; the right under Prince Maurice about 1,800 strong, and the left —the Northern Horse—under Sir Marmaduke Langdale,

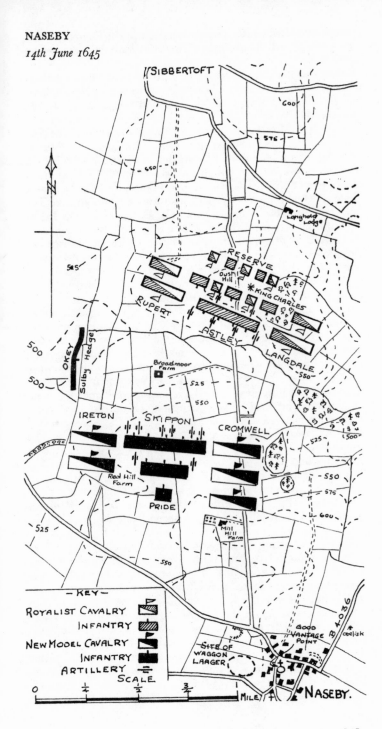

NASEBY
14th June 1645

SIBBERTOFT

600

575

550

525

Langhold Lodge

RESERVE

Dust Hill

KING CHARLES

RUPERT

ASTLEY

LANGDALE

500

OKEY

Sulby Hedge

500

Broadmoor Farm

525

550

IRETON

SKIPPON

CROMWELL

525

Red Hill Farm

500

550

PRIDE

575

525

600

Mill Hill Farm

550

— KEY —

ROYALIST CAVALRY

INFANTRY

NEW MODEL CAVALRY

INFANTRY

ARTILLERY

SCALE

B 4.036

GOOD VANTAGE POINT

obelisk

SITE OF WAGGON LAAGER

0   ¼   ½   ¾   MILE

NASEBY.

1,500 strong. Prince Rupert, though he was the General of the whole army, led his brother Maurice's men when the action began.

King Charles himself remained at the head of the reserve, a mixed body of horse and foot. The horse were his own Life-guard, a picked troop of 130 men and 800 horse from the garrison of Newark.

The New Model was drawn up in plainer order. The foot in the centre, some 6,000 strong, were commanded by Major-General Philip Skippon, an excellent officer who had risen from the ranks in the Dutch service. Cromwell commanded the right wing of not less than 3,000 horse, and Commissary-General Henry Ireton the left, also about 3,000 strong. The only reserve was the foot regiment of Colonel Thomas Pride. An unusual feature of the Parliamentarians' dispositions was the way in which Colonel John Okey's regiment of dragoons was placed in ambush along Sulby Hedge to fire into Rupert's flank as he charged. This idea is attributed to Cromwell.

Without wasting time and powder on a bombardment the Cavaliers advanced. Rupert halted half-way to the Roundhead line, no doubt to let Lord Astley catch up. Rupert's charge was not at once successful for he was seriously outnumbered. Astley, however, drove back the numerically superior Round-head foot and put them into some disorder, Skippon himself being dangerously wounded. Ireton, in an endeavour to relieve the foot, charged into the Duke of York's regiment on Astley's right, but was himself wounded and captured. Rupert's second line, under the Earl of Northampton, reinforced the Prince and drove Ireton's wing from the field. The Cavaliers pursued them as far as Fairfax's wagon train. Rupert summoned the wagon-laager to surrender but was repulsed by the firelocks who guarded it.

Thus far the Royalists had done well enough, but simul-taneously Cromwell's front line had routed Langdale's men, who were rallied with difficulty in rear of Prince Rupert's bluecoats. Cromwell now led his second line against Astley's left.

The King, sitting his horse on Dust Hill, could see the whole scene laid out before him. With a reserve of at least 930 horse —not counting Langdale's—and 700 foot, it was still in his power to change the fortunes of the day. A charge into Crom-well's wing now might have altered the course of history, but at the crucial moment the Earl of Carnwath seized the King's bridle, saying, 'Will ye go upon your death?' At the same moment some unknown officer gave the order 'March to your right!' and the Lifeguard galloped off along Dust Hill. They had gone a quarter of a mile in the wrong direction before they could be halted.

Meanwhile Prince Rupert, having dealt with Ireton fairly

successfully, rejoined the King. But some of the broken Roundhead left did manage to rally and rode cautiously back on to the field.

Okey now mounted his dragoons and charged the flank of Astley's foot killing some and taking, he says, 500 prisoners and a number of colours. Beset on three sides the valiant but outnumbered Royalist infantry began to surrender, though Rupert's regiment at least seems to have fought to the last.

After this success Fairfax and Cromwell were quick to form their men once more in battle array, and the King, seeing that he had lost the good moment for a counter-attack, rode speedily from the field to Leicester, 18 miles away. The Ironsides pursued vigorously and in their fanatic zeal tarnished their victory by massacring about a hundred of the Cavaliers' womenfolk whom they found with the baggage train.

The Royalists lost practically every man of their 4,000 foot, their 12 guns and all their train. Their cavalry too must have suffered severely. Little is known of the losses of the New Model, but they were probably fairly heavy in the centre and on the left; Skippon and Ireton themselves were among the casualties.

Naseby was a fatal blow to the King's cause. His veteran infantry was ruined. Regiments that had fought at Edgehill, Newbury and Lostwithiel were no more. The guns, including 2 demi-cannon which had been his heaviest pieces of ordnance since 1642, could not easily be replaced.

The battle destroyed 'the Oxford army'. Although King Charles did not surrender until 5 May 1646, the war was irretrievably lost on 14 June 1645.

P.Y.

FIRST and SECOND NEWBURY (B**); battles of, 20 September 1643 and 27 October 1644; **55**; First Civil War. In the first action, (south-west of the town) the Royalist army (14,000) failed to prevent the Roundheads (14,000) from returning towards London from Gloucester; in the second engagement (north of the town), King Charles's Cavaliers (9,000) fought off the larger Parliamentarian forces (17,500) under Manchester and Waller, and then retired to Oxford. See Young, P., and Adair, J., *Hastings to Culloden*, London, 1964.

NORTHAMPTON (B**); battle of, 10 July 1460; south of the town besides the river Nene; **44**; Wars of the Roses. The Earls of March and Warwick (7,000 Yorkists) drove the Duke of Buckingham's Lancastrians (5,000) from an entrenched position through the treachery of Lord Grey of Ruthin. See Sergeantson, R. R., 'The Battle of Northampton', in *Journal of Northants Natural History Society*, 1907.

PHILIPHAUGH (B**); battle of, 13 September 1645; near Abbotsford; **33**; First Civil War. The Covenanters under David Leslie (? 6,000) surprised the Marquis of Montrose (1,700) in a dawn attack and utterly destroyed his infantry. See Buchan, J. *Montrose*.

PINKIE CLEUGH (D*); battle of, 10 September 1547; near Musselburgh across the river Esk; **32**; Anglo-Scottish Wars. The Scottish army (23,000) of Arran and Huntly crossed the river to the east bank hoping to surprise and rout Protector Somerset's English army, but was fired on by English warships in the bay and then routed by the English force. See Oman, C. W. C., *The Art of War in the 16th Century*, New York, 1937.

Preston (B**)

Date: 17–19 August 1648.

Location: North-east of Preston in the suburb of Fulwood (17 August); at Winwick, near Warrington (19 August). **39.**

War and campaign: The Second Civil War (see p. 195).

Object of the action: Cromwell wished to halt the invasion of England by the 'Engagers'.

Opposing sides: (a) Oliver Cromwell in command of the Parliamentarian army. (b) The Duke of Hamilton commanding a force of Scots and English Royalists.

Forces engaged: (a) Parliamentarians: 6,000 foot; 3,000 horse; some guns. *Total*: 9,000. (b) Royalists: 16,000 foot; 3,600 horse; some guns. *Total*: 19,600.

Casualties: (a) Only a few Parliamentarians killed and wounded. (b) Details uncertain, but heavy.

Result: The Royalists were routed and in consequence the Second Civil War drew rapidly to a close.

Nearby accommodation: Preston or Warrington.

Suggested reading: General Work: Abbott, W. C., *The Writings and Speeches of Oliver Cromwell*, London, 1937–47. Biography: Young, P., *Oliver Cromwell*, London, 1962.

Hamilton crossed the border on 8 July and was joined by a number of English Royalists. Other Cavaliers seized Pontefract and Scarborough Castles.

Cromwell who had taken Pembroke Castle (11 July) marched thence to Pontefract in 27 days, and though compelled to mask the Yorkshire forces still had 'a fine smart army, fit for action'. Hamilton, who was no general, managed to get his army spread out over at least 30 miles. He was expecting nothing worse than the resistance of the Lancashire militia, when early on the morning of 17 August Cromwell (who had crossed the Pennines via A 59) came driving in on his flank.

The dour Yorkshire Cavalier, Sir Marmaduke Langdale, resisted bitterly against odds of three to one. Hamilton failed to support him, and the Cavaliers were driven back into Preston. Here the Duke counter-charged three times in vain. Leaving 4,000 prisoners in Cromwell's hands he swam the Ribble and fled south to Wigan.

In filthy weather Cromwell pursued relentlessly though the Scottish horse covered Hamilton's withdrawal quite well. On the 19th Cromwell caught up the Scots foot at Winwick, about 3 miles from Warrington.

After losing 1,000 killed General Baillie surrendered. Hamilton and some 3,000 horse made a bid to join Lord Byron in Nottinghamshire but Lambert forced him to surrender at Uttoxeter on the 25th. This victory and the surrender of Colchester to Sir Thomas Fairfax on the 28th put an end to the Second Civil War.

P.Y.

Prestonpans (B***)

Date: 21 September 1745.

Location: Fourteen and a half miles from North Berwick near the A 198 and B 6371 junction. **30.**

War and campaign: The Jacobite Rebellion of 1745 (see p. 195).

Object of the action: The Government forces were moving to intercept the Young Pretender.

Opposing sides: (a) Prince Charles Edward Stuart commanding the Jacobite forces. (b) General John Cope in command of the Government forces of George II.

Forces engaged: (a) Jacobites: 2,400 foot; 30–40 cavalry; a few guns. *Total*: 2,450. (b) Hanoverians: Some infantry, 2 regiments of dragoons; 6 guns. *Total*: 2,200.

Casualties: (a) 30 clansmen killed, 70–80 wounded. (b) 300 Hanoverians killed, 1,400–1,500 prisoners.

Result: The rout of the Government forces; a great improvement in Jacobite morale resulted, and their recruiting prospects improved.

Nearby accommodation: North Berwick.

Suggested reading: General Work: Taylor, A. and H., *The '45 and After*, London, 1935. Biographies: Lang, A., *Prince Charles Edward Stuart*, London, 1900. Tomasson, K., *Jacobite General*, London, 1961. On the Battle and Campaign: Tomasson, K. and Buist, F., *Battles of the '45*, London, 1962. Novel (on the period): Broster, D. K., *The Flight of the Heron*, London, 1949.

Charles entered Edinburgh on 17 September and after delaying for only 24 hours he marched south with some 2,500 men though totally without artillery. Meanwhile Cope had moved from Inverness to Aberdeen where he embarked by sea, landing at Dunbar on the 16th. Three days later he marched northwest along the coast road and on the 20th he made contact with the Highlanders who had halted on the brow of Falside Hill. Cope at once took up a seemingly unassailable position, well protected on three sides. To the north was the sea, almost the whole of the south side was covered by a marsh known as Tranent-Meadows while to the west were the 10-foot-high park walls of Preston House. The main Prestonpans–Longniddry road ran to the south of the marsh while two tracks between Tranent and Cockenzie crossed his position but were both too narrow and easily guarded to be a possible line of attack. When the rebels moved down from the hill to take up a position opposite the marsh, Cope, without weakening it, changed his position in order to present his front to the marsh. Despite believing the marsh to be impossible to cross he took considerable care in posting sentries.

Charles, however, learnt of a pathway, and modifying his original intention of marching his army round the east end of the marsh, he put it through during the evening and formed up for an attack in two lines in a position to the east and less than 200 yards from the English. While this was in progress the alarm sounded in the English camp, but as Cope was trying to form his line of battle with the infantry in the centre and the dragoons on the flanks the Highlanders attacked. Their oblique rush, as the left had outdistanced the right, first overwhelmed the English gunners, who were sailors, and then threw the dragoons into confusion. The infantry though now without flanking cover stood firm and maintained fire. The Highlanders, in order to avoid this, immediately closed and after a short skirmish routed the enemy. The whole action lasted barely 10 minutes but had a decisive effect upon the Highlanders' morale and helped recruitment for their cause.

H.G.M.

ST. ALBANS—I (VERULAMIUM) (D**); sack of, A.D. 61; 50; Boudicca's Rising. Following her victory over the IX Legion at Colchester (q.v.), Boudicca swept on towards London, burning Verulamium on her way. See Collingwood and Myers, *Roman Britain*, Oxford, 1936.

The Second Battle of St. Albans (B**)

Date: 17 February 1461.

Location: Between St. Peter's Church and Barnard's Heath. 51.

War and campaign: The Wars of the Roses (see p. 194).

Object of the action: The Lancastrian faction was attempting to recapture the town from the Yorkists.

Opposing sides: (*a*) The Duke of Somerset leading the Lancastrian army. (*b*) The Earl of Warwick leading the Yorkist army.

Forces engaged: (*a*) Lancastrians. *Total*: 12,000. (*b*) Yorkists. *Total*: 9,000.

Casualties: (*a*) Approx. 1,000 Lancastrians. (*b*) About 1,916 Yorkists.

Result: A Lancastrian victory, but its effect was speedily reversed at Towton (q.v.).

Nearby accommodation: St. Albans.

Suggested reading: General Work: Kendall, P., *The Yorkist Age*, London, 1962. Biography: Kendall, P., *Warwick the Kingmaker*, London, 1957. On the Battle: Young, P., and Adair, J., *Hastings to Culloden*, London, 1964. Article: 'Politics and the First Battle of St. Albans (1455)', in *Bulletin of Institute of Historical Research*, No. 87, 1960.

St. Albans was the scene of two battles in the Wars of the Roses. The first, in 1455, saw the defeat of the Lancastrians by the Duke of York. Most of the fighting took place in the streets of the town. The King's standard stood in the middle of St. Peter's Street. Visitors to the battlefield can still ascend the Bell Tower, which stands in the market place, where the alarm was rung before the battle.

Six years later the town was occupied by a Yorkist army under the Earl of Warwick, which had mustered to oppose the southern march on London. The Lancastrians under the Duke of Somerset, whose father had been killed in the First Battle of St. Albans, achieved surprise by capturing and killing an outpost of Yorkist archers in Dunstaple. They then marched down Watling Street and entered St. Albans in the early hours of 17 February. The vanguard, commanded by Andrew Trollope, was held up near the Bell Tower by a determined band of Yorkist bowmen whom Warwick had stationed in the town to guard his left flank. While the Lancastrians fell back to regroup, Warwick changed the front of his main forces on Barnard's Heath so that they faced towards the town.

By use of side roads and lanes the Lancastrians outflanked the Bell Tower and assembled their army in St. Peter's Street. After a volley of cannon-balls and arrows they attacked Warwick's waiting divisions. The battle waged furiously throughout the morning, but in the early afternoon the treachery of the Kentishmen in Warwick's army and the failure of reinforcements to arrive in time demoralised the Yorkist infantry, and they began to disperse.

Warwick escaped and joined the Earl of March, who had just won a Yorkist victory at Mortimer's Cross. Together they entered London in triumph, while Queen Margaret returned northwards.

J.E.A.

Sedgemoor (A***)

Date: 6 July 1685.

Location: Four miles south-east of Bridgwater to the north of the village of Weston Zoyland. 57.

War and campaign: Monmouth's Rebellion; the Rising in the West (see p. 195).

Object of the action: The Royalist forces were seeking to destroy the rebel army; the rebels wished to break away towards the important port of Bristol.

Opposing sides: (a) The Earl of Feversham in command of the Royalist army of James II. (b) The Duke of Monmouth in command of the West Country rebels.

Forces engaged: (a) Royalists: 6 infantry battalions; 4 cavalry squadrons; 17 guns. *Total*: 2,500. (b) Rebels: 5 infantry 'regiments'; 800 cavalry; 4 guns. *Total*: 3,700.

Casualties: (a) approx. 300 Royal troops. (b) approx. 1,000 rebels killed; 500 prisoners; and 3 guns taken.

Result: The total destruction of the rebel army and the end of Monmouth's Rebellion.

Nearby accommodation: Bridgwater or Taunton.

Suggested reading: General Work: Clark, G. N., *The Later Stuarts*, Oxford, 1939. On the Campaign: Fea, A., *King Monmouth*, London, 1902. On the Battle: Burne, A. H., *The Battlefields of England* (2nd Edn.), London, 1951. Article: McGuffie, D., 'The Sedgemoor Campaign', in *History Today*, July 1956. Work of Fiction: Conan Doyle, A., *Micah Clark*, London, 1889.

Although small in itself, the Battle of Sedgemoor is of importance as the last action fought on English soil. James Scott, the illegitimate son of the deceased Charles II, landed at Lyme Regis on 11 June 1685, to contest the accession of his Roman Catholic uncle, James II. After vainly attempting to seize Bristol with the 5,000 country-folk who rallied to his Protestant cause, Monmouth retraced his steps to Bridgwater (where he arrived on 3 July), hotly pursued by Feversham's smaller but better-trained army, which camped behind the Bussex 'rhine' (drainage ditch) near Weston Zoyland church.

As many of his men were deserting, Monmouth in desperation attempted a night attack on the Royalist camp. Leaving Bridgwater at dead of night, the rebels advanced silently along the bank of the Black Ditch (today the King's Sedgemoor Drain) shielded from the Royalist patrols by a convenient mist. The local guide missed the crossing of the Langmoor Rhine, and in the ensuing confusion a sentry at Chedzoy raised the alarm (1 am). Lord Grey and the rebel cavalry charged into the night hoping to reach the Bussex Rhine before the crossings were occupied, but they were forestalled by a Royalist patrol. Brigadier Churchill had meanwhile roused the camp, and a few well-directed volleys routed the untrained rebel horse who plunged through Monmouth's advancing infantry and swept away the reserve ammunition waggoners in their flight.

By the time Monmouth reached the north bank of the 'rhine' all 6 Royalist battalions were drawn up in line, and a brisk fire-fight developed. Churchill extended the formation to bring it precisely face to face with the rebels, and Bishop Mew of Winchester harnessed his coach-horses to several cannon—whose drivers had fled in the first confusion—and brought them into action against Monmouth's 3 guns and soon silenced them. At this juncture (3 am) Lord Feversham took control of the battle, wisely forbidding his men to advance before dawn. At 4.30 am the Royalist cavalry charged both rebel flanks simultaneously, supported by the infantry's pike and bayonet attack across the 'rhine'. Already desperately short of ammunition, the rebels broke, and the battle was soon over. One group, under Colonel Wade, fought to the last in a corn-field.

Monmouth fled the field but was captured three days later and executed on Tower Hill (15 July). Judge Jeffreys shortly afterwards held his notorious 'Bloody Assize' to wreak King James's vengeance on the West Country for their participation in Monmouth's Rebellion. The excesses that followed became a byword and contributed to the growing unpopularity of James which resulted in 'The Glorious Revolution' three year later.

D.G.C.

Stamford Bridge (B***)

Date: 25 September 1066.

Location: Stamford Bridge lies 7 miles east of York along the A 166 to Driffield. **38.**

War and campaign: The Danish Invasions of England—1066 (see p. 193).

Object of the action: King Harold planned to destroy Harold Hardrada's army before William of Normandy could land in the south.

Opposing sides: (a) King Harold at the head of the Anglo-Saxon army. (b) Harold Hardrada, King of Norway, leading a Norwegian force.

Forces engaged: (a) Part 'Huscarles' and part Fyrd. *Total*: possibly 7,000. (b) No details known.

Casualties: (a) Not known. (b) Not known, but both Hardrada and the traitor Tostig were slain.

Result: The complete defeat of Hardrada ended the invasions of the Norsemen; it also freed Harold's hands for meeting William of Normandy, but weakened his forces.

Nearby accommodation: York.

Suggested reading: General Works: Stenton, F. M., *Anglo-Saxon England*, Oxford, 1943. Garmonsway, G. N., *The Anglo-Saxon Chronicle* (Edn.), London, 1953. Work of Fiction: Muntz, H., *The Golden Warrior*, London, 1948.

In 1066 England under King Harold was threatened not only by William of Normandy but by Harold Hardrada, King of Norway. Early in September Harold who had concentrated his housecarls and the entire fyrd or militia of southern England in Sussex heard that his treacherous brother Tostig and Hardrada, after harrying the coast of Yorkshire, had sailed up the Ouse with 300 ships and anchored at Riccall. On 20 September Hardrada beat Edwin and Morcar at Fulford (2 miles south of York), captured York and waited for hostages at Stamford Bridge. Meanwhile Harold arrived at Tadcaster on 24 September with his housecarls and whatever militia he could collect, marched through York, which Hardrada had not defended, and took the Norwegians, as the *Chronicle* says, 'unawares'. Hardrada drew his troops up in a circular formation around his personal standard. The *Chronicle* records how a single Norwegian made a gallant effort to hold the vital bridge over the Derwent, but after he fell a long and bloody struggle went on until late in the day. A tale is told that during an attempt to parley, Harold merely offered Hardrada 6 feet of English earth in which to be buried. By the end of the day Hardrada and Tostig were both killed and the Norwegian army routed. They fled to their ships at Riccall. Here Hardrada's son Olaf (the Elegant) made peace with Harold and swore never to attack England again. The only indication of casualties is that whereas 300 ships brought the Norwegians, 24 took them away. On Thursday 28 September William landed at Pevensey.

D.D.R.

STIRLING BRIDGE (C**); battle of, 11 September 1297; **26**; Edward I's attempted conquest of Scotland. William Wallace (5,180) destroyed the advance guard of the Earl of Warrenne's army (5,400) after allowing it to cross the Forth. See Oman, C. W. C., *The Art of War in the Middle Ages*, Vol. 2 (2nd Edn.), London, 1924.

TEWKESBURY (B**); battle of, 4 May 1471; south of the town on A 38; **48**; Wars of the Roses. King Edward IV and the Yorkist army (9,000) stormed a deep ditch to rout Queen Margaret of Anjou and her Lancastrian forces (7,000) led by the Duke of Somerset. See Young, P. and Adair, J., *Hastings to Culloden*, London, 1964.

TOWTON (B**); battle of, 29 March 1461; 1 mile from the town on B 1217; **40**; Wars of the Roses. King Edward IV's Yorkist army (16,000) defeated the Duke of Somerset's Lancastrians (18,000) after the opportune arrival of Norfolk with reinforcements. See Young, P. and Adair, J., *Hastings to Culloden*, London, 1964.

WAKEFIELD (B**); battle of, 30 December 1460; near Sandal on A 61; **41**; Wars of the Roses. The Duke of York's army (8,000) was ambushed by Queen Margaret's Lancastrian army (10,000) and lost almost all of its leaders. See Mowat, R. B., *The Wars of the Roses*, London, 1914.

Worcester (A**)

Date: 3 September 1651.

Location: On the south-western, southern and eastern sides of the town and towards Powick. **46**.

War and campaign: Cromwell's War against Scotland (see p. 195).

Object of the action: Cromwell was determined to destroy Charles II's army.

Opposing sides: (a) Oliver Cromwell leading the Parliamentary army. (b) King Charles II at the head of the Anglo-Scottish Royalist army.

Forces engaged: (a) Parliamentarians: approx. 18,000 foot; 9,000 horse; some guns. *Total*: 28,000. (b) Royalists: approx. 8,000 foot; 4,000 horse; some guns. *Total*: 12,000 (five-sixths of the army was Scottish).

Casualties: (a) Cromwell claimed only 200 men were killed, but probably in error. (b) The Royalists were virtually wiped out; 6,000–7,000 became prisoners.

Result: A great Cromwellian victory, which virtually ended all armed resistance to his usurping rule. In due course it also led to the conquest of Scotland.

Nearby accommodation: Worcester.

Suggested reading: General Work: Abbott, W. C., *The Writings and Speeches of Oliver Cromwell*, London, 1937–47. Biography: Bryant, A., *King Charles II*, London, 1931. Biography: Young, P., *Oliver Cromwell*, London, 1962. On the Battle: Burne A. H., *Battlefields of Britain* (2nd Edn.), London, 1951. Fea, A., *The Flight of the King*, London, 1900. Young, P., and Adair, J., *Hastings to Culloden*, London, 1964.

Unable for lack of numbers to bring the war to a successful conclusion in Scotland, Cromwell decided to open the way to a Royalist invasion of England. This strategy is outlined in a letter of 4 August. By the 27th Cromwell had concentrated 28,000 men at Evesham and 5,000 militia at Coventry. Step by step he cast his net round the Royalists, who had thrown themselves into Worcester. Lambert took Upton Bridge on 28 August.

Cromwell was determined to operate on both banks of the Severn and had 20 great boats brought up so that he could build pontoon bridges across the rivers Severn and Teme. The bridges were put into position at dawn on 3 September, and Cromwell himself led the attack across them driving back Colonel Pitscotty's Highlanders.

From his observation post on the tower of Worcester Cathedral King Charles II watched the action develop. Seeing the crisis on the river Teme he galloped out to Powick Bridge to encourage the defenders. But after a long struggle they were driven back into the St. John's (western) suburb.

With Cromwell occupied on the west bank of the Severn, the King led a counter-attack to the east, his men pouring out from St. Martin's and Sudbury Gates against Red Hill. For 3 hours a doubtful struggle raged before Cromwell returned across his bridge of boats and turned the tide. In the dusk the Royalists were swept back into the town, where the old Earl of Cleveland by two gallant charges gave his King time to throw off his armour and start on the first stage of his dramatic escape to France.

The invading army was utterly destroyed. 'It is, for aught I know, a crowning mercy,' wrote Cromwell. It was his last battle.

P.Y.

The Yellow Ford (B****)

Date: 14 August 1598.

Location: Astride the Dungannon road, south of the Blackwater. 63.

War and campaign: Tyrone's Rebellion (see p. 194).

Object of the action: An English force was trying to relieve the Blackwater Fort.

Opposing sides: (a) Sir Henry Bagenal commanding the English army. (b) The Earl of Tyrone and Hugh O'Donnell commanding the Irish army.

Forces engaged: (a) English: 6 infantry regiments; 1 cavalry regiment; 4 guns. *Total*: 4,220. (b) Irish: between 4,000 and 6,000 foot; approx. 600 horse. *Total*: probably above 5,000.

Casualties: (a) About 2,000 English killed and missing. (b) Unknown, but far lighter.

Result: An overwhelming Irish victory, resulting in the surrender of Blackwater Fort and establishing Tyrone as the chief power in Ireland.

Nearby accommodation: Belfast or Armagh.

Suggested reading: General Work: Bagwell, R., *Ireland under the Tudors*, Vol. III, London, 1890. On the Battle: Falls, C., *Elizabeth's Irish Wars*, London, 1950. On the Period: Hamilton, E., *Elizabethan Ulster*, London, 1919.

During Tyrone's rebellion the English had established a fort on the south bank of the Blackwater, where the Armagh-Dungannon road crosses it, to give access to his territory. Though one attack on it had been repulsed with heavy loss, it had a grave disadvantage when revictualling. With Armagh abandoned, a long route had to be covered, and it required virtually the whole force available to the Earl of Ormonde, commanding-in-chief in an interregnum between viceroys. He would rather have had it 'razed, or yielded upon composition, than the soldiers to be left to the uttermost danger'; but this policy was rejected.

He entrusted the relief to Sir Henry Bagenal, the Marshal, who halted at Armagh and marched again on 14 August 1598,

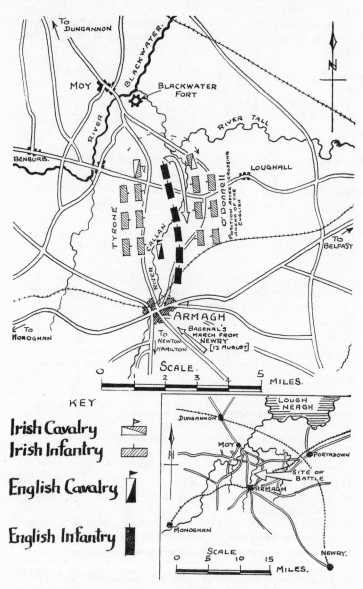

his 6 regiments in file, the distance between them being
unhappily too great. As the leading ones reached the ford—
which took its name from the colour of the banks—over the
Callan river, their left was attacked by Tyrone and their right

by O'Donnell, both avoiding close quarters but raking the column with the musketry fire of skirmishers. A gun with the third regiment lost a wheel, so that the gap with the leading troops widened and the whole force came under attack. Bagenal galloped to the front but was shot dead and the command passed to Sir Thomas Wingfield. A ghastly accident followed: a soldier replenishing his powder dropped his match into a barrel on the powder-cart, and the explosion inspirited Tyrone's men and scared into flight some of the English and their Irish auxiliaries.

Confusion followed as retreating regiments turned back to aid those in adversity. Three were virtually destroyed. The rearguard and the cavalry fought admirably and, aided by artillery fire, brought the remnant back to the relative safety of Armagh, but in a low state of morale. Tyrone allowed not only them but the garrison of the fort to march out. Blame must fall largely on Ormonde, a first-class soldier but intent on defending his own estates, threatened by risings in Leinster. Elizabeth fortunately forgave him: otherwise Ireland would have been lost.

This was the worst disaster ever suffered by English troops in Ireland and might have been fatal but for Tyrone's hesitation. Munster rose in revolt and soon almost the whole province but for the walled towns was in the hands of the rebels. It was four and a half years before Lord Mountjoy ended the revolt.

C.F.

Holland

Alkmaar (B***)

Date: 21 August–8 October 1573.

Location: The town lies 23 miles north-west of Amsterdam. **3.**

War and campaign: The Campaign of 1573; the Eighty Years' War (or Dutch Revolt against Spain) (see p. 194).

Object of the action: The Spaniards were determined to capture Alkmaar, key to north Holland, and make an example of its inhabitants in order to discourage the Dutch Patriots.

Opposing sides: (a) The Patriot garrison of Alkmaar. (b) Don Frederic in command of the Spanish army.

Forces engaged: (a) Dutch: 800 trained soldiers; 1,300 citizen militia. *Total*: 2,100. (b) Spaniards: approx. 5 *tercios* *; numerous artillery. *Total*: 16,000.

Casualties: (a) 24 Dutch soldiers and 13 burghers killed. (b) At least 1,000 Spaniards killed in the assaults (attempted storming of 18 September only).

Result: The successful defence of the city and the consequent blow to the Spanish military reputation vastly increased the morale of the Dutch 'Patriot' insurgents.

Nearby accommodation: Alkmaar.

Suggested reading: General Work: Motley, J. L., *The Rise of the Dutch Republic*, Vol. II, (Edn.), London, 1906. On the Campaign: Oman, C. W. C., *The Art of War in the 16th Century*, London, 1937. Biography: Wedgwood, C. V., *William the Silent*, London, 1944. On the Rebellion: Geyl, P., *The Netherlands Revolt*, London, 1947.

* *Special Note:* See glossary p. 192.

Following the successful reduction of Haarlem (q.v.), the Duke of Alva selected the town of Alkmaar as the next recipient of Spanish attentions. The opening of the siege was considerably delayed by dissensions and mutinies within the Spanish army over arrears of pay, but on 21 August Don Frederic, son of the great Alva, at last appeared outside the walls at the head of an army of veterans. Alva was determined to make a terrible example of Alkmaar, hoping thereby to cow the resistance of the stubborn 'Patriots' throughout the Netherlands. 'If I take Alkmaar,' he wrote to Philip II of Spain, 'I am resolved not to leave a single creature alive; the knife shall be put to every throat.'

Faced by such a discouraging prospect there is little wonder that the burghers of Alkmaar resolved to offer a stout defence. Although they had originally hesitated to admit the small garrison of regular troops sent to organise the defence by Prince William of Orange, every man now rallied to the burgher militia. Faced by adversaries of such experience and reputation, however, their best hope lay in letting in the sea to flood the surrounding countryside. A carpenter named Van der Mey volunteered to smuggle letters to the Prince of Orange and Diedrich Sonoy, Patriot Governor of North Holland, through the Spanish lines, containing plans for cutting the dykes and opening the Zyp sluices. This mission he successfully accomplished.

After several inconclusive skirmishes beyond the walls, Don Frederic at length decided to attempt a *coup-de-main*. The selected day—18 September—opened with a twelve-hour bombardment against the walls, and when it was over a strong force attempted to storm both the Frisian Gate and the Red Tower simultaneously. Every citizen was on the walls to repel the assault, and after three costly attacks the discomfited Spaniards were compelled to draw off as dusk approached. The following day Don Frederic ordered a new attempt; 700 shots were fired at the breach, but when the moment to advance arrived, the demoralised Spanish infantry refused to move forward. Threats and entreaties proving equally useless, the Spanish commander had no option but to prosecute the siege by less direct means.

Governor Sonoy had already opened some of the dykes, and the ground near the Spanish camp was rapidly becoming sodden when a Spanish picquet surprised Van der Mey as he attempted to re-enter the town, and although he made good his escape he lost his hollow stick containing the Prince of Orange's reply, authorising the total flooding of the area. Shaken by this information, Don Frederic's resolution wavered, and rather than see his army drowned he abandoned the siege and retired to Amsterdam. This success put fresh heart into the Patriot cause.

D.G.C.

Arnhem (A****)

Date: 17–25 September 1944.

Location: On the north bank of the Neder Rijn, some 9 miles north of Nijmegen. **6.**

War and campaign: The Second World War; the North-west Europe Campaign of 1944–5 (see p. 197).

Object of the action: The Allies were attempting to achieve a rapid breakthrough to the Ruhr, thus turning the north flank of the German Siegfried Line.

Opposing sides: (*a*) Field-Marshal Montgomery in command of 21st Army Group. (*b*) Field-Marshal Model commanding German Army Group 'B'.

Forces engaged: (*a*) 1st British Airborne Division; 1st Polish Parachute Brigade; 101st U.S. Airborne Division; British 30th Corps. (*b*) 11th S.S. Panzer Corps, comprising 9th and 10th S.S. Panzer Divisions; 4 battalions; various battle groups; parts of 1st Paratroop Army.

Casualties: (*a*) 1st Airborne Division lost 1,200 killed and 6,000 prisoners of war including 3,000 wounded. (*b*) Perhaps 3,300 Germans killed and wounded.

Result: The failure of the final stage of 'Operation Market Garden'; however the possession of Nijmegen gave the Allies a sallyport into Germany.

Nearby accommodation: Arnhem.

Suggested reading: General Works: Wilmot, C., *The Struggle for Europe*, London, 1951. Montgomery of Alamein, *Memoirs*, London, 1958. Horrocks, B., *A Full Life*, London, 1960. On the Battle: Hibbert, C., *The Battle of Arnhem*, London, 1962. Saunders, H. St. G., *The Red Beret*, London, 1950.

From the end of the Battle of Normandy in the last week of August 1944 and throughout September, Eisenhower and Montgomery failed to see eye to eye, the former adhering to a plan made the previous May for an advance all along the front to the Siegfried Line, and the latter pressing for a single full-blooded thrust into the heart of Germany.

Faced by a supply crisis and the opening of the German V2 offensive in early September, Eisenhower authorised Montgomery to mount an attack towards Arnhem and gave him the 1st Allied Airborne Corps for the purpose. This went some way towards meeting Montgomery's demand for a single thrust, but it was too late.

His plan, ' Market Garden ', envisaged one drop by the 101st U.S. Airborne Division to seize the Eindhoven area; another by the 82nd U.S. Airborne Division to get the bridges over the Maas at Grave and the Waal at Nijmegen; and finally

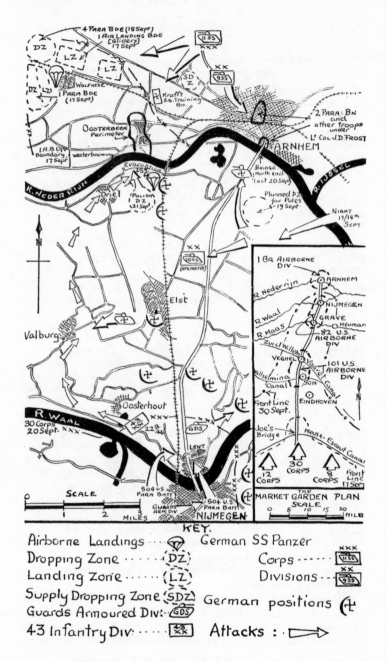

KEY.

Airborne Landings · · · ·   German SS Panzer

Dropping Zone · · · · · · (DZ)   Corps · · · · ·

Landing Zone · · · · · · (LZ)   Divisions · ·

Supply Dropping Zone (SDZ)   German positions

Guards Armoured Div: (GDS)

43 Infantry Div · · · ·   Attacks : ⟹

the capture of the Arnhem bridge over the Neder Rijn by the British 1st Airborne Division. Simultaneously, the 30th Corps, under Lieutenant-General Brian Horrocks, was to thrust forward 64 miles from the Albert Canal and link up with the airborne troops. Eventually Montgomery hoped to establish his 2nd Army between Arnhem and the sea and then advance into Germany.

By 17 September the German armies had to some extent recovered from the collapse in Normandy. Von Runstedt had been reinstated as C.-in-C. West. Model, commanding Army Group 'B', faced the Allies on the Albert Canal with Student's Parachute Army, his 15th Army prolonging the front to the west. Unknown to the Allies, the 11th S.S. Panzer Corps, under Colonel-General Bittrich, had been sent to the Arnhem area on 3 September to reorganise. There was also a battalion of young soldiers under Major Krafft in the suburb of Oosterbeek. Altogether on 17 September there were some 2,500 German troops in the immediate area of Arnhem and considerable reinforcements close at hand.

Unfortunately, there were insufficient aircraft available to put down all three airborne divisions in one lift. Without a free run to Nijmegen, the 30th Corps could never hope to link up with the 1st Airborne Division at Arnhem. Of necessity, therefore, Major-General Urquhart, the commander of this division, had to accept a plan which although it enabled the two American divisions to come down in one drop, provided only sufficient aircraft to land his 1st Parachute Brigade, some divisional troops and part of his glider-borne brigade on the first day. The rest had to follow on succeeding days. The ideal dropping zone for the quick capture of Arnhem bridge would have been the open polders immediately south of it but this had to be ruled out after R.A.F. objections. The open ground north and south of the railway at Wolfheze, 6 miles west of Arnhem bridge, was therefore chosen instead.

The attack by the Airborne Corps went in at 1 pm on Sunday 17 September. Both American divisions met little resistance and secured their objectives with the exception of Nijmegen bridge. The Guards Armoured Division thrust through Student's Parachute Army on a narrow front and by nightfall had advanced 6 miles. Eindhoven fell to the 101st U.S. Airborne Division on 18 September and on the same day the Guards Armoured Division linked up with the 82nd Airborne Division at Grave. Their dashing attack on the afternoon of the 20th secured the Nijmegen road bridge over the Waal.

Ill luck, however, dogged the 1st Airborne Division from the start. Krafft's battalion and a battle group of the 9th S.S. Panzer Division delayed the advance of the 1st Parachute Brigade from Wolfheze and it was not till 8 pm that Lieutenant-

Colonel Frost's 2nd Parachute Battalion reached the northern end of the Arnhem bridge. In fact, surprise was lost from the start. Model himself was having lunch at the Tafelberg Hotel in Oosterbeek at the time of the drop and only escaped by the skin of his teeth. General Bittrich, the commander of the 11th S.S. Panzer Corps, quickly sized up the situation and by 3 pm had issued orders for the quick annihilation of the 1st Airborne Division, the securing of Arnhem bridge and the seizure of Nijmegen bridge. That afternoon an American glider shot down near the headquarters of General Student's Parachute Army was found to contain the complete Allied plan on one of the bodies. In full knowledge of the Allies' strength and intentions from the very outset and with the excellent communications of the German Air Force at their disposal, Model and Bittrich proceeded rapidly to build up strength in the Arnhem area and to launch attacks with armour from east and west against the Allied corridor between Son and Veghel.

The situation of the 1st Airborne Division went from bad to worse. Bad flying weather hampered the arrival of reinforcements. Most of the supplies dropped fell into enemy hands. Major-General Urquhart became personally involved in the fighting and was cut off from his headquarters for a whole day. Uncertainty as to his whereabouts and intentions added to the confusion, and within Arnhem the Germans soon got the upper hand. The complete breakdown of communications kept the 30th Corps from finding out where the airborne division actually was and what its commander intended to do.

The 21st was the crucial day. At first light the heroic resistance of the 2nd Parachute Battalion finally came to an end. Major-General Urquhart withdrew what was left of his division into a close perimeter at Oosterbeek. The Westerbouwing, which commanded the ferry crossing to Driel on the south bank, was lost. In the afternoon, the Polish Parachute Brigade was dropped in confusion in the face of anti-aircraft fire near Driel. An attempt by the Guards Armoured Division to break out of the Nijmegen bridgehead was halted before Oosterhout about a mile north of the Waal. On the German side, 45 Tiger tanks, a Panzer grenadier battalion and a considerable number of infantry arrived at Arnhem.

Enemy attacks on the corridor made it impossible for the 30th Corps to launch the 43rd Wessex Division from the Nijmegen bridgehead till the following day. Seven armoured cars of the Household Cavalry slipped through to join the Poles at Driel in the morning mist. The 43rd Wessex Division struck stiff opposition at Oosterhout, but by the afternoon their leading troops, 5th D.C.L.I. riding on the tanks of 4/7th Royal Dragoon Guards, after a clash with German armour at Valburg, got through to Driel. Meanwhile the Germans had built up considerable strength along the main concrete road from Arnhem to Nijmegen. A bitter struggle for Elst developed, ending in its capture by the 43rd Wessex Division. Attempts by this division and some of the Poles to cross the river on 23/24 and 24/25 September failed in the face of the strong current and fierce enemy fire.

On 25 September Montgomery decided to withdraw what was left of the 1st Airborne Division and this was done that night by the 43rd Wessex Division. Over 2,000 were evacuated.

The failure to make good the bridgehead at Arnhem must primarily be attributed to inadequate planning and bad intelligence. The likely German reaction was ignored. In particular, their recovery in morale was not appreciated. The estimate of the speed with which the relief column, advancing down a narrow corridor along which tanks could not operate off the road, was unrealistic. At least, one parachute brigade should have been dropped on the polders immediately south of Arnhem bridge. As it was, the first troops to land were slow off the mark, and next day the weather turned against the Allies. Nevertheless, the courage of the airborne troops was of a high order.

The last hope of capturing the Ruhr in 1944 was lost at Arnhem. Montgomery took a great risk with his eyes open and, for once, luck was against him. If Eisenhower had backed his plan for a single thrust a fortnight earlier, before the Germans had time to recover from the debacle in Normandy, the results might have been very different. None the less, the possession of the crossings over the Maas and Waal was to serve as a valuable corridor for a later advance to the Rhine.

H.E.

BERGEN (B**): battle of, 19 September 1799; between Bergen and Oudkarspel, north of Alkmaar; 2; French Revolutionary Wars. The Duke of York's Anglo-Russian army (40,000) was repulsed by General Brune's Franco-Dutch forces (20,000). See Fortescue, J. W., *History of the British Army*, Vol. IV (2nd Edn.), London, 1910.

BRILLE (C**); battle of, 1 April 1572; west of Rotterdam; 7; Eighty Years' War or Dutch Revolt against Spain. La Marck at the head of 200 'Sea Beggars' induced the Spanish authorities to flee by a ruse. See Geyl, P., *The Netherlands Revolt*, London, 1947.

HAARLEM; siege of, 18 December 1572 to 12 July 1573; 15 miles west of Amsterdam; **4**; Eighty Years' War. Ripperda's gallant garrison and burghers (4,000) defeated all attempts at assault by Don Frederic's Spanish army (30,000), but was eventually starved into surrender. See Motley, J. L., *The Rise of the Dutch Republic*, Vol. II (Edn.), London, 1908.

HEILIGER-LEE (C**); battle of, 23 May 1568; near Winschoten; **1**; Eighty Years' War. Louis and Adolphus of Nassau lured Aremberg's Spanish army (5,000) into swamps by feigning defeat, and thereafter slaughtered 1,500 of them, including their commander; this victory represented the first success of the Dutch patriots and their allies. See Motley, J. L., *The Rise of the Dutch Republic*, Vol. II, (Edn.), London, 1906.

ZUTPHEN (D*); battle of, 11 November 1586; 17 miles north-west of Arnhem; **5**; Eighty Years' War or Dutch Revolt against Spain. The Duke of Parma's Spanish army inflicted heavy casualties on the English army of the Earl of Leicester (in alliance with the Dutch), including the death of Sir Philip Sidney, eventually raising the siege of Zutphen. See Geyl, P., *The Netherlands Revolt*, London, 1947.

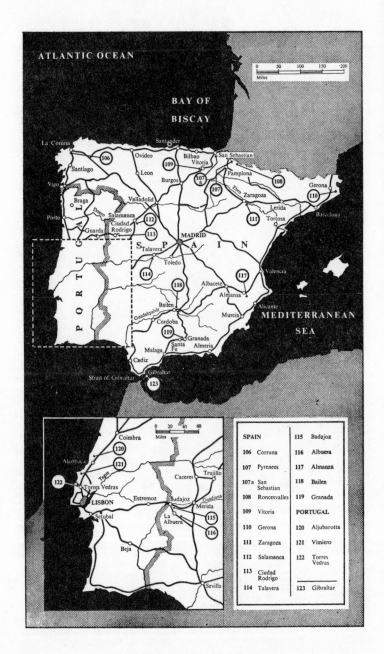

ATLANTIC OCEAN

BAY OF BISCAY

0 50 100 150 200
Miles

La Coruña
Santander
Santiago
Oviedo
106
Bilbao
San Sebastian
109
Vitoria
Vigo
Leon
Pamplona
Braga
Burgos
107a
108
Porto
Valladolid
107
Gerona
Zaragoza
110
Douro
Salamanca
Lerida
112
Barcelona
Guarda
Ciudad
Tortosa
Rodrigo
111
113
MADRID
Talavera
S P A I N
Toledo
114
Valencia
117
118
Albacete
Bailen
Almansa
Guadalquivir
Alicante
Murcia
MEDITERRANEAN
Cordoba
SEA
119
Granada
Santa
Almeria
Malaga
Fe
Cadiz
Gibraltar
Strait of Gibraltar
123

P O R T U G A L

Coimbra
0 20 40 60
Miles
120
Alcobaça
121
Trujillo
Caceres
122
Tagus
Torres Vedras
Estremoz
Badajoz
Guadiana
LISBON
Merida
115
Setubal
La
Albuera
116
Beja
Sevilla

SPAIN		115	Badajoz
106	Corruna	116	Albuera
107	Pyrenees	117	Almanza
107a	San Sebastian	118	Bailen
108	Roncesvalles	119	Granada
109	Vitoria	**PORTUGAL**	
110	Gerona	120	Aljubarotta
111	Zaragoza	121	Vimiero
112	Salamanca	122	Torres Vedras
113	Ciudad Rodrigo		
114	Talavera	123	Gibraltar

Portugal

Aljubarotta (B***)

Date: 14 August 1385.

Location: Five miles east-north-east of Alcobaça towards Batalha, west of Road N 1. **120.**

War and campaign: The War of the Portuguese Succession (see p. 194).

Object of the action: Rival claimants for the throne of Portugal were settling the issue by battle.

Opposing sides: (*a*) King João I of Portugal and the Great Constable, Nuño Alvarez Pereira. (*b*) King Juan I of Castile in command of a Castilian army.

Forces engaged: (*a*) Portuguese: 4,000 infantry; 800 cross-bowmen; 2,000 cavalry. *Total*: 6,800. (*b*) Spaniards: 10,000 infantry; 20,000 cavalry (including 2,000 French). *Total*: 30,000.

Casualties: No reliable figures available for either side.

Result: The rout of the Spanish army decided the independence of Portugal.

Nearby accommodation: Alcobaça or Leira.

Suggested reading: General Work: Livermore, H. V., *A History of Portugal*, London, 1947. On the Battle: Oman, C. W. C., *The Art of War in the Middle Ages*, Vol. II (2nd Edn.), London, 1924. Poetry: Camoens, L. de, *Os Lusiadas*, Lisbon, 1572; trans. into English by Fanshawe as *The Lusiad*, Harvard and Oxford, 1940.

The death of Fernando I in 1383 left no lawful successor to the throne of Portugal, since his daughter, the Infanta Dona Brites, had forfeited her right of succession by marrying Don Juan I, King of Castile. However, Fernando had left a bastard, and when the Cortes met at Coimbra, this nobleman's claims were so ardently supported that he was unanimously elected

King, as João I. Most Portuguese were anxious to avoid a union with Castile. During the interregnum prior to this election, the King of Castile, claiming Portugal in the right of his wife Brites, invaded Portugal and advanced on Lisbon.

On the afternoon of 14 August 1385 he encountered the Castilian army at Canoeira, the site of Batalha monastery. The Castilian centre was at Cruz da Legoa, and their rear stretched beyond Aljubarotta. Facing them at the foot of the ridge was the Portuguese army, its left wing commanded by the Great Constable. Its right wing and the centre, led by King João in person, had 700 horsemen and the main infantry force. A rearguard stood a good distance behind.

At first the fire from 10 pieces of Castilian artillery caused some panic in the Portuguese ranks, but the King and Constable displayed exemplary valour; indeed, at one point the King was unhorsed by a Spanish knight and would have been killed but for a prompt rescue. Their troops soon pressed back the enemy's centre at Cruz da Legoa and clinched the victory at Aljubarrota. Local tradition has it that the baker's wife here killed seven Spaniards with her *pá*, a long wooden shovel.

When the standard of Castile was captured, King Juan fled from the battlefield, his tent and treasure falling into Portuguese hands.

A.B.-J.

The Lines of Torres Vedras (A***)

Date: October 1810–March 1811.

Location: The forward line, supported by two more, stretched from Alhandra on the Tagus to the mouth of the river Zizandre on the coast. **122.**

War and campaign: The Napoleonic Wars; the Peninsular War, Campaign of 1810 (see p. 196).

Object of the action: The British and Portuguese forces were protecting the great base of Lisbon from the French armies, in order to retain a foothold in the Peninsula.

Opposing sides: (a) Wellington in command of an Allied army. (b) Marshal Masséna, Prince of Essling, and the French 'Armée de Portugal'.

Forces engaged: (a) 34,000 British, 24,500 Portuguese, 8,000 Spaniards and 11,000 militia and volunteer artillery; 15,000 irregulars outside the lines; 14 R.N. gunboats and a transport brig. *Total*: 92,500. (b) French: approx. 55,000 infantry and 8,000 cavalry. *Total*: 63,000.

Casualties: (a) Allies: full details unknown, but approx. 95 between 11 and 14 October. (b) French: approx. 270.

Result: The French confronted the Lines for a month without attacking. Faced with starvation they retired on 14 November. Wellington's army followed.

Nearby accommodation: Torres Vedras or Sintra.

Suggested reading: General Work: Oman, C. W. C., *A History of the Peninsular War*, Vol. III, Oxford, 1902. On the Lines: Porter, W., *History of the Corps of Royal Engineers*, Vol. I, London, 1889.

After the battle of Talavera (q.v.) Wellington realised that he would have to rely on his slender British force and his Portuguese allies, and largely discount the Spanish armies. A defensive policy to protect his base at Lisbon must be the first consideration, and he had to be prepared, if need arose, to embark his army. So in October 1809 he chose positions for the famous defensive Lines, and placed Colonel Richard Fletcher in charge of the work, with a dozen Engineer officers, some artificers and up to 7,000 Portuguese peasants. Over 50 miles of defences were built, not as a continuous wall but as a series of redoubts and earthworks scientifically positioned to afford cross-fire. Ravines were blocked by massive stone walls and abattis; rivers were dammed to make valleys into swamps; bridges were mined, houses demolished, trenches dug across the slopes, scarps cut on hill brows, vineyards and olive groves pulled up, trees felled, and any possible cover removed.

Wellington's plan was to entrust the defence of the actual Lines to Portuguese militia, posted in over 150 works, containing garrisons of 50 to 500 men and 2 to 6 guns each, and to keep his 7 British divisions and 3 Portuguese brigades behind, ready to reinforce any danger point or to fight a battle in the open if the Lines were pierced.

The secret was marvellously kept. After his victory at Busaco Wellington retreated across Portugal, the Portuguese carried out something of a 'scorched earth' policy, and the French, expecting 'undulating accessible plateaux', were unaware of even the ranges of hills, and did not discover the Lines until 11 October. Several bitter skirmishes were fought near Sobral, but the French commanders wisely decided against any full-scale assault.

A.B.-J.

VIMIERO (C**); battle of, 21 August 1808; between Lourinha and Torres Vedras; **121**; Peninsular War. Sir Arthur Wellesley's Anglo-Portuguese army (16,778) beat off three attacks by General Junot's French 'Armée de Portugal' (13,000), thus demonstrating that British linear tactics and skirmishers could defeat Napoleon's columns. See Napier, W. F. P., *History of the War in the Peninsula*, Book II (new Edn.), London, 1851.

Spain

ALBUERA (C**); battle of, 16 May 1811; 14 miles south-east of Badajoz on N 432; **116**; Peninsular War. Marshal Beresford's Allied army (34,450) narrowly defeated Marshal Soult (24,260) when the French army attempted to interfere in the siege of Badajoz. See Napier, W. F. P., *History of the War in the Peninsula*, Book XII (new Edn.), London, 1851.

Almanza (B***)

Date: 25 April 1707.

Location: To the south of the town, reached from Albecate (N 430) after 40 miles. **117**.

War and campaign: The War of the Spanish Succession; the Spanish Campaign of 1707 (see p. 195).

Object of the action: The Allies were attempting a march on Madrid from Valencia.

Opposing sides: (*a*) Marshal Berwick in command of a Franco-Spanish army. (*b*) Generals Galway and Das Minas leading the army of the Grand Alliance.

Forces engaged: (*a*) French: 72 battalions; 76 squadrons; approx. 40 guns. *Total*: 30,000 (but only part engaged). (*b*) Allies: 25 battalions; 17 squadrons; approx. 30 guns. *Total*: 15,000.

Casualties: (*a*) Probably 2,000 killed and 4,000 wounded. (*b*) 4,000 killed; 3,000 prisoners (later augmented by 2,000 more).

Result: The rout of the Allied army and the failure of Galway's march on Madrid.

Nearby accommodation: Almanza.

Suggested reading: General Work: Churchill, W. S., *Marlborough, his Life and Times*, Book II, London, 1947. On the Campaign: Parnell, A., *The War of the Spanish Succession in Spain*, London, 1888. Work of Fiction (on the period): Woodruff, P., *Colonel of Dragoons*, London, 1951.

The year 1707 proved full of disasters for the armies of the Grand Alliance, and nowhere was this more obviously so than in Spain. Although the major fighting of the war took place in central Europe and north Italy, a series of bitter, if smaller, campaigns were fought in the Iberian Peninsula. General Galway—an exiled French Huguenot—took over command of the Allied army from Peterborough in late 1706, and early next year set out to march on Madrid from Valencia to capture the capital of Philip V, the grandson of Louis XIV.

The Allies initially disposed of 30,000 men, but the success of the proposed march was severely compromised when half the army was diverted to occupy Aragon and Catalonia. The defence of Madrid had been entrusted to the capable British Catholic exile, Marshal the Duke of Berwick, in command of 25,000 Frenchmen and Spaniards. Hearing that a further 8,000 French were on their way to reinforce Berwick, Galway decided to risk a battle, and at dawn on 25 April his army advanced on the town of Almanza from Villena. Unfortunately for the Allies, however, the bulk of the reinforcements had already reached Berwick's camp, still further aggravating the numerical disparity between the two armies. Galway was particularly short of cavalry.

Berwick drew up his men in two lines to the south of the town —Spanish cavalry on the right, infantry in the centre, the French horse on the left. Galway placed Das Minas and the Portuguese cavalry on his right, massed the infantry in the centre, but was forced to supplement the scanty English squadrons with infantry detachments on his left.

At 3 pm the battle opened in the west, when the English squadrons charged and routed the first line of Spanish horse. Heartened by this success, the Allied infantry fell upon the Franco-Spanish centre with such *élan* that it, too, was forced back to the walls of Almanza. The Portuguese cavalry on the right, however, failed to advance in concert with their comrades, and fled at the approach of the French squadrons which promptly fell upon the flank and rear of the exposed Allied centre. The battle became desperate; Galway was temporarilly incapacitated by a head wound, and the French switched their best units to reinforce the Spanish cavalry, which in turn swept the English squadrons from the field. Both flanks gone, the Allied centre was attacked from all sides, but the bandaged Galway led up his small reserve to cover the centre's retreat. Miraculously he succeeded in extricating 3,500 men, and a further body of 3,000 also made good their escape along a different route under Count Dohna and Major-General Shrimpton. Three days later, however, Shrimpton was forced to surrender with 2,000 men in the mountains, while Galway fell back to Valencia.

The disaster of Almanza was a major blow to the Grand Alliance: as Marlborough wrote: 'This ill-success in Spain has flung everything backwards.'

D.G.C.

Badajoz (A***)

Date: 16 March–6 April 1812.

Location: On the Spanish-Portuguese frontier, due east of Lisbon. **115.**

War and campaign: The Napoleonic Wars; the Peninsular War—Campaign of 1812 (see p. 196).

Object of the action: Wellington wished to capture the frontier fortress and thus open the way for a campaign in French-occupied Spain.

Opposing sides: (*a*) Wellington commanding a British, German and Portuguese army. (*b*) General Phillipon in command of the French garrison.

Forces engaged: (*a*) Allies: 4 divisions engaged in the siege; 3 divisions to the south and 1 to the east covering the operations. *Total*: approx. 32,000. (*b*) French: 4,333 French combatants; 667 sick and servants. *Total*: 5,000.

Casualties: (*a*) About 4,000 British and 1,000 Portuguese. (*b*) About 1,500 French killed and wounded besides 3,500 prisoners.

Result: The capture of the fortress-town induced Soult to retreat back to Andalusia and Marmont towards Salamanca, whither Wellington followed him.

Nearby accommodation: Badajoz.

Suggested reading: General Work: Jones, J. T., *Journal of the Sieges carried on in Spain*, Vol. I (3rd Edn.), London, 1846. On the Siege: Fortescue, J., *A History of the British Army*, Vol. VIII, London, 1917. Eyewitness Account: Bell, G., *Soldier's Glory*, London, 1956. Grattan, W., *Adventures with the Connaught Rangers* (new Edn.), London, 1902. Work of Fiction: Heyer, G., *The Spanish Bride*, London, 1940.

The town was invested on 16 March. By night on the 24th 500 volunteers stormed Fort Picurina, an outlying bastion on the east side, the capture of which enabled Wellington's gunners to begin bombarding the south-east—and weakest—

corner of the wall enclosing the town. By 6 April three breaches had been made and that night the assault took place. The 4th and Light Divisions were to storm the breaches, Picton's 3rd Division would if possible scale the 100-foot wall and seize the castle, while the 5th Division and some Portuguese troops were to distract the garrison with a feint attack. The powerful defences, supported by artillery fire and sharpened with mines, *chevaux de frise*, crows' feet and other devices, were formidable, and the British losses scarcely less so.

The soldiers could not penetrate the breaches, and after two hours of slaughter by the light of fireball, exploding powder barrel and flaming carcass, in which hundreds were blown to pieces, or hurled from ladders or drowned in a flooded ditch, Wellington called off the attack. But unknown to him as yet, Picton's men had fought their way at terrible cost into the castle, and although from there they were unable to reach the town, they had captured Phillipon's reserves of ammunition and food—his means of prolonging the defence. Meanwhile, part of the 5th Division on the south side had, after heavy fighting on the walls, broken into Badajoz; and their appearance through the streets and behind the breaches so disconcerted the French there that they gave up the struggle. The survivors of the 4th and Light Divisions attacked again, only to find the breaches deserted.

Wellington wrote: 'The capture of Badajoz affords as strong an instance of the gallantry of our troops as has ever been displayed, but I anxiously hope that I shall never again be the instrument of putting them to such a test.' As at Ciudad Rodrigo, the victorious soldiers went wild for three days.

A.B.-J.

BAILÉN (B***); battle of, 21–2 July 1808; at the junction of the N IV and the N 323; **118**; Spanish War of Independence. General Dupont's French army (24,000) failed to break out through General Castaños' Spanish army (47,000) and was eventually forced to surrender. See Oman, C. W. C., *A History of the Peninsular War*, Vol. I, Oxford, 1902.

CIUDAD RODRIGO (B***); siege of, 7–19 January 1812; on the N 620 from Salamanca; **113**; Peninsular War. Wellington (35,000) undertook a winter siege of the town, defended by Général de Brigade Baron Barrié (1,890); two breaches were made, and the town was successfully stormed on 19 January; disgraceful excesses ensued. See Fortescue, J., *A History of the British Army*, Vol. VIII, London, 1917.

CORUNNA (B***); battle of, 16 January 1809; on the Betanzos side of the town; **106**; Peninsular War. At the conclusion of his retreat, Sir John Moore (approx. 15,000) turned to face his pursuers whilst awaiting the Fleet's arrival, and inflicted a sharp check on Marshal Soult (16,000); Moore died of wounds, but his men escaped. See Hibbert, C., *Corunna*, London, 1962.

GERONA (C**); siege of, 4 June–12 December 1809; Catalonia; **110**; Peninsular War. Governor Alvarez de Castro (30,000) held out heroically against General Verdier's French investing army (35,000), and was eventually defeated by famine and disease rather than action. See Napier, W. F. P., *History of the War in the Peninsula*, Books I and IX, London, 1851.

Granada (A****)

Date: April 1491–2 January 1492.

Location: Southern Spain. **119**.

War and campaign: The War of Granada—the final campaign (see p. 194).

Object of the action: The Christian forces wished to capture the capital of the Moorish kingdom.

Opposing sides: (*a*) King Ferdinand V of Castile (II of Aragon) and Queen Isabella of Castile. (*b*) King Abdallah of Granada, also known as 'Boabdil' and 'El Rey Chico'.

Forces engaged: (*a*) Christians: approx. 50,000 horse and foot. (*b*) Moors: the population of Granada had swollen to 200,000; perhaps one-quarter were combatants.

Casualties: No accurate figures known for either side.

Result: The capture of Granada concluded a war commenced ten years before, and terminated the Moorish Empire in Spain after almost eight centuries.

Nearby accommodation: Granada.

Suggested reading: General Work: Prescott, W. H., *History of the Reign of Ferdinand and Isabella*, London, 1837. On the War and Siege: Irving, W., *A Chronicle of the Conquest of Granada*, London, 1829. On the Siege: Lucena, L. S. de, *Practical and Art Guide of Granada*, Granada, 1911. Poetry: Lockhart, J. G., *Ancient Spanish Ballads* (trans.), London, 1823.

Since 1251 Moorish power in Spain had been confined to the southernmost kingdom of Granada. The union of Aragon and Castile under Ferdinand and Isabella, coupled with serious dissensions within the Moorish state, afforded an opportunity to achieve Ferdinand's aim of expelling the last Moors from Spanish soil. Already in 1486 he had captured King Abdallah (Boabdil) and compelled him to promise neutrality and, more important, the surrender of his capital, Granada, in the event of capitulation by Guadix and Baza to the east and Almeria on the south coast. By 1490 these towns had fallen, and Boabdil was summoned to keep his promise and evacuate Granada. He declined, on the grounds that he was no longer his own master and that the inhabitants insisted on defending their city from behind the massive walls which were flanked by 1,030 towers. In fact, many members of Boabdil's council advised him to seek honourable terms or to throw himself upon Ferdinand's mercy, but sterner counsels prevailed.

Having devastated the cultivated plain right up to these city walls, Ferdinand spent the winter preparing for war, and in April 1491 led his army to besiege Granada. First he sent a strong force to ravage the mountainous districts to the south which served the beleaguered city as a granary. Then he encamped his army on the banks of the Genil river, near the fountain of Los Ojos de Huescar, 3 miles south-west of Granada. The cautious Ferdinand, having decided that to storm the fortifications would be too costly, determined to reduce the city by famine and to cut off from external aid this last retreat of Moorish power in Spain.

Realising that the Spaniards were not going to attack, Muza, the active commander of the Moors, harassed the edges of the Christian camp with his cavalry, until Ferdinand had it ringed with trenches and bulwarks. Then Muza urged his warriors to challenge the Christian knights to single or group combat, and there were many such encounters, until Ferdinand worked out his losses and forbade acceptance of such challenges. The Moors next tried bravado, sending insolent taunts and hurling insults tied to their lances; but the King's prohibition prevented retaliation, until one day a daring Moor came so close that he sent his lance quivering into the earth near the royal pavilions. As the Queen had been insulted, a knight named Fernando Perez del Pulgar was allowed to take a small detachment, fight his way into Granada, nail a Christian tablet to the door of the chief mosque and then make good his escape, leaving the city in uproar. A particularly savage fight was provoked by Queen Isabella's visit to a forward position from which to view the fortifications, and on this occasion the Moors suffered about 2,000 casualties.

One July night the Queen was at prayer when a lamp set light to the hangings in her pavilion, and gusts of wind swept the flames from tent to tent, from one soldier's bivouac of branches to the next, until the entire camp was burning. The royal family escaped injury. Cavalry kept watch in case the

GRANADA
April 1491 to 2nd January 1492

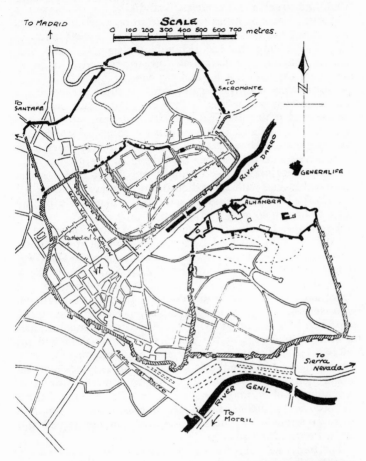

KEY

The Granada town wall is shown thus :-
① Portion still standing in 1910 :-
② Position of walls destroyed prior to 1910:-

Moors sallied forth to take advantage of the wild confusion, but suspecting a stratagem, they remained within their defence works. Next morning, however, as if to exploit the blow which Allah had struck at his enemies, Boabdil led his soldiers out to do battle. Fierce fighting took place in orchard and garden, with the Christians gaining possession of several outlying towers. Suddenly the Moorish infantry panicked and fled, leaving Boabdil, who had shown great personal courage, in danger of capture, but he and his companions were able to gallop to safety within the gates, while artillery prevented the Spaniards from advancing farther, and Muza and his horsemen retired reluctantly into the city. This proved to be the last Moorish sortie of a long war in the course of which they had suffered one disaster after another, lost every other town and fortress one by one, yet had disputed the ground with obstinate resolution. Even during this final siege, Muza inspired his men with the exhortation: 'We have nothing left to fight for but the ground we stand on. When this is lost, we cease to have a country and a name.'

To obviate the risk of another conflagration, Isabella had the flimsy camp replaced by a proper town of stone houses surrounded by walls and towers. After 80 days the work was finished, and she named the new camp Santa Fé, or Holy Faith. This symbol of Spanish determination and permanence depressed the already despondent inhabitants of Granada, who were suffering from the rigorous blockade, dreading the approach of winter, and living on increasingly tenuous hopes of relief from Egypt or the Barbary Coast. Boabdil and his advisers realised that, in the face of Spanish interception of all communication from outside, Granada could not be held much longer without starvation: the city was almost destitute of provisions, and of 7,000 horses only 300 had not been killed for food. So in October secret negotiations were opened, and after numerous conferences the capitulation was signed and ratified on 25 November.

The terms were liberal: the Moors were to be allowed the free exercise of their religion and the use of their mosques; their laws and customs were to be respected; of weapons of war, only the artillery had to be relinquished; Christian captives were to be released without ransom; Boabdil was to rule over a small but fertile region near Purchena, on condition that he paid homage to the Castilian crown; all who chose to remove themselves to Africa within 3 years would be provided with a free passage; finally, the city was to be surrendered within 60 days.

Eventually the public outcry and demonstrations against these terms became so violent in Granada that Boabdil was obliged to advance the date of surrender to 2 January 1492. Amid scenes of pageantry he handed over the keys of the

Alhambra, whereupon Ferdinand and Isabella entered Granada in a great procession, troops having discreetly occupied the city beforehand. That same day Boabdil, riding south to his new domain, paused on a hillock for one last glimpse of Granada and the Alhambra. He burst into tears, and his mother reproached him with the words: 'Thou dost well to weep like a woman for that which thou hast not defended like a man.' The place is known as 'El Ultimo Suspiro del Moro' (on the N 323 between Armilla and Padul).

The news of the capture of Granada was received with rejoicing throughout Christendom, and in London Henry VII caused a special *Te Deum* to be sung. For Spain the year 1492 was also marked by the departure on 3 August of Christopher Columbus on his great trans-Atlantic voyage of discovery. As for Boabdil, he soon tired of his tiny kingdom, which was sold back to Ferdinand, and went to Africa, where, 40 years later, he died fighting for the King of Fez.

A.B.-J.

The Pyrenees (C**)

Date: 25 July–2 August 1813.

Location: An area of the Pyrenees between Pamplona and St. Jean Pied de Port. **107.**

War and campaign: The Napoleonic Wars; the Peninsular War—the Pyrenees Campaign (see p. 196).

Object of the action: The French were trying to drive Wellington beyond the Ebro and recapture lost ground in northern Spain, relieving Pamplona.

Opposing sides: (a) Wellington commanding a British, German, Portuguese and Spanish army. (b) Marshal Soult commanding the reorganised relics of 4 French armies.

Forces engaged: (a) Allies: approx. 40,000 (or half the Allied army). (b) French: approx. 77,500 troops (out of 88,000 available).

Casualties: (a) 876 British and Portuguese killed; 5,464 wounded; 706 missing. (b) 1,908 killed; 8,545 wounded; 2,710 prisoners.

Result: Soult's costly failure to relieve Pamplona and drive the British beyond the Ebro shook French morale and enabled Wellington to improve his position in the Pyrenees.

Nearby accommodation: Pamplona.

Suggested reading: General Work: Oman, C. W. C., *A History of the Peninsular War*, Oxford, 1902. On the Campaign: Beatson, F. C., *With Wellington in the Pyrenees*, London, n.d. An Infantry View: Bell, G., *Soldier's Glory*, London, 1956. An H.Q. View: *The*

Private Journal of F. Seymour Larpent, Judge-Advocate General, Vol. 2, London, 1852. Work of Fiction: Gleig, G. R., *The Subaltern*, Edinburgh, 1845.

On learning of the disaster at Vitoria (q.v.) while in Germany, Napoleon dispatched Soult to restore the situation if he could. Quickly, skilfully, the Marshal rallied and reorganised the available troops, and on 24 July took the offensive. He aimed to relieve besieged Pamplona and even recapture Vitoria. There were two passes across the Pyrenees into Spain, Col de Maya and Roncesvalles (half-way between St. Jean Pied de Port and Pamplona), and he sent a column by each. Count d'Erlon and 20,000 troops attacked the first, took the British under Hill by surprise, captured 4 guns, and then lost some initial gains to a bold British charge.

At the second pass, 20 miles away, Byng's 5,000 had to oppose 18,000 Frenchmen under Soult, while a similar French force went past their flank. The divisions of Picton and Cole were forced back beyond Zubiri, and so Hill, his right flank now exposed, retired from the Col de Maya to Irurita. With both mountain passes in French hands, the situation had become critical.

Wellington, visiting the besiegers of San Sebastian (q.v.) when he learnt of Soult's incursion, galloped off to find Picton and Cole on ridges in front of Huarte and Villaba, barely 3 miles from Pamplona. A Portuguese battalion recognised the lone horseman, and their welcoming shout of 'Douro!', taken up by the British soldiers, made the cautious Soult, just across the valley by Sorauren, defer his impending attack till next day. By that time another division had reached Wellington, and Soult was defeated. On 28 July the Frenchman tried again, and the battle was 'fair bludgeon-work', to quote Wellington; but the outnumbered Allies held their ground at a cost of 2,600 casualties.

Thwarted in his drive on Pamplona, Soult next turned against Hill and with 20,000 men attacked half that number on 30 July. Hill had to fall back to avoid his flank being turned, but meanwhile Wellington had forced the French left to relinquish Sorauren and retreat, with a loss of many prisoners as well as 2,000 killed and wounded. Soult now had no option but to withdraw into France, and he only just avoided being cut off in the process.

A.B.-J.

RONCESVALLES (B**); battle of, August 778; **108**; Charlemagne's Offensive against the Saracens. The rearguard of Charlemagne's army, led by Roland, became separated from the main body in the Nive valley and was trapped and massacred by the local Basque population. See Winston, R., *Life of Charlemagne*, London, 1956.

SALAMANCA (A***); battle of, 22 July 1812; south-south-east of the city towards Los Arapiles; **112**; Peninsular War. Wellington's Allied Army (48,569) defeated Marshal Marmont (50,000) when the French rashly marched across the Allied front, erroneously believing that Wellington was retiring. See Bryant, A., *The Age of Elegance*, London, 1950.

SAN SEBASTIAN (C**); siege of, 9 July-9 September 1813; northern coast of Spain; **107a**; Peninsular War. Sir Thomas Graham's Allied force (approx. 10,000) conducting the siege against a French garrison (3,000) stormed the breach on 31 August but sustained heavy casualties (3,700 July-September); the castle surrendered nine days later. See Brett-James, A., *General Graham Lord Lynedoch*, London, 1959.

TALAVERA (B**); battle of, 27–28 July 1809; below the Sierra de Montalban; **114**; Peninsular War. Sir Arthur Wellesley and the Spaniard, General Cuesta (jointly 55,000), fought off the attacks of King Joseph and Marshal Jourdan (46,138). See Napier, W. F. P., *History of the War in the Peninsula*, Book VIII (new Edn.), London, 1851.

Vitoria (B****)

Date: 21 June 1813.

Location: North-west Spain. **109**.

War and campaign: The Napoleonic Wars; the Peninsular War—Campaign of 1813 (see p. 196).

Object of the action: Wellington wished to crush the forces of King Joseph of Spain and drive the French out of the Peninsula once and for all.

Opposing sides: (*a*) The Marquess of Wellington commanding a British, Portuguese and Spanish force. (*b*) King Joseph and Marshal Jourdan with the French army.

Forces engaged: (*a*) infantry: British 27,372, Portuguese 27,569,

Spanish 6,800; cavalry: 8,317; 90 guns. *Total*: 70,058. (*b*) **French:**
43,000 infantry; 7,000 cavalry; 153 guns. *Total*: 50,000.
Casualties: (*a*) Allies: 740 killed; 4,174 wounded; 266 missing.
(*b*) French: approx. 756 killed; 4,414 wounded; 2,829 missing.

Result: The defeat of the French terminated Joseph Bonaparte's
reign as King of Spain, drove the French forces back into the
Pyrenees, and induced Austria to join the Coalition against France.

Nearby accommodation: Vitoria.

Suggested reading: General Work: Bryant, A., *The Age of
Elegance*, London, 1950. A Cavalry Account: Tomkinson, W., *A
Diary of a Cavalry Officer*, London, 1894. An H.Q. Account: *The
Private Journal of F. Seymour Larpent, Judge Advocate-General*, 2 vols.,
London, 1852. Work of Fiction: Heyer, G., *The Spanish Bride*,
London, 1940. Poetry: Roberts, D., *The Military Adventures of
Johnny Newcome*, London, 1815 (new Edn. 1904).

Wellington, steadily reinforced during the spring of 1813, had
a stronger, healthier army than ever before when, late in May,
he and Hill led 30,000 troops against Salamanca, while
Graham took the rest northwards 200 miles through the
mountainous Tras os Montes region across the Douro and
Esla rivers, and so behind the French defences. By 3 June
Wellington had his entire force north of the Douro. For 10
days the army marched over the flat corn-fields of Castile, a
cavalry screen hustling the French at so respectful a distance
that the Allied infantry seldom glimpsed their opponents.
Enemy efforts to quicken the withdrawal were hampered by
the caravan of courtiers, wives, mistresses and otiose officials
who, trailing in the wake of King Joseph, cluttered the road
with their carriages and baggage wagons.

Wellington, declining to launch a frontal attack on French
positions prepared south of the Ebro, sent a third of his troops
northwards on another outflanking march, this time among
the Cantabrian Mountains, along tracks deemed impassable
by the French. King Joseph and Marshal Jourdan, levered off
the Ebro line, eventually drew up their forces behind the
Zadorra river covering Vitoria, and then cast away a natural
advantage by failing to destroy all the bridges.

The battle was fought across a country of ripe wheat-fields
nearly as high as a soldier's head, vineyards, deep wide ditches,
hamlets, a ridge of hills on the southern flank, and the winding
river. It was to gain possession of this ridge that Hill, crossing
the Zadorra early on 21 June, sent off a flanking column of
Spaniards, supported by Cadogan's brigade. Soon after 8 am
this force met Gazan's troops who had also climbed to the
crest. Once this had been captured and his flank thus secured,
not without serious casualties, Hill pushed another brigade
along the foothills. Skirmishing went on all the morning as the
French, allowing their attention to be too much engrossed by

this threat, vainly sought to regain the heights. As for their repeated attempts to retake the village of Subijana de Alava, these failed also, after a fierce struggle for the churchyard.

Just before noon a peasant told Wellington that the French had omitted to guard the Tres Puentes bridge across the river. At once Kempt's brigade was sent to secure positions on the far side—a movement hidden from the French by convenient high ground.

VITORIA
21st Juen 1813

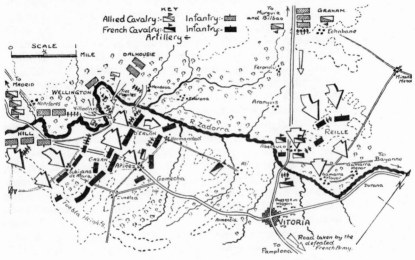

Also about midday the 3rd Division came up, and its commander, Picton, exasperated at being without orders and then hearing orders intended for Lord Dalhousie's 7th Division, which was still not on the scene, having been delayed in rough country to the west, took it upon himself to lead his men over the river. Opposed to him were 2 French divisions and well-sited guns, but Wellington had Kempt's brigade attack them. This caused the French artillerymen to pull back after firing a few rounds only. The 4th Division and the rest of the Light Division also crossed the Zadorra—against Gazan's front, which had already been depleted in the centre by the struggle for the Puebla heights. Gazan formed a defensive line to hold the knoll by Ariñez, but soon after 3 pm Picton, Kempt and one of Dalhousie's brigades, all under Wellington's direct command, stormed and seized both knoll and village. Soon

187

the French decided to abandon the valley and began withdrawing towards Vitoria in orderly fashion.

Meanwhile Sir Thomas Graham, commanding the left of the army, had moved forward along the Bilbao road from Murguia towards Vitoria. Besides 2 British-Portuguese divisions, he had a Spanish force under Colonel Longa which kept in front to persuade the French for as long as possible that this was nothing but the movement of some partisan corps unsupported by British troops. Longa did his job well. The French were holding hills to cover the villages of Gamarra Mayor and Menor and Abechuco as well as the Zadorra bridges. Graham ordered a strong British-Portuguese force to turn and capture the heights, and no sooner had this been achieved than the village of Gamarra Mayor was stormed. Another column now assaulted Abechuco, which fell into our hands, though at the same time the French tried desperately to recapture Gamarra Mayor. Their every effort proved vain. However, Graham found it impossible to cross the river towards Vitoria, as 2 reserve French divisions still held some high ground on the left of the Zadorra and did not relinquish their hold until Wellington's main body of troops advanced in the centre. Graham had nevertheless achieved his main objective, namely to intercept the enemy's retreat direct via Tolosa to Bayonne in France. The French were obliged instead to use the Pamplona road.

They left the battlefield to a litter and confusion seldom paralleled. Paintings, church plate, libraries, uniforms, women's dresses, treasure chests, choice wines—all these and more were abandoned. To quote one officer: 'The battle was to the French like salt on a leech's tail. The plunder of Spain was disgorged at one throw.' And Wellington remarked: 'Well, they have always abused me for want of trophies. I hope we have enough today.' One of these trophies was Jourdan's *bâton*, which was sent to the Prince Regent.

Pursuit of the vanquished French was delayed by heavy rain, by slack leadership of the cavalry, above all by plundering which engaged the zeal of some 4,000 British and Portuguese soldiers and caused Wellington to write his celebrated letter in which occur the phrases: 'We have in the service the scum of the earth as common soldiers . . . The officers of the lower ranks will not perform the duty required from them for the purpose of keeping their soldiers in order . . . As to the non-commissioned officers, they are as bad as the men.'

By the beginning of July the French armies were behind their own frontiers, and, with minor exceptions, all that remained to them in Spain were the garrisons defending San Sebastian and Pamplona. A furious Napoleon sacked Jourdan and said caustically of his brother Joseph: 'Spain had a general too little and a king too much.'

A.B.-J.

ZARAGOZA (SARAGOSSA) (C**); siege of, 20 December 1808 to 20 February 1809; south bank of the river Ebro; **III**; Peninsular War. General José Palafox (25,000) conducted a heroic defence against the French army (35,000), successively commanded by Moncey, Mortier, Junot and Lannes; pestilence and starvation eventually forced the city to surrender. See Southey R., *History of the Peninsular War* (3 vols.), London, 1823–32.

Glossary of Military Terms

ARQUEBUS: early type of musket, often discharged by use of a lighted match, and frequently supported on a forked rest.

BASHI-BAZOUKS: mercenary soldiers raised by the Turks for service in their irregular forces.

BOMBARD: early type of cannon, usually firing stone missiles or large iron darts.

CHEVAUX DE FRISE: wooden barricades studded with steel spikes and sword-blades.

CIRCUMVALLATION (lines of): trenches and fortifications used by a besieging army to protect its camp from attack by relieving forces.

COHORT: unit of the later Roman legions; each comprised 360 men, and usually there were 10 in all.

CONTRAVALLATION (lines of): trenches and fortifications used by a besieging army to isolate a beleaguered fortress.

ENCEINTE: the line of continuous fortifications forming the perimeter of a defended place.

FÉDERÉS: the original French volunteers who rallied to the defence of their country at the outset of the Revolutionary Wars.

FYRD: force of Anglo-Saxon troops raised by mobilising all men on a regional basis.

GENDARMERIE: part of the crack Household troops of the French monarchy, including the Red and Black Musketeers.

GLACIS: area of sloping ground in front of a fort, on which attackers are exposed to fire.

HOPLITE: heavily armed foot soldier of Ancient Greece, often armed with a long spear.

HUSCARLE: member of the personal escort and household of the Danish and late Anglo-Saxon monarchs.

IAYLARS: Moslem fanatics famed for their ferocious courage, employed in the Turkish armies.

IMMORTALS: members of the Shah's bodyguard in Ancient Persia, employed on a long engagement.

JANISSARY: member of the Turkish Sultan's bodyguard and 'corps d'élite'; originally recruited from Christian slave-boys.

MAISON DU ROI: part of the crack Household troops of the French monarchy.

MÊLÉE: mixed fight or skirmish; frequently used to describe hand-to-hand fighting.

PHALANX: deep formation of hoplites used in Ancient Greece.

PRAETOR: high-ranking Roman officer, frequently a commanding general; later an elected public official.

RAVELIN: outwork with two faces used in fortification to protect bastions and salients.

SCHILTRON: dense formation of spearmen employed by the Scots and the Swiss.

SERGEANT: in the Middle Ages this term denoted a personal attendant serving a knight: approximately a squire.

TARGE or TARGET: small round shield, normally carried by infantry.

TERCIO: Spanish infantry formation, combining musketeers and pikemen, 2,000–3,000 strong.

Campaign Chronology

The purpose of this section is to place the battles and sieges treated in this book in their correct chronological sequence from 1200 B.C. to 1945. If a reader wishes to follow up any particular war or period a quick reference to the following pages will reveal which relevant subjects are to be found in the National Sections. Those battles marked with an asterisk (*) appear in Volume 1; those without an asterisk in Volume 2.

I. Ancient Wars: 1200 B.C. to A.D. 500

On account of the difficulty of placing an exact day or month to the subjects belonging to this period, in most cases only the relevant year is shown.

Date	Name of Action	National Section	War
1200 B.C. approx.	Siege of Troy	Turkey	Trojan Wars
490	Marathon	Greece	Greco-Persian Wars
480	Thermopylae	Greece	Greco-Persian Wars
479	Plataea	Greece	Greco-Persian Wars
415–413	Siege of Syracuse	Italy	Peloponnesian War
396	Siege of Veii	Italy	Roman conquest of Etruria
321	Caudine Forks	Italy	Second Samnite War
225	Telamon	Italy	Gallic Invasion of Italy
218	Trebbia	Italy	Second Punic War
217	Lake Trasimene	Italy	Second Punic War
216	Cannae	Italy	Second Punic War
207	Metaurus	Italy	Second Punic War
*58	Mülhausen	France	Caesar's Gallic War
*52	Siege and Battle of Alesia	France	Caesar's Gallic War
48	Pharsalia	Greece	Second Roman Civil War
42	First and Second Philippi	Greece	Third Roman Civil War
9 A.D.	Teutoburger Wald	W. Germany	Roman Conquest of Germany
*61	Camulodunum (Colchester)	Gt. Britain	Boudicca's Revolt
*61	Verulamium (St. Albans)	Gt. Britain	Boudicca's Revolt
*84	The Grampians	Gt. Britain	Roman Conquest of Britain
*122–128	Hadrian's Wall	Gt. Britain	Roman Conquest of Britain
324	Adrianople	Turkey	Civil War of the Emperors
409	Sack of Rome (I)	Italy	Gothic Invasion of N. Italy
*451	Châlons-sur-Marne	France	Hun Invasion of Gaul

II. Mediaeval Wars: A.D. 500 to A.D. 1500

Date	Name of Action	National Section	War
*732 10 Oct.	Tours	France	Saracen Invasions
*778 Aug.	Roncesvalles	Spain	Charlemagne's War against the Saracens
*878	Ethandune	Gt. Britain	Danish Invasions
*887	Montfaucon	France	Danish Invasions
*1016 18 Oct.	Assandune	Gt. Britain	Danish Invasions
*1066 25 Sept.	Stamford Bridge	Gt. Britain	Danish Invasions

*1066	14 Oct.	Hastings	Gt. Britain	Norman Conquest
*1106	28 Sept.	Tinchebrai	France	English Conquest of Normandy
1191	6 May	Amathus	Cyprus	Third Crusade
*1214	27 July	Bouvines	France	English Invasion of France
*1264	14 May	Lewes	Gt. Britain	Baronial Wars
*1265	4 Aug.	Evesham	Gt. Britain	Baronial Wars
1289	11 June	Campaldino	Italy	Wars of the Ghibellines and Guelphs
*1297	11 Sept.	Stirling Bridge	Gt Britain	Anglo-Scottish Wars
*1298	22 July	Falkirk (I)	Gt.. Britain	Anglo-Scottish Wars
*1302	11 July	Courtrai	Belgium	Flemish Revolt against France
*1314	24 June	Bannockburn	Gt. Britain	Anglo-Scottish Wars
1315	15 Nov.	Mortgarten	Switzerland	Confederation against Austria
*1346	26 Aug.	Crécy	France	Hundred Years' War
*1356	19 Sept.	Poitiers	France	Hundred Years' War
*1385	14 Aug.	Aljubarotta	Portugal	War of Portuguese Succession
1386	9 July	Sempach	Switzerland	Swiss War of Independence
1388	9 Apr.	Nafels	Switzerland	Swiss War of Independence
1410	15 July	Tannenberg (I)	Poland	Wars of Teutonic Order
*1415	25 Oct.	Agincourt	France	Hundred Years' War
1426	5 July	Khirokitia	Cyprus	Lusignian Wars
*1428	12 Oct.–8 May 1429	Siege of Orléans	France	Hundred Years' War
1444	26 Aug.	St. Jakob an der Birs	Switzerland	Armagnac Invasion
1453	5 Apr.– 29 May	Siege of Constantinople	Turkey	Wars of Islam against Byzantium
*1460	10 July	Northampton	Gt. Britain	Wars of the Roses
*1460	30 Dec.	Wakefield	Gt. Britain	Wars of the Roses
*1461	17 Feb.	Second St. Albans	Gt. Britain	Wars of the Roses
*1461	29 Mar.	Towton	Gt. Britain	Wars of the Roses
*1471	14 Apr.	Barnet	Gt. Britain	Wars of the Roses
*1471	4 May	Tewkesbury	Gt. Britain	Wars of the Roses
1476	22 June	Morat	Switzerland	Burgundian War
1480	23 May– 20 Aug.	Siege of Rhodes	Greece	Wars of Mahomet II
*1485	22 Aug.	Bosworth	Gt. Britain	Wars of the Roses
*1491	Apr.–2 Jan. 1492	Siege of Granada	Spain	War of Granada
1499	22 July	Dornach	Switzerland	Swabian War

III. Modern Wars: A.D. 1500 to A.D. 1945

Date		Name of Action	National Section	War
*1513	9 Sept.	Flodden	Gt. Britain	Anglo-Scots War of 1513–14
1515	13–14 Sept.	Marignano	Italy	French Reconquest of Milan
1525	25 Feb.	Pavia	Italy	Wars between Francis I and Charles V
*1545	17 Feb.	Ancrum Moor	Gt. Britain	Anglo-Scots Wars
*1547	10 Sept.	Pinkie Cleugh	Gt. Britain	Anglo-Scots Wars
1565	19 May– 8 Sept.	Siege of Malta	Malta	Wars of Islam
*1568	23 May	Heiliger Lee	Holland	Eighty Years' War
1568	21 July	Jemmingen	W. Germany	Eighty Years' War
1570	25 July– 9 Sept	Siege of Nicosia	Cyprus	Wars of Islam
1570	18 Sept.–6 Aug. 1571	Siege of Famagusta	Cyprus	Wars of Islam
*1572	1 Apr.	Brille	Holland	Eighty Years' War
*1572	18 Dec.–12 July 1573	Siege of Haarlem	Holland	Eighty Years' War
*1573	21 Aug.– 8 Oct.	Siege of Alkmaar	Holland	Eighty Years' War
*1586	11 Nov.	Zutphen	Holland	Eighty Years' War
*1589	21 Sept.	Arques	France	French Religious Wars
*1590	14 Mar.	Ivry	France	French Religious Wars
*1594	7 Aug.	Ford of the Biscuits	Gt. Britain	O'Donnell's Revolt
*1598	14 Aug.	Yellow Ford	Gt. Britain	Tyrone's Rebellion
*1601	5 July–14 Sept. 1604	Siege of Ostend	Belgium	Eighty Years' War

*1601	26 Dec.	Kinsale	Eire	Tyrone's Rebellion
*1626	Nov.–28 Oct. 1627	Siege of La Rochelle	France	French Religious Wars
1631	17 Sept.	Breitenfeld	E. Germany	Thirty Years' War
1632	16 Nov.	Lutzen	E. Germany	Thirty Years' War
1634	5–6 Sept.	Nordlingen	W. Germany	Thirty Years' War
1636	4 Oct.	Wittstock	E. Germany	Thirty Years' War
*1642	23 Oct.	Edgehill	Gt. Britain	First English Civil War
*1643	19 May	Rocroi	France	Thirty Years' War
*1643	18 June	Chalgrove	Gt. Britain	First English Civil War
*1643	20 Sept. and 27 Oct. 1644	First and Second Newbury	Gt. Britain	First English Civil War
*1644	2 July	Marston Moor	Gt. Britain	First English Civil War
*1644	21 Aug. and 2 Sept.	Lostwithiel	Gt. Britain	First English Civil War
*1645	14 June	Naseby	Gt. Britain	First English Civil War
*1645	13 Sept.	Philiphaugh	Gt. Britain	First English Civil War
*1648	17–19 Aug.	Preston	Gt. Britain	Second English Civil War
*1649	10 Sept.	Drogheda	Gt. Britain	Cromwell's Irish Campaign
*1650	3 Sept.	Dunbar	Gt. Britain	Cromwell's Scottish War
*1651	3 Sept.	Worcester	Gt. Britain	Cromwell's Scottish War
*1658	3 June	The Dunes	France	Franco-Spanish War
1664	1 Aug.	St. Gotthard-on-the-Raab	Hungary	Turkish Wars
1675	27 July and 1 Aug.	Sasbach and Altenheim	W. Germany	European War of 1672–9
1683	14 July–12 Sept.	Siege of Vienna	Austria	Great Turkish War
*1685	6 July	Sedgemoor	Gt. Britain	Monmouth's Rebellion
1687	12 Aug.	Mohács	Hungary	Great Turkish War
*1689	17 Apr.–30 July	Siege of Londonderry	Gt. Britain	Jacobite War
*1689	27 July	Killiecrankie	Gt. Britain	William III's Scots War
*1690	1 July	Fleurus	Belgium	War of the League of Augsburg
*1690	11 July	Boyne	Gt. Britain	Jacobite War
*1691	12 July	Aughrim	Eire	Jacobite War
1691	19 Aug.	Szlankamen	Hungary	Great Turkish War
*1691	Sept.–Oct.	Siege of Limerick	Eire	Jacobite War
*1692	3 Aug.	Steenkirk	Belgium	War of the League of Augsburg
*1693	28 July	Landen	Belgium	War of the League of Augsburg
1697	11 Sept.	Zenta	Yugoslavia	Great Turkish War
1700	20 Nov.	Narva	U.S.S.R.	Great Northern War
1704	13 Aug.	Blenheim	W. Germany	War of the Spanish Succession
*1706	23 May	Ramillies	Belgium	War of the Spanish Succession
1706	7 Sept.	Turin	Italy	War of the Spanish Succession
*1707	25 Apr.	Almanza	Spain	War of the Spanish Succession
*1708	11 July	Oudenarde	Belgium	War of the Spanish Succession
1709	28 June	Pultava	U.S.S.R.	Great Northern War
*1709	11 Sept.	Malplaquet	Belgium	War of the Spanish Succession
*1712	24 July	Denain	France	War of the Spanish Succession
1714	19 Oct.–20 Oct. 1715	Siege of Stralsund	E. Germany	Great Northern War
1716	5 Aug.	Peterwardein	Yugoslavia	Turkish Wars
1717	16 Aug.	Belgrade	Yugoslavia	Turkish Wars
1734	29 June	Parma	Italy	War of Polish Succession
1734	19 Sept.	Guastalla	Italy	War of Polish Succession
1741	10 Apr.	Mohwitz	Poland	War of Austrian Succession
1743	27 June	Dettingen	W. Germany	War of Austrian Succession
1744	11 Aug.	Velletri (I)	Italy	War of Austrian Succession
*1745	11 May	Fontenoy	Belgium	War of Austrian Succession
*1745	21 Sept.	Prestonpans	Gt. Britain	Jacobite Revolt of the '45
*1746	17 Jan.	Falkirk (II)	Gt. Britain	Jacobite Revolt of the '45
*1746	17 Apr.	Culloden	Gt. Britain	Jacobite Revolt of the '45

1746	15 June	Piacenza	Italy	War of Austrian Succession
*1746	11 Oct.	Rocoux	Belgium	War of Austrian Succession
*1747	2 July	Laffeldt	Holland	War of Austrian Succession
1747	19 July	Col de l'Assiette	Italy	War of Austrian Succession
1756	1 Oct.	Lobositz	Czechoslovakia	Seven Years' War
1757	6 May	Prague	Czechoslovakia	Seven Years' War
1757	18 June	Kolin	Czechoslovakia	Seven Years' War
1757	26 July	Hastenbeck	W. Germany	Seven Years' War
1757	5 Nov.	Rossbach	E. Germany	Seven Years' War
1757	5 Dec.	Leuthen	Poland	Seven Years' War
1758	23 June	Crefeld	W. Germany	Seven Years' War
1758	14 Oct.	Hochkirch	E. Germany	Seven Years' War
1759	13 Apr.	Bergen	W. Germany	Seven Years' War
1759	1 Aug.	Minden	W. Germany	Seven Years' War
1760	31 July	Warburg	W. Germany	Seven Years' War
1760	3 Nov.	Torgau	E. Germany	Seven Years' War
*1761	7 April–8 June	Belle Isle	France	Seven Years' War
*1779	24 June–7 Feb. 1783	Siege of Gibraltar	Gibraltar	War of American Independence (European involvment)
*1792	20 Sept.	Valmy	France	French Revolutionary Wars
*1793	6 Sept.–19 Dec.	Siege of Toulon	France	French Revolutionary Wars
1796	10 May	Lodi	Italy	French Revolutionary Wars
1796	30 May	Borghetto	Italy	French Revolutionary Wars
1796	27 June–2 Feb. 1797	Siege of Mantua	Italy	French Revolutionary Wars
1796	15–17 Nov.	Arcola	Italy	French Revolutionary Wars
1797	14–15 Jan.	Rivoli	Italy	French Revolutionary Wars
1798	10 June	Valetta	Malta	French Revolutionary Wars
1799	19 Sept.	Bergen	Holland	French Revolutionary Wars
1799	25 Sept.	Second Zurich	Switzerland	French Revolutionary Wars
1800	14 June	Marengo	Italy	French Revolutionary Wars
1800	3 Dec.	Höhenlinden	W. Germany	French Revolutionary Wars
1805	2 Dec.	Austerlitz	Czechoslovakia	Napoleonic Wars
1806	4 July	Maida	Italy	Napoleonic Wars
1806	14 Oct.	Jena-Auerstadt	E. Germany	Napoleonic Wars
1807	8 Feb.	Eylau	U.S.S.R.	Napoleonic Wars
1807	14 June	Friedland	U.S.S.R.	Napoleonic Wars
*1808	21–2 July	Bailén	Spain	Napoleonic Wars (Peninsula)
*1808	21 Aug.	Vimiero	Portugal	Napoleonic Wars (Peninsula)
*1808	20 Dec.–20 Feb. 1809	Siege of Zaragoza	Spain	Napoleonic Wars (Peninsula)
*1809	16 Jan.	Corunna	Spain	Napoleonic Wars (Peninsula)
1809	21–2 May	Aspern-Essling	Austria	Napoleonic Wars
*1809	4 June–12 Dec. 1809	Siege of Gerona	Spain	Napoleonic Wars (Peninsula)
1809	5–6 July	Wagram	Austria	Napoleonic Wars
*1809	27–8 July	Talavera	Spain	Napoleonic Wars (Peninsula)
*1810	Oct.–Mar. 1811	Siege of Torres Vedras	Portugal	Napoleonic Wars (Peninsula)
*1811	16 May	Albuera	Spain	Napoleonic Wars (Peninsula)
*1812	7–19 Jan.	Siege of Ciudad Rodrigo	Spain	Napoleonic Wars (Peninsula)
*1812	16 Mar–6 Apr.	Siege of Badajoz	Spain	Napoleonic Wars (Peninsula)
*1812	22 July	Salamanca	Spain	Napoleonic Wars (Peninsula)
1812	7 Sept.	Borodino	U.S.S.R.	Napoleonic Wars
1812	28 Nov.	Beresina	U.S.S.R.	Napoleonic Wars
*1813	21 June	Vitoria	Spain	Napoleonic Wars (Peninsula)
*1813	9 July–9 Sept.	Siege of San Sebastian	Spain	Napoleonic Wars (Peninsula)
*1813	25 July–2 Aug.	Pyrenees	Spain	Napoleonic Wars (Peninsula)
1813	26–7 Aug.	Dresden	E. Germany	Napoleonic Wars
1813	16–18 Oct.	Leipzig	E. Germany	Napoleonic Wars
*1814	10 Apr.	Toulouse	France	Napoleonic Wars
*1815	18 June	Waterloo	Belgium	Napoleonic Wars
1847	23 Nov.	Gisikon	Switzerland	Sonderbund Civil War
1849	23 Mar.	Novara	Italy	First War of Italian Independence
1849	Apr.–June	Siege of Rome (II)	Italy	French Intervention

1849	19 May	Velletri (II)	Italy	War between Naples and the Roman Republic
1854	20 Sept.	Alma	U.S.S.R.	Crimean War
1854	28 Sept.–8 Sept. 1855	Siege of Sebastopol	U.S.S.R.	Crimean War
1854	25 Oct.	Balaclava	U.S.S.R.	Crimean War
1854	5 Nov.	Inkerman	U.S.S.R.	Crimean War
1859	4 June	Magenta	Italy	Second War of Italian Independence
1859	24 June	Solferino	Italy	Second War of Italian Independence
1866	24 June	Custozza	Italy	Austro-Prussian War
1866	3 July	Sadowa	Czechoslovakia	Austro-Prussian War
*1870	6 Aug.	Spicheren-Wörth	France	Franco-Prussian War
*1870	16–18 Aug.	Mars-la-Tour and Gravellote	France	Franco-Prussian War
*1870	1 Sept.	Sedan	France	Franco-Prussian War
*1870	20 Sept.–28 Jan. 1871	Siege of Paris	France	Franco-Prussian War
1877	17 July–9 Jan. 1878	Schipka Pass	Bulgaria	Russo-Turkish Wars
1877	20 July–10 Dec.	Siege and Battle of Plevna	Bulgaria	Russo-Turkish Wars
1912	28 Oct.–1 Nov.	Lüleburgaz	Turkey	Balkan Wars
*1914	23 Aug.	Mons	Belgium	First World War
1914	26–31 Aug.	Tannenberg	Poland	First World War
*1914–18		Flanders (a summary)	Belgium and N.E. France.	First World War
1915	25 Apr.–10 Jan. 1916	Gallipoli	Turkey	First World War
*1916	21 Feb.–20 Dec.	Verdun	France	First World War
*1916	1 July–18 Nov.	Somme	France	First World War
*1917	16–30 Apr.	Chemin-des-Dames	France	First World War
1917	24 Oct.–7 Nov.	Caporetto	Italy	First World War
*1917	20 Nov.–5 Dec.	Cambrai	France	First World War
*1918	26 Sept.–11 Nov.	Argonne	France	First World War
1918	24 Oct.–4 Nov.	Vittorio Veneto	Italy	First World War
*1940	21 May	Arras	France	Second World War
*1940	26 May–3 June	Dunkirk	France	Second World War
1941	20 May–1 June	Crete	Greece	Second World War
*1942	19 Aug.	Dieppe	France	Second World War
1942	22 Aug.–2 Feb. 1943	Siege and Battle of Stalingrad	U.S.S.R.	Second World War
1943	9 July–17 Aug.	Etna	Italy	Second World War
1943	9–18 Sept.	Salerno	Italy	Second World War
1943	19 Nov.–3 Dec.	River Sangro	Italy	Second World War
1944	17 Jan.–18 May	Cassino	Italy	Second World War
1944	22 Jan.–22 May	Anzio	Italy	Second World War
*1944	6 June	D-Day	France	Second World War
*1944	6 June–25 July	Caen Area	France	Second World War
*1944	24–28 July	St. Lô	France	Second World War
*1944	17–25 Sept.	Arnhem	Holland	Second World War
1944	4 Oct.–1 Dec.	Aachen	W. Germany	Second World War
*1944	19–22 Nov.	Belfort	France	Second World War
*1944	16 Dec.–1 Feb. 1945	Ardennes	Belgium	Second World War
1945	7 Mar. and 8 Feb.–21 Mar.	Remagen and the Rhineland	W. Germany	Second World War

Index